Other Books Written or Edi

The Oxford Handbook of Evangelical Theology

The Baker Pocket Guide to World Religion:
What Every Christian Needs to Know

Understanding Jonathan Edwards:
Introducing America's Theologian

Claiming Christ:
A Mormon-Evangelical Debate (with Robert Millet)

God's Rivals:
Why God Allows Different Religions—Insights from
the Bible and the Early Church

Jonathan Edwards Confronts the Gods:
Christian Theology, Enlightenment Religion, and Non-Christian Faiths

Can Evangelicals Learn from Non-Christian Religions?
Jesus, Revelation and the Religions

One Holy and Happy Society:
The Public Theology of Jonathan Edwards

Seeing God:
Jonathan Edwards and Spiritual Discernment

Cancer:
A Medical and Theological Guide for Patients and Their Families
(with William A. Fintel, M.D.)

The Great Theologians
A Brief Guide

Gerald R. McDermott

IVP Academic

An imprint of InterVarsity Press
Downers Grove, Illinois

InterVarsity Press
P.O. Box 1400, Downers Grove, IL 60515-1426
World Wide Web: www.ivpress.com
E-mail: email@ivpress.com

InterVarsity Press® is the book-publishing division of InterVarsity Christian Fellowship/USA®, a movement of students and faculty active on campus at hundreds of universities, colleges and schools of nursing in the United States of America, and a member movement of the International Fellowship of Evangelical Students. For information about local and regional activities, write Public Relations Dept., InterVarsity Christian Fellowship/USA, 6400 Schroeder Rd., P.O. Box 7895, Madison, WI 53707-7895, or visit the IVCF website at <www.intervarsity.org>.

Scripture quotations, unless otherwise noted, are from The Holy Bible, English Standard Version, *copyright © 2001 by Crossway Bibles, a division of Good News Publishers. Used by permission. All rights reserved.*

Chapter two: the selection on pp. 27-28 taken from Origen: An Exhortation to Martyrdom, Prayer and Selected Works *is reprinted by permission of Paulist Press, Inc., www.paulistpress.com.*

Chapter six: the selection on pp. 94-95 taken from Martin Luther, Christian Liberty *is used by permission of Augsburg Fortress Publishers.*

Design: Cindy Kiple
Images: Saint Thomas Aquinas by Bernadino Mei at Coll. Chigi-Saracini, Siena, Italy. Scala/Art Resource, NY

ISBN 978-0-8308-3875-2

Printed in the United States of America ∞

Library of Congress Cataloging-in-Publication Data

McDermott, Gerald R. (Gerald Robert)
  The great theologians: a brief guide / Gerald R. McDermott.
    p cm.
  Includes bibliographical references and index.
  ISBN 978-0-8308-3875-2 (pbk.: alk. paper)
  1. Theology—History. 2. Theologians. I. Title.
  BT21.3.M33 2010
  230.092'2—dc22

                                                                                    2009042069

P *28 27 26 25 24 23 22 21 20 19 18 17 16 15 14 13 12 11 10 9 8 7 6 5 4 3 2 1*
Y *34 33 32 31 30 29 28 27 26 25 24 23 22 21 20 19 18 17 16 15 14 13 12 11 10*

To Magdalen Marie

Our third grandchild

Contents

Acknowledgments

As with every other book I have written, Jean has been a source of ideas, inspiration and comfort. She tolerates my single-minded concentration on thinking and writing that sometimes lets important matters slip, and helps me manage my busy life so that I can find time and relative relaxation to write.

Thanks are due to Andy LePeau for encouraging this project from the beginning. My editor, Gary Deddo, has been an insightful guide, especially in his lengthy comments on the original draft. The detailed suggestions from my two anonymous readers have made this book better than it would have been and kept me from egregious mistakes. My hat goes off to Michael McClymond, who must have set a record for this sort of book by penning sixty-three pages of detailed criticisms and suggestions. I have not been able to accommodate all of his ideas, but he will find that many—perhaps most—have slipped into the following pages in some form or other. They are far more interesting and historically informed as a result of training his penetrating and encyclopedic mind on them.

I received significant help from Paul Hinlicky for my Luther chapter, Chris Hackett for my Balthasar chapter and Ned Wisnefske for my Barth chapter. Other readers who helped improve this book were Alan Pieratt, Tom Oster, Ryan McDermott, Kim Burgess, Michael Kelly and Bill Fintel. Bob Benne was an intellectual companion throughout and suggested ways to solve problems in more than a few chapters. Judi Pinckney's wonderfully cheerful and helpful services as department secretary speeded the production process.

A research grant from Roanoke College helped me clear space to write, and a grant from the Baylor Institute for Studies of Religion enabled me to concentrate most of a summer on this manuscript. I am especially appreciative to Byron Johnson for his encouragement and support for my scholarship.

Diane Kelly's proofreading saved me from embarrassment. Other mistakes and omissions are mine alone!

1

Why Study Theology?

The question was a familiar one. The young businessman had grabbed me after the service in which I had preached. My sermon had referred to Saint Augustine and Martin Luther.

"Is there any way I can get a handy introduction to these theologians you and the other pastors talk about all the time? I wish I could go to seminary, but that's impossible. And I am afraid I won't understand a big textbook. All I want is a little handbook to give me the basics of each of these great theologians."

Like so many Christians who have said something very similar to me and other pastors over the years, this young man wanted to learn about "the greats"—but not too much, thank you. Too much would be overwhelming in terms of time and complexity.

That's why I wrote this book. I wanted to be able to provide a short and accessible introduction to some of the greatest theologians—so that any thinking Christian could get a ballpark idea of what is distinctive to each. And at a level they could understand. Challenging but not overwhelming. Provocative but not frustrating. An introduction that could inform and provide a gateway to deeper study if so desired.

WHY STUDY THEOLOGY?

Many Christians think theology is for pointy-headed professors and students in the seminaries. Many people in the pews also think they can't understand most of what is in theology books, but that it wouldn't matter anyway because it is irrelevant to the real world.

What they don't realize is that they already do theology. You see, the word *theology* comes from two Greek words—*theos*, which means "God," and *logos*, which means "reason" or "word" and therefore "speaking." So anyone who thinks and speaks about God is doing theology.

People who speak or think about God a *lot* have a framework to put God into. That framework is their theology. It is the lens through which they read the Bible, listen to sermons, read books about God, think about and pray to God. When they read anything about God, they are reading someone else's theology and using what they read to adjust their own theology—whether they realize that or not.

Therefore, there is no faith without theology. There is no reading of the Bible without a theology that is used—wittingly or unwittingly—to interpret the Bible. There is no hearing a sermon without theology that is both being modified in some way and at the same time helping to analyze the sermon.

So every thinking Christian has some theology. The question is not *whether* we do theology and use theology, but *which* theology we do and use. This begs the question, How do we know that our theology—which means our view of God—is the right one?

Let me try to answer this question with an illustration. Suppose you know there is a great woman of God in your church who has read the Bible and theology for forty years. She not only has deep knowledge of Scripture and how to interpret it for life and culture, but she also walks a holy life. People often remark on her humility and love.

What if you were to take the attitude, "I'm going to construct my theology [which, remember, is your view of God] on my own, simply reading the Bible and theology books by myself."

Wouldn't that be odd, when you have a godly theologian in your midst? In fact, doesn't this seem to illustrate sinful pride? It calls to mind the warning of Proverbs: "Fools despise wisdom and instruction" (Prov 1:7).

Ignoring the great and godly minds of the church—who have been ruminating on God for thousands of years—when we have them at our fingertips through books and even the Internet seems to be a kind of arrogance and presumption. It ignores the biblical reminder that there is wisdom in "the multitude of counselors" (Prov 11:14 KJV).

It also forgets another biblical observation that learning from other godly minds and comparing our thoughts with theirs is like iron sharpening iron (Prov 27:17), making our thinking about God sharper and clearer.

The result will be deeper knowledge of God, which Jesus said is "eternal life" (Jn 17:3).

This is the beginning of an answer to the question, How do we know which theology is best? The best way is to study the theologies of the greatest minds of the church. That's what we will begin to do in this book.

WHY THESE THEOLOGIANS?

No doubt you will wonder why I chose these eleven. (I like the fact that the number is odd because it rightly suggests that theology is provisional and incomplete.)

Generally, these are the eleven I consider to have had the most influence on the history of Christian thought. Origen's way of reading shaped Bible interpretation for the next fifteen hundred years. Athanasius saved the church from degenerating into a little sect of Greek philosophy. Augustine was perhaps the most influential of all theologians—East or West—teaching us all, for instance, the meaning of grace. Thomas Aquinas was declared by the Catholic Church to be its foremost Doctor (teacher), and he showed us how faith relates to reason and the meaning of "sacrament." Luther's efforts to reform the Catholic Church were the principal stimulus to the rise of Protestantism. Calvin was the first and greatest teacher of that second great Protestant tradition, the Reformed movement. Edwards was the greatest religious thinker to grace the American continent and also the premier Christian thinker about how God relates to beauty. Friedrich Schleiermacher was the father of liberal theology. John Henry Newman was the great reformer of the Church of England who famously became a Catholic and showed us how doctrine develops through time. Barth was the most influential of all twentieth-century theologians, and von Balthasar, a contemporary of Barth, is fast becoming the most important Catholic theologian for this new century.

There were others who also had great influence, and a future list maker might prove that one or more of my eleven were edged out by one or more with even greater influence.

Who are some of those others? To list just a few, I have left out the Cappadocians (Basil the Great, Gregory of Nazianzus and Gregory of Nyssa) and other Eastern theologians, Irenaeus, Clement of Alexandria, Anselm, Teresa of Ávila, and such "moderns" as John Wesley, Charles Hodge,

Henri de Lubac, Dietrich Bonhoeffer, C. S. Lewis (not usually considered a theologian but one with remarkable influence on Christian thought nonetheless), Edith Stein, Sergei Bulgakov, Simone Weil, H. Richard Niebuhr, John Paul II and Benedict XVI. Perhaps, if this book does well, I might write another book devoted to some or all of these.

But all the theologians in this book have had great influence on the development of Christian thought. That doesn't mean that the theology of every one has been good. In fact, some have done damage to Christian thinking. For example, Schleiermacher, the father of liberal theology, has caused multitudes to question orthodoxy by saying that theology and creeds are simply words used to depict inner feelings, which suggests that Christian faith is more about what is inside us than objective reality outside us. But I include him in this book because his influence has been enormous. Anyone who has any interest in modern Christian theology must understand Schleiermacher if she or he is to comprehend the strange turns modern theology has taken.

Are these eleven the *greatest*? As I have just suggested, I am not sure. I must confess that my own personal interests have influenced me. For example, some colleagues would not agree that Newman was the most significant theologian of the nineteenth century. I included him not only because of his huge influence on both Protestants and Catholics but also because I find him so personally intriguing.

But if these eleven are not indisputably the most significant theologians of the last two millennia, they are nevertheless all very important and exceedingly influential. Anyone trying to become acquainted with Christian theology will get a handy overview of the last two thousand years by learning what is distinctive to each.

THE FORMAT

I think it is important when coming to theology for the first time to get a big and personal picture first before diving into the theological details. So each chapter starts with a biographical sketch of the theologian, telling a story about that theologian's life or important events in his life. Then it briefly introduces the main themes of that person's thinking.

The third and most important section of each chapter zeroes in on one theme that is distinctive to that thinker and examines it in some detail. It is not always the only theme that the theologian is famous for. But it is distinctive to his theology and has had particular impact on the Christian church.

After the discussion of an important distinctive theme, I highlight several lessons I think we can learn from the theologian. At the end of each chapter there are two further helps to the new student of theology. The first is a short selection—typically two to four hundred words—from the theologian's works, which elucidates one of the theologian's most important themes—usually one discussed in the chapter.

At the end of each chapter is a list of books. One is by the particular theologian and one or more are *about* that theologian. These are suggestions for those readers who want to go further.

There are also questions for discussion at the end. These are ideal for Sunday school classes or home study groups. This book can then be the focus for a thirteen-week series—one chapter a week.

Once you finish this book, you will be able to nod appreciatively and even critically when a pastor—or a writer—refers to one of these "greats." You won't feel out to lunch, but will know that you have joined what has been called "the Great Conversation."

Happy reading and thinking.

QUESTIONS FOR REFLECTION AND DISCUSSION

1. Why do *you* want to study the great theologians?

2. In what way does everyone have a theology?

3. Why is it important to study the great theologians while reading the Bible?

2

Origen

Oft-Reviled but
"The Greatest Teacher After the Apostles"

Born in A.D. 185 to Christian parents, probably in Alexandria, Origen (185-253) was something of a child prodigy. Encouraged by his father, the boy not only memorized huge portions of the Bible but eagerly probed their deeper meaning. His father, delighted by his son's love for the Lord and the Bible, would go to the sleeping boy at night and kiss his breast "as if it was the temple of a divine spirit," blessing God for being given such a promising child.[1]

When Emperor Septimius Severus launched a persecution of the church in 202, seventeen-year-old Origen begged his father not to waver: "Mind you, don't change your mind on our account."[2] His father apparently listened to his son, for he perished in the attacks. Origen was prevented from fulfilling his desire for martyrdom only when his mother hid his clothes, preventing him from appearing in public.

Because of his prodigious ability and the loss of his teachers to persecution, Origen was made head of the church's catechetical school within a year of his father's death. By night he studied the Bible and by day he prepared his students for martyrdom.

---

[1]Eusebius *The History of the Church from Christ to Constantine* 6.2., trans. G. A. Williamson (Harmondsworth, U.K.: Penguin, 1965). Joseph W. Trigg doubts the authenticity of this story, but adds that "even if not reliable, such stories indicate the impression Origen made on others" (Joseph W. Trigg, *Origen* [New York: Routledge, 1998], p. 3).
[2]Eusebius *History of the Church* 6.2.

For not only when they were in prison, or were being cross-examined, up to the final sentence, but even when they were afterwards led away to execution, he was at the side of the holy martyrs, displaying astonishing fearlessness and meeting danger face to face. As he boldly approached and fearlessly greeted the martyrs with a kiss, again and again the maddened crowd of pagans that surrounded him was on the point of stoning him.[3]

Moving from house to house to avoid those plotting against him, Origen fasted both food and sleep in his effort to grow closer to God. For several years he went without shoes, abstained from wine and subsisted on a minimum of nourishment. After a time he started a school similar to Justin Martyr's in Rome,[4] teaching Greek philosophy to all who cared to learn. Thousands flocked to hear him. Those familiar with philosophy remarked that his knowledge of the classics was unparalleled.

When Origen was nearly thirty, he was asked by two bishops in Palestine to move there to preach and teach. While there the bishop of Alexandria excommunicated Origen, probably because he was jealous of Origen's renown.

In 249, when Decius unleashed his cruel persecution of Christians, Origen was granted his wish to suffer for Christ. Eusebius writes of the sixty-five-year-old's "agony in iron and the darkness of his prison; how for days on end his legs were pulled four paces apart in the torturer's stocks—the courage with which he bore threats of fire and every torture devised by his enemies," and the "messages full of help for those in need of comfort."[5] Origen was released from prison before he died, but his health was broken. Death came shortly after.

BAD REPUTATION

Despite his holiness, devotion and theological influence, Origen's reputation has suffered under a cloud to this day. There are two reasons for this. First, in a fit of teenage religious zeal, he castrated himself. Eusebius explains that this was an attempt, in an uncharacteristically literalist reading, to fulfill his Savior's observation that some "made themselves eunuchs for

---

[3]Ibid., 6.3.
[4]Justin Martyr (c. 100-c. 165) opened a school in Rome to teach "Christian philosophy," which he said was the fulfillment of whatever truth was taught in other philosophies.
[5]Eusebius *History of the Church* 6.39.

the sake of the kingdom of heaven" (Mt 19:12).[6] The other reason is that some of his teachings were later judged to be heretical. The most notorious was his suggestion that all creatures might eventually be saved, including the devil himself. There is also dispute about whether he suggested the possibility of the transmigration of souls (reincarnation).

Origen, however, never advanced these, or any other irregular ideas, as dogmatic doctrines.[7] For one thing, the editor of Origen's principal theological treatise confessed he had altered Origen's text.[8] So we don't know if these views were actually taught by Origen. Second, Origen "put forward his views for discussion, not as settled dogmas."[9] Origen feared heresy, arguing it would destroy the church. Eusebius tells us Origen kept "from his earliest years the rule of the Church and 'abominat[ed]'—the very word he uses somewhere himself—all heretical teachings."[10] He advanced new ideas only tentatively, always acknowledging the church's right to condemn them if they were contrary to the rule of faith. Some of his ideas were later condemned as heretical, but he was never formally branded a heretic because his erroneous opinions were always concerning questions that at the time had not been settled. He was bound, he said, to church teaching. "But[, for instance,] what existed before this world, or what will exist after it, has not yet been made known openly to the many, for no clear statement on the point is set forth in the Church teaching."[11]

His questionable teachings were usually developed in attempts to undermine other heresies. For example, Origen emphasized human freedom in order to combat the Gnostics, who said there is nothing you can do to change your eternal fate. Origen imagined that freedom must be an eternal constant—hence the freedom of even the devils and the damned to change their minds. Long after Origen's death, the church condemned this idea. But should we discount everything else this teacher of the church

---

[6]Ibid., 6.8. Eusebius tells us that Origen later regretted this, and, even later, argued against such a literal reading of the Gospel text (ibid.). Some historians have cast doubt on the authenticity of Eusebius's story, but Trigg says "it seems" that this is what happened (Trigg, *Origen*, p. 14).

[7]Dogmatic doctrines are propositions that must be believed in order to remain orthodox.

[8]Rufinus, preface to Origen *On First Principles*, intro. Henri de Lubac (Gloucester, Mass.: Peter Smith, 1973), p. lxiii.

[9]G. W. Butterworth, introduction to *On First Principles*, by Origen (Gloucester, Mass.: Peter Smith, 1973), p. xxxvii.

[10]Eusebius *History of the Church* 6.2.

[11]Origen *On First Principles* preface 7.

wrote because he tentatively explored questions that the church had not yet settled?

Origen declared himself to be a *vir ecclesiasticus* (man of the church) and insisted that he would never knowingly violate any church doctrine. In fact, if the church decided that any part of his teaching was in error, he hoped the church would condemn it.

> I bear the title of priest and, as you see, I preach the Word of God. But if I do anything contrary to the discipline of the Church or the rule laid down in the Gospels—if I give offence to you and to the Church—then I hope the whole Church will unite with one consent and cast me off.[12]

THE GREATEST TEACHER AFTER THE APOSTLES

The fourth-century biblical scholar Jerome said Origen was the greatest teacher of the church after the apostles.[13] Origen's *De Principiis (On First Principles)* was the first systematic theology, the first Christian attempt at a coherent interpretation of Christianity as a whole. Over the course of his career, Origen wrote somewhere between one and two thousand works, most of which were tragically destroyed by the same man (Emperor Justinian) who built in Constantinople (now Istanbul) Hagia Sophia, the greatest church building of the first millennium. Origen's impact on later Christian thinking was profound, influencing Eusebius and the Cappadocian theologians (Basil the Great, Gregory of Nazianzus and Gregory of Nyssa), Maximus the Confessor, Hilary of Poitiers and Ambrose of Milan. He who "tower[ed] above the Greek fathers as Augustine tower[ed] above the Latins,"[14] has also been called the "ancestor of the great monastic movement of the fourth century."[15]

But Origen was not just a theologian. Above all, he was a teacher of the Bible, with a pastor's heart. The pastoral challenges he faced sound remarkably similar to those facing pastors in the twenty-first century. Immersed in a culture more interested in undemanding pantheism than rig-

---

[12]Origen *Homily on Joshua* 7.6, cited in Jean Danielou, *Origen*, trans. Walter Mitchell (New York: Sheed & Ward, 1955), p. 8.

[13]Later in his life, when Origen's work came under suspicion of heresy, Jerome changed his mind.

[14]Butterworth, introduction to *On First Principles*, p. xxvii.

[15]Danielou, *Origen*, p. vii.

orous discipleship, many Christians gave scant attention to their own religion, were more concerned with pleasure and commerce, and even when in church wanted to be titillated with amusing stories rather than difficult strictures from the Scriptures. Listen to an excerpt from one of Origen's sermons.

> The Lord has entrusted me with the task of giving his household their allowance of food [Bible teaching] at the appointed time [Lk 12:42]. . . . But how can I? Where and when can I find a time when you will listen to me? The greater part of your time, nearly all of it in fact, you spend on mundane things, in the market-place or the shops; some of you are busy in the country, others wrapped up in litigation. Nobody, or hardly anybody, bothers about God's Word. . . . But why complain about those who are not here? Even those who are, those of you who have come to church, are paying no attention. You can take an interest in tales that have become worn out through repetition, but you turn your backs on God's Word and the reading of Holy Scripture.[16]

Origen complained that some stood in the corner of church and gabbed while the Bible was being read or preached. He lamented that although he urged the young men to study the Bible, he had wasted his time. "None" seemed to take his suggestion.

ORIGEN'S GREATEST CONTRIBUTION

Origen laid the foundations for the ways we think about the Trinity (by, among other things, suggesting that Jesus was eternally generated by the Father and therefore different from all other created beings) and about the relation between Christ's human and divine natures (by pointing out that Scripture applies the properties of either nature to the other).

His model of spirituality became standard for the medieval church and later: a *mysticism* of ascent in which the believer is led heavenward to seeing and enjoying the infinite splendors of the Logos. *Mysticism* means having direct communion with God. *Logos* is Greek for "Word" and refers to the second person of the Trinity, Jesus Christ, who Origen said fills the whole cosmos of human beings and angels imparting life, light, trust and resur-

---

[16]Origen *Homilies on Genesis* 10.1 in ibid., p. 42. A full English translation is *Homilies on Genesis and Exodus/Origen*, ed. and trans. Ronald Heine (Washington, D.C.: Catholic University of America Press, 1992).

rection. The Logos is incarnated in three ways—in his resurrected body in the Eucharist (Communion), in the church which is his body and in Scripture. Origen emphasized the necessity of personal holiness for making progress in this upward pilgrimage, including the use of Scripture. Here he said believers can find the real presence of Christ, but only if they are seeking holiness and the spiritual sense of the text.

Before we discuss the impact this model of spirituality had on the later church, let's pause to reflect that we see several themes in Origen that will reappear in later Christian theology. The first is asceticism, the idea that it is helpful in our pilgrimage to the heavenly city to deprive ourselves of the pleasures of the flesh. Origen slept on the floor and went without shoes and wine; he avoided martyrdom in his teen years, but his constant pursuit of prayer and study were a kind of living martyrdom. Jonathan Edwards (see chap. 8) was similar; he worked in his study twelve to fourteen hours every day and purposely cut back on food and drink and sleep to keep himself sharp and in a state of self-denial. In Edwards we see also an Origen-like emphasis on seeing God by something like mystical vision. Edwards himself spoke of being "rapt up" to heaven and being "swallowed up" by God. Interestingly, both prized the Song of Songs; Origen wrote three commentaries on it in ten volumes, and Edwards commented on it extensively with delight. Both saw it as an erotic poem whose first meaning was to portray the love between God and his people.

But now let's get back to Origen's spirituality and stress on the Bible's spiritual meaning. It was this emphasis on the spiritual sense of the biblical text—for the purpose of mystical ascent—that left what was perhaps Origen's greatest mark on the history of Christianity. Origen unfolded a "spiritual interpretation of the Bible" that became the "unanimous interpretation" of the church in its first fifteen hundred years. Its aim was to discern in the Old Testament the sense that the gospel gave to it.[17]

Origen believed this was the way Jesus and the apostles read the Old Testament. Paul was his principal teacher. In 1 Corinthians 10 ("Our fathers . . . drank from the spiritual Rock that followed them, and the Rock was Christ. . . . Now these things . . . were written down for our instruction") and Galatians 4 ("Abraham had two sons, one by a slave woman and

---

[17]Robert Wilken, foreword to Henri de Lubac, *Medieval Exegesis*, vol. 1, *The Four Senses of Scripture* (1959; reprint, Grand Rapids: Eerdmans, 1998), pp. ix-x.

one by a free woman. . . . [T]his may be interpreted allegorically: these women are two covenants") Paul teaches that all of the Old Testament must be read in the light "of the prodigious new fact of Christ." In the words of Henri de Lubac, the great historian of biblical hermeneutics, for Origen "Jesus Christ brings about the unity of Scripture because he is the endpoint and fullness of Scripture. Everything in it is related to him. In the end, he is its sole object. Consequently, he is, so to speak, its whole exegesis."[18]

Of course the Old Testament never refers to Jesus by name. So how are we to understand the Bible as always referring to Jesus Christ?

The first thing to notice is that Jesus himself seemed to believe this was the case. Luke tells us that he "interpreted to [the disciples on the road to Emmaus] in all the Scriptures the things concerning himself" (Lk 24:27). By "the Scriptures" Luke meant the Old Testament, the only Scriptures at that time.

Origen taught that in order to see Christ in the Old Testament (and therefore the highest meaning of this Testament), we must realize there is not just a single meaning to a biblical passage. This was the mistake of the Gnostics, against whom Origen battled. I might add that this is a common mistake today as well, made by both orthodox and nonorthodox. Origen was convinced—and the church followed his lead for fifteen hundred years—that just as Jesus saw both the literal meaning of an Old Testament text and its spiritual meaning as referring to himself, and just as Paul could say that when Deuteronomy commands us not to muzzle the ox when it is treading out the grain (Deut 25:4), it really means we should pay our pastors (1 Cor 9:9-12), the proper conclusion is that most Scripture passages therefore have more than one layer of meaning. If we assume each passage has only one meaning, and that it is restricted to the original intent of the human author of that passage, then we will miss the rich and beautiful biblical drama that was created not by the human authors but by the divine Author behind the human authors.

THE FOURFOLD SENSE OF SCRIPTURE

Origen developed what later became known as the *four*fold sense of the Bible.[19] The first is the *literal* or *historical* sense, which means, in the case

---

[18]de Lubac, *Medieval Exegesis*, 1:237.
[19]Origen spoke most often of three senses, corresponding to what he thought to be the three parts of the human person—body, soul and spirit. Cassian (c. 360-c. 430) then developed

of the Old Testament, "what happened" in the text. Let's say the passage is Genesis 22, the story of Abraham's near-sacrifice of Isaac. "What happened" is that Abraham offered Isaac as a sacrifice to God, in obedience to God's command. At the last minute God intervened to stop Abraham from slaying his son, and provided a ram instead for the sacrifice. These events constitute the literal or historical sense.

Then there is the *allegorical* sense or "what you should believe." This is the most important part of the spiritual understanding, the part that shows us Christ. For Origen, both the ram and Isaac represent, or are *types* (that is, Old Testament people or things that point to New Testament realities) of, Christ, who was the perfect sacrifice on our behalf. The ram represents the flesh of Christ, which was killed on Calvary. But Isaac stands for "Christ according to the Spirit," who "remained incorruptible." The ram perished, but Isaac did not. What is the allegorical or spiritual lesson here? "Abraham offered to God his mortal son, who did not die, and God gave up his immortal Son who died for all of us."[20]

The third layer of meaning is the *moral* or *tropological*—"what you should do." In other words, what instruction does this give us for living our Christian lives? In this case, Origen would say we should respond in gratitude and praise for God's sacrifice of Christ for us, and in turn we should offer our own lives up as a sacrifice to God.

The last layer is the *anagogical*, which is Greek for "leading up." It refers to "what we should aim for" in heaven. Origen might say this passage reminds us that in heaven we will have the beatific vision of the "Lamb who was slain" from the foundation of the world (Rev 13:8), and that all our lives should be led in anticipation of that blessed sight.

Although this way of interpreting the Old Testament was not new, Origen developed the various layers of meaning in profound ways, and used them extensively in his many biblical commentaries. Preachers and theologians used and learned from these commentaries for many centuries. They found that layers of meaning gave meaning to parts of the Old Testament whose value seemed otherwise puzzling. For example, Origen said the stories of Israel's wars against Canaanites were full of lessons for Christians about their inner wars against the world, the flesh and the devil.

Origen's layers of meaning into a carefully elaborated fourfold sense.

[20]Origen *Homilies on Genesis and Exodus*, p. 144.

But Origen added that not every believer will be able to understand all these layers of meaning. Just as humans are made up of body, soul and spirit, so too Scripture has corresponding layers. The most simple believer will discern only the body of Scripture—its literal or historical sense. Those a bit more advanced will be able to see the soul of Scripture—perhaps its moral (tropological) meaning. The most mature will discern in a passage the "secret and hidden wisdom of God"—the allegorical and anagogical meanings. Origen believed Paul had something like this in mind in 1 Corinthians 2:6-7 when he said, "Among the mature we do impart wisdom. . . . [A] secret and hidden wisdom of God," and in 1 Corinthians 3:1 when he referred to "people of the flesh, . . . infants in Christ."

Origen developed this multiple sense of Scripture in his battles with the Gnostics, who said the gods of the Old and New Testaments are two different gods. The first is irrational and cruel, and the second is kind and loving. The Gnostics said the Father of Jesus would never have given the law to the Jews. They pointed to Old Testament events and prescriptions that to them seemed ridiculous or cruel.

Origen's response was to appeal to the early church's "rule of truth," which was eventually developed into the Nicene and Apostles' creeds. He said this "rule" came down from the apostles and that it affirmed the unity of the two Testaments. So both Testaments came from the Father of Jesus Christ. The New Testament was the hermeneutical key to the Old Testament, which contained the "shadows" and "types" of the New.

One of the Gnostics might have been a teacher named Paul, who came to Alexandria from Antioch. Origen said he was a heretic. Apparently Paul was a powerful speaker, for he attracted large numbers to his talks, both heretics and orthodox. Origen says he "loathed" this teacher's doctrine and refused to join in his prayers.[21]

In his treatise written against Marcion, a heretic who was influenced by Gnosticism to reject both the Jewish God and the Old Testament, Origen wrote that Marcion and others like him speak of a Christ different from that of the New Testament. Hence there are "two Christs." One is that of the heretics, who reject the Christ's prefigurings (shadows and types) in

---

[21]Trigg, *Origen*, pp. 7-8.

the Old Testament and the whole Testament altogether. The other is the true Christ who is the true subject of both Testaments.

Origen's pursuit of the spiritual sense of Scripture has been criticized for its tendency to all but abolish the literal meaning of the Old Testament. For example, Origen wrote that the Levitical command to eat only animals that chew the cud really means that believers are to meditate on the law of God. There is spiritual insight in this reflection, but it would be dangerous to abandon all historical-critical study of the Bible. We would have far less understanding of Jesus and Israel if we had not studied the Dead Sea Scrolls, second-temple Judaism and Greco-Roman customs. All these areas of research were stimulated by a desire to understand the literal meaning of the Bible.

Ironically, the same Origen who stressed so heavily the spiritual sense of the Bible also produced the *Hexapla*, the most important work of biblical criticism before the modern era. This was a sixty-five hundred-page book that put side-by-side six different renditions of the Old Testament, one in Hebrew and five in Greek. His purpose was to use it for interreligious discussions with Jews and others. He also made extensive notes on variant readings of the New Testament.

Origen fought fiercely for true doctrine. He believed that false doctrine was worse than bad morality, perhaps because the former leads people away from the true God (and true morality as well). Heretics, he said, call Jesus their master and embrace him, but their kiss is the kiss of Judas.[22] Origen is noted in the history of apologetics for his *Contra Celsum*, a massive work of careful reasoning that uses a Greek philosophical framework to argue boldly for the incarnation of God in Jesus. It is widely regarded as the capstone of ancient Christian apologetics (before Augustine's *City of God*, which appeared after paganism had started to recede).

WHAT WE CAN TAKE AWAY

What can we learn from Origen's approach to the Bible? Three things, I believe.

1. A new way of seeing the Bible's unity. It is one book, finally, because there is one author—the Holy Spirit. Too often we have let modern his-

---

[22]de Lubac, introduction to *Origen on First Principles*, pp. xiii-xiv.

torical criticism dominate our understanding of Scripture. Its purpose and sometimes its results are helpful, for they illuminate a book's historical and cultural background, which helps us in turn hear the message of the book. But too often its results suggest the Bible is but a collection of contradictory messages. In addition, its restriction of focus on background historical issues leaves us feeling dry and unsatisfied. And it is no wonder, for its practitioners often presume they know what can and cannot happen—so that biblical miracles and prophecies are assumed to be spurious. These scholars remind us of the professors whom John of Salisbury (c. 1115-1180) described as proud of their scientific knowledge but rather unspiritual:

> In the chariot of the eunuch of the Queen of Ethiopia they discuss and read the Scriptures with eyes closed, and they disdain or are unable to see him who is "led like a lamb to the slaughter" (Isaiah 53). . . . In any case, although they are seated on the wheels of Scripture, and are borne by a motion of winged animals, their tongue, when they discuss higher things, licks at the earth; nor do they understand the Scriptures, because the Lord of every kind of knowledge does not open their hearts.[23]

Such an approach fails to explain how the psalmist could say, "Oh [LORD,] how I love your law" (Ps 119:97). But seeing Origen's passion for the Bible, which he saw as the location for the real presence of the Logos in every passage, helps us imagine how the Scriptures can have a single message—Jesus Christ. As Origen put it, "All Divine Scripture is the Gospel."[24]

2. A new appreciation for the profundity of Scripture. For Origen, and those whose vision was fired by his,

> Scripture is like the world: "undecipherable in its fullness and in the multiplicity of its meanings." [It is] a deep forest, with innumerable branches, "an infinite forest of meanings": the more involved one gets in it, the more one discovers that it is impossible to explore it right to its end. It is a table arranged by Wisdom, laden with food, where the unfathomable divinity of the Savior is itself offered as nourishment to all. Treasure of the Holy Spirit, whose riches are as infinite as himself. True labyrinth. Deep heavens, unfathomable abyss. Vast sea, where there is endless voyaging "with all sails set." Ocean of mystery.[25]

---

[23]Quoted in de Lubac, *Medieval Exegesis*, 1:265-66.
[24]Quoted in ibid., 1:246.
[25]de Lubac, *Medieval Exegesis*, 1:75. The quotations are from, in order, Jonah of Orleans, Jerome,

So Origen can help us gain or renew a vision for the infinite beauty of Scripture, and a reverence for its mystery. We can drop behind us the Enlightenment's false presumption that it can reduce the Bible to being a product of history or sociology or power politics, and nothing more. More important, we may be able to see afresh that, as Origen put it, behind every letter of the Bible is the ineffable goodness of God.[26]

3. A new openness to Scripture's role in our spiritual formation. For Origen, knowledge of Scripture was less for polemical purposes and far more for knowledge of God. But knowledge of God, while it starts with intellectual apprehension of the words of Scripture, must end with a tabernacling of the Word in our hearts. We are to be formed into God's image—or more specifically, the image of Christ. The medieval devotion to the *imitatio Christi* was indebted largely to Origen.

Origen is also the fountainhead of an immense stream of Christian tradition that aims at divinization (also called "deification")—the idea that believers participate in the divinity of Christ. Origen pointed often to 2 Peter 1:3-4 ("His divine power has granted to us . . . his precious and very great promises, so that through them you may become *partakers of the divine nature*" [italics added]), saying that we are not to be merely imitators of Christ but actually share in his very nature. While teaching that we can share in the divine nature, he warned that this still means there is an infinite difference between Christ and the saint—Christ is divine by nature, but the saint is divine only by participation. We will see in the pages that follow that divinization played an important role in the thought of other great theologians such as Athanasius and Edwards. We may have trouble thinking about this, but it is a helpful reminder that Scripture's purpose is not just to impart head knowledge but to enable us to share in the very life of the Trinity.

A SELECTION FROM ORIGEN'S WORKS

And Paul in addressing the Corinthians as "babes" and as people "behaving like ordinary men" (cf. 1 Cor. 3:1, 3) says, "I fed you with milk, not solid food; for you were not ready for it; and even yet you are not ready, for you are still of the flesh" (1 Cor. 3:2-3). And in Hebrews he says, "You need milk, not solid food; for everyone who lives on milk is unskilled in the word of righteousness, for he is a

---

Gregory, Richard of St. Victor, John of Salisbury, Jerome, Autpertus, Ambrose and Origen.
[26]Ibid., 1:76.

child. But solid food is for the perfect, for those who have their faculties trained by practice to distinguish good from evil" (Heb. 5:12-14). And I think that the verse, "One believes he may eat anything, while the weak man eats only vegetables" (Rom. 14:2) refers not primarily to his corporeal food, but to the words of God that nourish the soul. The first one, who is most faithful and perfect, can partake of all of them, as is indicated by "one believes he may eat anything." But the other one, who is weaker and less perfect, is content with the simpler teachings and with those that do not produce much vigor, as Paul wishes to indicate when he says, "The weak man eats only vegetables."

And I think that what is said by Solomon in Proverbs teaches that the one who cannot receive the more vigorous and greater teachings because of his simplicity and yet does not stumble in his thinking is better than the one who is quicker and sharper and applies himself to these matters more fully, but does not see clearly the meaning of peace and of the harmony of the universe. This is what the verse says, "Better is a dinner of vegetables with friendship and grace than a fatted calf with hatred" (Prov. 15:17). And so we often accept a common and more simple dinner with a good conscience, when we are entertained by those unable to offer us any more, in preference to words lifted on high against the knowledge of God (cf. 1 Cor. 10:5), which proclaim with great persuasiveness a teaching foreign to the Law and the prophets given by the Father of our Lord Jesus (cf. Mt. 5:17, 7:12, 22:40; Lk. 16:16). Therefore, lest we should be sick through lack of food for the soul or die because of a famine of the Lord's Word (cf. Amos 8:11; Rom. 14:8; Gal. 2:19), let us ask the Father for the "living bread," who is the same as the "daily bread." Let us obey our Savior as teacher, believing and living more worthily.[27]

FOR REFLECTION AND DISCUSSION

1. What is most inspiring about Origen's life?

2. What did Origen mean when he said he was a *vir ecclesiasticus* (man of the church)? Should we be the same?

3. Is it encouraging or discouraging to see the problems in Origen's church (for example, that Christians even then did not always pay attention to sermons)? Why?

---

[27]From *Origen: An Exhortation to Martyrdom, Prayer and Selected Works*, trans. and intro. Rowan A. Greer, pref. Hans Urs von Balthasar (New York: Paulist Press, 1979).

4. Ask someone in your group to rehearse for everyone the fourfold sense. Try to use it on the parable of the good Samaritan.

5. How does the idea of the unity of the Bible help our thinking when we come upon two passages that seem to contradict each other? For example, Paul says we are "not justified by works of the law but through faith in Jesus Christ" (Gal 2:16), and James says that "a person is justified by works and not by faith alone" (Jas 2:24).

6. Origen believed the Bible was an ocean of mystery. Does this perspective help us approach the Word of God with more respect and reverence?

FOR FURTHER READING

Origen *On First Principles*. Introduction by Henri de Lubac. Gloucester, Mass.: Peter Smith, 1973.

————. *Homilies on Genesis and Exodus/Origen*. Edited and translated by Ronald Heine. Washington, D.C.: Catholic University of America Press, 1992.

Chadwick, Henry. *Origen: Contra Celsum*. Cambridge: Cambridge University Press, 1953.

Clark, Elizabeth A. *The Origenist Controversy*. Princeton, N.J.: Princeton University Press, 1992.

Eusebius. *The History of the Church from Christ to Constantine*, pp. 239-48, 255-74. Translated by and introduction by G. A. Williamson. Harmondsworth, U.K.: Penguin Books, 1965.

Trigg, Joseph W. *Origen*. London and New York: Routledge, 1998.

3

Athanasius

The Black Monk Who Saved the Faith

Athanasius (c. 296-373) was a short, swarthy Egyptian (hence the epithet "black dwarf" given him by his enemies) who repeatedly outwitted and out-thought his Arian opponents. They often beat him in the short-term—his battles with them lasted almost fifty years, and he was exiled five times during those years. He never lived to see his cause prevail. Yet eventually, after his death, the orthodox position he tirelessly championed finally won the day.

The risks were huge. As C. S. Lewis put it, if Athanasius had not fought so bravely and persistently, orthodox Christianity might have disappeared from history.[1]

> His epitaph is *Athanasius contra mundum*, "Athanasius against the world." We are proud that our own country has more than once stood against the world. Athanasius did the same. He stood for the Trinitarian doctrine, "whole and undefiled," when it looked as if all the civilized world was slipping back from Christianity into the religion of Arius—into one of those "sensible" synthetic religions which are so strongly recommended to-day [*sic*] and which, then as now, included among their devotees many highly cultivated clergymen. It is his glory that he did not move with the times; it is his reward that he now remains when those times, as all times do, have moved away.[2]

---

[1] Of course Jesus promised "the gates of hell shall not prevail against" his church (Mt 16:18). But we could say that God used Athanasius's lone finger in the dike, as it were, to prevent a flood of heresy from drowning orthodoxy—if not forever, at least for a time.

[2] C. S. Lewis, introduction to Athanasius *On the Incarnation: The Treatise "De Incarnatione Verbi*

The future saint and "Doctor" (Latin for "teacher") of the Eastern Church grew up in a little village on the banks of the Nile. He spoke Coptic—the language of ordinary Egyptians—and probably came from a lower-class family. When he was only five years old, the emperor Diocletian launched the most ferocious persecution of the first three centuries of the church. It didn't stop until Athanasius was fourteen, in 311, under the new emperor Maximin. (But later, Maximin renewed the persecutions.)

Athanasius survived, and it strengthened his faith. Moved by the courage of the martyrs, he was drawn to serious discipleship. His friend Gregory of Nazianzus—another Doctor of the Eastern Church—said the young man Athanasius "meditate[ed] on every book of the Old and New Testament, with a depth such as none else has applied even to one of them." [3] Athanasius had at least one excellent mentor. He wrote later in his *Life of Saint Antony (Anthony)* that when he (Athanasius) was a young man, he would often go out into the desert to help care for and learn from the old Antony, who lived as a holy hermit in prayer and meditation.

When he was thirty, Athanasius attended the famous Council of Nicaea (325) in what is now Turkey. As a deacon Athanasius had no vote, but the proceedings made a deep impression on him. He became rock-hard in his conviction that the essence of Christianity is the presence of God as a human being among men and women in the person of Jesus of Nazareth, and that nothing short of that divine dwelling in human flesh could save human beings from corruption and death. He likened this divine visitation to the visit of a king to a city. Because of his visit the city gains new honor and is protected against attacks by bandits. So too we humans have been visited by God himself. He has joined our race and now protects us from attacks by the evil one. Now we are free to become what God intended us to be in the first place—creatures who share his very life.

Just three years later Athanasius was made—against his wishes—bishop of Alexandria, one of the greatest cities of the empire. That same year Emperor Constantine revoked the sentence banishing Arius from Alexandria. Arius had taught that Jesus was more than just a man but less than

---

Dei, trans. and ed. "A Religious of C.S.M.V." (Crestwood, N.Y.: St. Vladimir's Seminary Press, 1996), pp. 8-9.
[3]Gregory of Nazianzus *Oration* 21, 6; cited in Thomas G. Weinandy, *Athanasius: A Theological Introduction* (Burlington, Vt.: Ashgate, 2007), p. 1.

fully God, and the Council at Nicaea had declared Jesus' full deity. As a result, Arius had been prevented from returning to his former ministry as a deacon in Alexandria.

But now that Constantine had given the Arian cause new life, the followers of Arius were emboldened. They circulated rumors that Athanasius dabbled in magic. A synod in Tyre (now Lebanon) accused him of having murdered another bishop by the name of Arsenius. They also charged that he had cut off Arsenius's hand for use in special magical rites.

Tradition has it that when Athanasius came to a hearing at Tyre, he brought with him a man whose head was covered by a hood. Because Athanasius knew there were bishops at Tyre who had known Arsenius personally, he waited until the bishops were present before he removed the man's hood. There were audible gasps when the man turned out to be Arsenius himself, very much alive.

Some protested, "Yes, but maybe Athanasius really did cut off his hand." Athanasius then held up the bishop's one hand.

Others yelled, "Show us his other hand!" Athanasius then held up the bishop's other hand and asked, "What do you think this man is—a monster with three hands?" Everyone laughed. The plot against Athanasius was foiled, but only for a while.

Some time later Athanasius went to Constantinople (now Istanbul) to argue his case before Emperor Constantine. The emperor's Arian advisers, however, would not let him in. So on a day when Athanasius knew the emperor was going for a ride on his horse, the little bishop bolted out of hiding and grabbed the reins of the emperor's horse, forcing it to stop. The emperor was angry. So when one of Athanasius's rivals told the emperor in 335 that Athanasius had threatened to cut off Egyptian grain shipments to Rome, Constantine banished him to Trier (in today's Germany). By this time Athanasius had become so popular with the people of Alexandria that riots broke out there on his behalf.

In 337 Constantine died, and his three sons, ruling jointly, permitted all exiled bishops to return. Athanasius started to approach Alexandria, but riots again threatened, so he went to Rome instead. There he was able to convince Julius, the bishop of Rome, that Arius was wrong and Nicaea was right—Jesus was fully God and not simply a divine emissary.

Yet Arianism was still on the march. It seemed to have won the war when in 351 a council of bishops gathered at Sirmium (in today's Serbia) and openly rejected the decision at Nicaea.

That ecclesiastical victory seemed to be sealed politically when in 353 Constantius, one of Constantine's sons, gained sole possession of the empire. The new emperor was rigorously pro-Arian. By threats and force he compelled most of the bishops to accept Arianism. He tried to compel Athanasius as well. When the latter was celebrating communion one night in Alexandria, the church was suddenly surrounded by five thousand soldiers armed with swords, bows, clubs and spears. The general in charge forced his way in and commanded all the people to come out. Amid cries of desperation, Athanasius ordered the congregation to sing Psalm 136, with the refrain "For his mercy endures forever." The soldiers pushed their way through the crowd, trying to get at their bishop, but he announced he would not leave until all the congregation had escaped. His clergy formed a circle around him, he fainted, and in the ensuing commotion they somehow spirited him out of the building and away from the soldiers.

For the next five years Athanasius lived in the desert with legions of scattered monks, moving whenever word came that troops were approaching. Back in the cities of the empire, Arianism seemed to have triumphed. As Jerome put it, "The whole world groaned and was astonished to find itself Arian."[4]

But then Constantius died in 360 and Julian the Apostate ascended the throne. Athanasius was able to return to his home, but only for a while. Julian, like his predecessors, was threatened by Athanasius's position and banished him again. During this exile, when Athanasius once more was trying to elude the authorities, he was traveling up-river on the Nile, with an imperial ship about to overtake him. Soldiers on the imperial ship called out, "Have you seen Athanasius?"

Athanasius answered truthfully, "Yes, he is just ahead of you. But if you hurry, you can catch him."

The great theologian died in 373, his cause apparently lost. It would be another eight years before the universal church regained its footing at the Second Ecumenical Council in 381, when it reaffirmed Nicene orthodoxy—repudiating Arianism once and for all.

---

[4]Jerome *Dialogue Against the Luciferians* 19; Weinandy, *Athanasius*, p. 6.

WHY THE INCARNATION WAS NECESSARY

Athanasius is known for more than just his battle against Arianism. His *Life of Antony* had a huge impact on the development of monasticism, for example. Without it, we may not have had a St. Benedict, who is often called the father of Western monasticism, and it is difficult to imagine Western civilization without the Benedictine monasteries that preserved the Western classics of philosophy and theology.

The *Life of Antony* was also a first in terms of spiritual biography. Athanasius had no model to follow when writing the life of a surviving saint (there *were* models for writing about martyrs). So Athanasius's story of Antony's battling the devil and demons in the desert, and dispensing divine healing and wisdom to all comers, created a new paradigm. It presented the saint as one who proceeds heavenward (this recalls Origen's model of ascetic ascent) by steps on a spiritual ladder. The saint uses spiritual weapons to ascend, such as making the sign of the cross and praying with groans. Each step upward risks a greater fall because, after each victory by the saint, the devil always returns with a stronger temptation. But the saint draws on Christ's very life and grace, which Christ in turn has received from the Father.[5]

The story of Antony was also connected to Athanasius's lifelong war with Arianism. In words that reminded readers of Moses, Athanasius wrote that Antony "came down from the mountain" in the desert to go to Alexandria and contend with the Arians, warning Christians "neither to go near them nor to share their erroneous belief." Antony said publicly "that the whole creation itself is angered at [the Arians], because they number among the creatures the Creator and Lord of all, in whom all things were made."[6]

Athanasius also played a role in the ancient debates over the date of Easter, and he made important arguments for the divinity of the Holy Spirit as an equal member of the Trinity.

But it was his work on the person of Jesus as the Word of God that made his lasting mark on the church. He insisted that it was Jesus' work as God incarnate that brought healing to a sick world, and that this work was

---

[5]Athanasius Athanasius: *The Life of Antony and The Letter to Marcellinus*, trans. Robert C. Gregg (New York: Paulist Press, 1980).
[6]Athanasius *Life of Antony* sec. 69.

crystallized at the cross. There, at a scene the world despised, "He overturn[ed] the pomp and parade of idols, and quietly and hiddenly w[on] over the mockers and unbelievers to recognize Him as God."[7]

Athanasius's long career of fighting for the deity of Christ was focused on two overall arguments: first, that the cross and incarnation were *necessary* for human salvation; and second, that Jesus Christ *was* indeed the incarnation of God in human flesh. Let's take a look now at the first argument about the necessity of the incarnation.

Athanasius contended that Jesus *had* to be God in order to solve three dilemmas: humans had irreparably corrupted the image of God originally placed in them, their inner beings had become diseased, and they had incurred a debt they could not repay.

These three dilemmas had arisen because of sin—which Athanasius defined as an abuse of freedom. God originally gave his human creatures the ability to know him by looking at the creation (and seeing its otherwise inexplicable order and harmony) and noticing the image of the Word within themselves. But they turned away from the signs of God in creation and in themselves, and turned instead to things of this world and worshiped them. The three dilemmas were the result—the image of God in us became horribly disfigured, our souls became sick, and we owed a debt we could not settle.

Therefore, Athanasius reasoned, forgiveness is not enough. (This, by the way, is an important argument against Jewish and Muslim assertions that God can forgive sins without the incarnation or cross.) Since human nature had been polluted by sin, forgiveness by itself would not remove the corruption. God could forgive our lust, and we could repent, but that alone would not check our compulsion to lust.

> Had it been a case of trespass only, and not of a subsequent corruption, repentance would have been well enough; but when once transgression had begun, men came under the power of the corruption. . . . [Christ had to] bring again the corruptible to incorruption.[8]

In addition, sin was ruining our nature more and more. The forces of death were gradually spreading through our souls and bodies, and would

---

[7]Athanasius *On the Incarnation*, p. 25.
[8]Ibid., p. 33.

lead to both physical and spiritual death. Forgiveness was not enough to stop that process.

The result is soul sickness. We are diseased. We need a divine physician to cure us. Only by the infusion of new life could the sickness of death coursing through our souls be arrested and destroyed: "If death was within the body, woven into its very substance and dominating it as though completely one with it, the need was for Life to be woven into it instead, so that the body by thus enduing itself with life might cast corruption off."[9]

These are just three of the innumerable benefits of the cross and incarnation: "So many are the Savior's achievements that follow from His Incarnation, that to try to number them is like gazing at the open sea and trying to count the waves."[10]

The key to understanding *how* God is able to accomplish all this through the incarnation of his Son is the principle of "solidarity." This is the idea, familiar to the ancients but foreign to the developed West today, that we can be joined to a person in such a way that whatever happens to that person also happens as a result to us. This is why ancient and medieval peoples naturally followed the religious choices of their kings and fathers—because they believed that they were joined to their corporate heads at the level of being, and so the new god or reality which was shared by their head was now also shared with them. This was also why Adam's sin could spread to us so easily, because we were joined to him by solidarity. Athanasius explains this is why Christ's defeat of death destroyed death's power not only over himself but also over *us:* "For the solidarity of mankind is such that, by virtue of the Word's indwelling in a single human body, the corruption which goes with death has lost its power over all."[11]

The power has been crippled and the spell has been broken because death's demands have been met. Humanity's sin demanded punishment. But when the Word joined itself with the human race and allowed that punishment for sin (death) to be fully executed on himself—and therefore by the principle of solidarity on the whole race—death no longer had traction in humanity. It was stripped of its ability to corrupt and destroy the race.

---

[9]Ibid., pp. 80-81.
[10]Ibid., p. 93.
[11]Ibid., p. 35.

Thus, taking a body like our own, because all our bodies were liable to the corruption of death, He surrendered His body to death in place of all, and offered it to the Father. This He did out of sheer love for us, so that in His death all might die, and *the law of death thereby be abolished because, when He had fulfilled in His body that for which it was appointed, it was thereafter voided of its power for men.*[12]

So death's power over us, which means its power to keep us in fear and destroy us forever, has been put to death. But we are joined as a race not only to Christ on the cross but also to Christ in his resurrection. That means, for Athanasius, that believers are joined to Christ's resurrection life, which gradually restores our sick souls from a state of corruption to a state of increasing incorruption. Our sick souls are being healed by Jesus' resurrection life.

A big part of that gradual healing comes from listening to our Savior's words and acting on them. Sin has marred our thinking about how to live and think. We need to be retaught and redirected. Studying the words of Jesus and the apostles will help us grow in the *knowledge* of God, which is not only intellectual but always involves intellectual understanding of the teachings of Scripture.[13]

The result will be what Athanasius and the Eastern Orthodox churches today call *theopoiēsis*—"divinization." Building on the promise of 2 Peter 1:4 Origen believed that by trusting in the promises of God we can "become partakers of the divine nature" (see chap. 2). Athanasius understood this to mean the transformation of a person into deity. He probably was influenced by the earlier theologian Irenaeus (c. 130-c. 200) who had written famously that "[Christ] became as we are that we might become as He is."[14] By this Irenaeus and Athanasius did not mean that we become God but that God's very nature and life transform and infuse us. We grow from grace to grace, not by our own will and thinking but by the will and mind of Christ which have come into us and started to change us into his likeness.

This view of divinization as participation in Christ connected to Athanasius's view of the Trinity and in fact later Christian development of

---

[12]Ibid., p. 34, italics added.
[13]Weinandy, *Athanasius*, p. 45.
[14]Irenaeus *Against Heresies*, Ante-Nicene Fathers 1, ed. Alexander Roberts and James Donaldson (Grand Rapids: Eerdmans, 1993), 3.19.

trinitarianism. Athanasius emphasized that the Father gave his full divinity to his Son, and the Son gives his divinity to us. Therefore salvation means that the Son of God shares with us his own sharing in the Father's being and life. We participate in Christ's participation in the Father's life and being.

This view of salvation as participation in divinity has several implications for the Christian doctrine of the Trinity.

1. It means that God is not only one but also a community. Because God is a community of Persons who share with one another, and in turn with us, we are able to be saved and share that salvation with others in community. This also means that we are made for community (and not to be isolated individuals), just as God *is* a community.

2. This shows that God is fundamentally giving. The Father gives the gift of himself to the Son, and the Son gives the gift of himself to believers. The Father also gives the gift of the Spirit to believers, so that we can have the Son. Salvation is a gift. So is human existence itself!

3. Historians of the doctrine of the Trinity often say the doctrine was most importantly worked out by the Cappadocians (Basil the Great, Gregory of Nazianzus and Gregory of Nyssa). But these three great minds built on the foundation which Athanasius had laid.

Athanasius said the result of divinization (participation in God's own nature) will be disciples who do not fear death, who lay down their lives for the gospel, and who grow into the divine likeness. This occurs as they turn away from the deceptions of sin and the devil, and lead holy lives of virtue.[15]

One more thing. We have examined why the incarnation was necessary to do things that could not be accomplished by God's forgiveness alone. Athanasius also argued that if Jesus was merely a creature, as Arius supposed he was, then we are not saved at all. For then we are joined in solidarity not to God and God's nature, but to another creature with a creaturely nature. The latter cannot destroy the power of death, since it is itself under that power. Another creature has no capacity to heal sickness of soul, since all of creation is under a curse. And no creature can pay the infinite debt owed by humans, because a creature cannot be infinite and so cannot pay an infinite debt. So if Jesus was not God, then not only are we

---

[15]Ibid.

not saved but we are still lost and broken and diseased and debt-ridden. We are also worshiping a creature—which is idolatry.

THE INCARNATION REALLY DID HAPPEN

Arius and his followers did not believe in the incarnation. They assumed, along with most contemporaries in the Hellenistic world, that the Father alone was fully divine. Arius figured that if the Father alone is God and is one, then any sharing of his nature with another person (the Son) would destroy his oneness. Then there would be two gods. Advocates of Nicaea often used the analogy of one torch lighting another to illustrate the Father's sharing his essence with the Son, but Arius took from this that now there were two torches—hence two different gods, which was an impossibility for a committed monotheist. God's oneness would be compromised.

Since the Father by himself had all that was necessary to be God, Arius concluded that the Son must have been created by the will of the Father at some point. (There were also biblical passages that seemed to him to suggest this, but at this point his philosophical reasoning alone was enough to bring him to this conclusion.) Hence the Son was not coeternal with the Father. God was not always a Father (in Arius's thinking), and "there was a time when the Son was not." The Son was a creature—the first and far greater than a mere human being—but a creature nonetheless.

For Arius this meant, in turn, that the Son's nature was different from the Father's. He had a different kind of being. God had no beginning and created all things, but the Son had a beginning and was only the mediator of the creation. These were two entirely different kinds of beings. If the Son is God in any sense, he is so only by grace as a gift, not by direct participation in the Father's being.

And because the Father alone is God, and God was understood by all Greeks to be ineffable (unable to be comprehended or described), Arius said even the Son cannot comprehend the Father.

Furthermore, all those familiar with Greek philosophy knew that God—by definition—is immutable (does not change). Any change would mean change from perfection, which then becomes imperfection. Since God is perfect, said Arius, he cannot be imperfect. Thus he cannot change.

The problem for Arius and all his followers was that the incarnation seemed to require change. God seemed to change into a human. But since God cannot change, and the incarnation would require God to change, the incarnation must not have really happened.

Finally, the portraits of Jesus in the Gospels seemed to Arius and his followers to demean God. They picture a man, Jesus, who is forsaken by God on the cross, is ignorant of the last day, asks to receive glory and prays to God. Arius asked, How could God have such human weaknesses? The cross seemed to be the epitome of weakness! As Athanasius paraphrased Arius, "How can he be Word or God who slept as a man, and wept, and inquired [asked questions]?"[16]

How Athanasius Defeated the Arians

Now we will look at the arguments Athanasius used to rebut all of these charges and answer all these questions.

First, he refused to let philosophy determine the ground rules. Arius and his followers assumed the Father alone is "ungenerate" (not produced, made or begotten by anyone or anything) and ineffable, that there is an infinite gulf between the Father and every other person and thing, and that the Father alone has everything that pertains to God.

Athanasius insisted that these are philosophical terms and assumptions, and that the biblical story of salvation—not philosophers—should determine presuppositions and establish ground rules. For starters, *ungenerate* and *ineffable* are philosophical and not biblical terms. Scripture does *not* show an infinite gap between the Father and every other person—that is, no such gap is shown between the Father and the Son. And the Bible indicates the Son has complete knowledge of the Father. So the Father is not ineffable to *every* conceivable person.

Athanasius and the orthodox at Nicaea developed their own distinction between "making" and "begetting." This was important because the Bible says Jesus was the "only-begotten Son," which seemed to imply that Jesus was made a son just as we are made sons and daughters of God. But Athanasius said that while we were "made," Jesus was "begotten." "Making" produces something of a *different* sort, while "begetting" produces something of the *same* kind. Bees make beehives but beget bees. Ants make

---

[16]Athanasius *Contra Arianos* 3.27, cited in Weinandy, *Athanasius*, p. 59.

anthills but beget ants. Humans make houses but beget other human beings. The Father made the world but begets the Son from eternity—so that there *never* was a time when the Father was *not* begetting the Son. And since the Father was begetting in this case and not making, what he begets is the Son identical to his very own nature and being. Hence the Son is fully divine.

This is why the Council of Nicaea said the Son was *homoousios* (of the same nature as) the Father. The Arians complained that this was not a biblical word. Athanasius later replied that they themselves used far more unbiblical words, but that the more important issue was not unbiblical *words* but unbiblical *concepts*. Sometimes it is necessary to use an unbiblical word such as *Trinity* to teach properly and clearly a biblical *concept*. This is also why theology is necessary and the Bible alone is not enough—it needs an orthodox community and tradition to interpret it. Arius and his followers were adept at using Scripture to support their position. The orthodox had to use new words—words not found explicitly in the Bible, such as *homoousios*, to defend biblical *concepts*. The use of biblical words alone was not enough to defeat heresy and clearly teach the biblical *message*.

But "one of the most important breakthroughs and one of the most significant insights in the whole history of Christian doctrine" was Athanasius's rejection of the Greek assumption that the Father by himself has and is all that is God.[17] In place of this definition of God, Athanasius produced his own—that God is by nature, from eternity, Father. This means that he has *always* had a Son. The Son could not have been created at some point in time, such that there was a time when he was not. For then God would not have been God, who by definition and nature is Father.

Therefore when we call God "Father," we at once signify the Son's existence. In the same way, Athanasius argued, when we speak of the sun, we assume the sun's radiance. Or when we talk about a fountain, we immediately picture water springing from it. Therefore "the whole being of the Son is proper to the Father's *ousia* [being], as radiance from light and a stream from a fountain."[18]

This preserves the distinction of persons in the Trinity while retaining the oneness. It shows that the Father and the Son are not identical in *who*

---

[17]Weinandy, *Athanasius*, p. 64.
[18]Athanasius *Contra Arianos* 3.3, cited in Weinandy, *Athanasius*, p. 70.

they are, but they are identical in *what* they are. They are two different persons (the Spirit is the third) but the same one God: the same being.

Athanasius went on to respond to other philosophical challenges thrown down by Arius. The most important was that the incarnation requires the immutable God to change, which appeared to be a contradiction in terms. Athanasius replied that when the Word became flesh, God the Son remained the same in his divine nature. He argued that *become* does not mean "change into." The incarnation does not mean God changed but that he descended to the world of humans.

Athanasius likened the incarnation to Aaron's putting on his high-priestly robe, while still remaining who he was as Aaron. He robed himself in his priestly flesh, just as God the Word remained God but robed himself in his priestly flesh for the incarnation. He is the unchanged God who is truly human.[19]

THE BIBLICAL CHALLENGE

The Arians marshaled an arsenal of biblical texts that showed Christ's weakness, ignorance, suffering and growth. For example, "The Lord created me at the beginning of his work" (Prov 8:22);[20] "God made him Lord and Christ" (Acts 2:36); "[He was] the first-born of many brethren" (Rom 8:29); "The Father is greater than I" (Jn 14:28).

Athanasius said that these texts and others like them refer to the Son not in his divinity but in his humanity. They all must be interpreted in the light of the overall story of Scripture, which is that God took on human flesh and walked among us. Since God became human, not a counterfeit human but a real human, we should not be surprised that he shows the characteristics of all humans—ignorance, weakness and even despair. But the biblical story does not stop there; it gives us a "double" account of the Savior. He was at all times God and Savior, but at the same time had flesh and blood and was fully human.

---

[19]Weinandy, *Athanasius*, pp. 84-87. Some historians have noted that another way that Athanasius responded to the Greeks' charge that God changed in the incarnation was to say that Christ "assumed" human nature in an act of "inhomination." That is, he did not change in his deity but simply took on human nature (*hominis* is Latin for "of a human being"). Thanks to Gary Deddo for this information.

[20]For centuries the early church had seen Jesus as Wisdom described as co-creator with the Father in Proverbs 8.

So when the Bible says Christ suffered, he suffered not as the Word insofar as he was God, but insofar as he was a man with human flesh. "God, being impassible [unaffected by the world], had taken passible flesh [flesh that was affected by the world]."[21]

> Suffering and weeping and toiling, these things which are proper to the flesh, are ascribed to him together with the body. If then he wept and was troubled, it was not the Word, as being the Word, who wept and was troubled, but it was proper to the flesh. If he also pleaded that "the cup might pass away," it was not the Godhead that was in terror, but this passion too was proper to the manhood. And the words "Why hast thou forsaken me?" are his, according to the explanation offered above, though He suffered nothing, for the Word was impassible. This is nonetheless declared by the evangelists, since the Lord became man and these things are done and said as from a man, that he might himself lighten these sufferings of the flesh, and free it from them.[22]

The Arians also asked why Jesus wondered where Lazarus was buried and didn't know when the Last Day would come. Athanasius replied this was to be expected, given the divine plan for God to take on a fully human existence, which always involves a degree of ignorance. "The Word as man was ignorant of [the Last Day], for ignorance is proper to man, and especially ignorance of these things."[23] Of course the Word as God knew everything about the Last Day, but as man chose to let go of that knowledge.

WHAT DID ATHANASIUS TEACH THE CHURCH?

1. Athanasius was a thoroughly biblical theologian who recognized that the Bible will be misinterpreted if it is interpreted primarily from our own experience as creatures. Instead, he insisted, we must use God's own words and examples in history to understand the meaning of the biblical text. We must not, he said, "think from a center in ourselves," which is what he said the Arians were doing. They thought of the sonship of the Son by starting from human sonship and then working their way back to the Father-Son relationship. Athanasius said that any think-

---

[21] Athanasius *Contra Arianos* 3.55, cited in Weinandy, *Athanasius*, pp. 89-90.
[22] Ibid., 3.56, cited in Weinandy, *Athanasius*, p. 90.
[23] Ibid., 3.43, cited in Weinandy, *Athanasius*, p. 93.

ing that begins with creatures risks replacing theology with "mythology." Academics and even church leaders sometimes follow the Arian method, reinterpreting biblical narrative and church doctrine by analogy with our experience as creatures rather than the divine models we have been given in revelation.

Athanasius also saw the critical importance of doctrine. The Scriptures, and therefore the historic church, are all about doctrine. Doctrine is teaching about who the triune God is and what he means for us. That means a host of *truths* that are to shape both our minds and our hearts. They are necessary to *see* the true Father and Son and Holy Spirit. Only with knowledge of biblical doctrine can we share the life of the Trinity. In his first epistle John says we can have fellowship with the Father and Son only if we accept what he tells us he saw and heard: "That which we have seen and heard we proclaim also to you, so that you too may have fellowship with us; and indeed our fellowship is with the Father and with his Son Jesus Christ" (1 Jn 1:3). Doctrine is like a map. With a bad map, travelers won't reach their destination. Athanasius knew that with false doctrine about Jesus, we will never reach the true God.

Athanasius also shows us that biblical understanding must trump philosophical understanding. Philosophy is necessary for theology, but philosophy that serves theology must be shaped and informed by the vision of Scripture. In our day we are faced with the call to name God as Mother as much as we call God Father. It is also suggested that we baptize in the name of the Creator, Redeemer and Sanctifier. Athanasius would say that these innovations come not from biblical concepts but from recent cultural assumptions built on rival philosophies. He would add, no doubt, that the new words for God point not to the true God of Scripture and church tradition but to "another Jesus," "a different Spirit" and "a different gospel" (2 Cor 11:4).

2. Athanasius showed us who Jesus is. Jesus' question to Peter is just as compelling today: "Who do you say that I am?" Athanasius's answer was, "None other than the eternal Son of God." He showed us that the hermeneutical key to Christology is what the theological tradition has called the communication of idioms (or unique properties). This means that both human and divine attributes are assigned to Jesus of Nazareth. So we can say God himself cried as a baby in the manger and was a teenager for a few

years. We can also say that the man who said he didn't know the Last Day was also the Son of God who decided to lay that knowledge aside during his incarnation. The payoff is that we in our humanness—with all of our fears and weaknesses—were taken up with the Son of God to the cross for our sins, and then through the resurrection to eternal life in the Trinity. This is what it means to be saved. It could be done only by a God who was also fully human. Apart from this, there is no salvation. And because of this, we know that God himself really does understand when we suffer and struggle. For since he was a man (and the Word still *is* the God-man!), he suffered the same temptations and weaknesses and struggles that we do. What's more, he both understands and overcame those weaknesses because he took our place, suffering our sufferings but overcoming them in his resurrection.

3. Athanasius showed us that sometimes it is not right to compromise—when core theology is at stake. There are matters of ego and nonessentials on which it is proper and Christian for us to compromise. But when the heart of the gospel is at stake, it is time to be like Athanasius and refuse to bend, even when we are criticized for not being a "team player."

At several key points in the long debate, Arians and semi-Arians (even some believers who were otherwise orthodox but confused) tried to get Athanasius and others to find middle ground between *homoousios* (Jesus is of the *same* nature and being as the Father) and *homoiousios* (Jesus is of a *similar* nature to the Father's). More often they simply proposed the latter, *homoiousios*, as a compromise between the two parties, Arian and orthodox. Athanasius consistently refused to consider compromise. He rightly insisted that to say Jesus was of a "similar" nature to the Father or anything short of the "same" nature as the Father was to fail to accept Jesus as *fully* God. And only if Jesus was and is fully God can we have assurance that we are saved. Any being other than God is incapable of saving us—which would mean that if Jesus was not fully God, we would still be in our sins and on the road to damnation.

This is how Athanasius saved the faith of the church. Without his flint-like determination, Christianity might have become a little, obscure sect of Greek philosophy, lost in the mists of time. Or we would still be worshiping Jesus among a variety of other minor gods, with the Father viewed as a distant, inaccessible deity.

A SELECTION FROM ATHANASIUS'S WORKS

What was God to do in face of this dehumanising of mankind, this universal hiding of the knowledge of Himself by the wiles of evil spirits? Was He to keep silence before so great a wrong and let men go on being thus deceived and kept in ignorance of Himself? If so, what was the use of having made them in His own Image originally? . . .

What, then, was God to do? What else could He possibly do, being God, but renew His Image in mankind, so that through it men might once more come to know Him? And how could this be done save by the coming of the very Image Himself, our Saviour Jesus Christ? Men could not have done it, for they are only made after the Image; nor could angels have done it, for they are not the images of God. The Word of God came in His own Person, because it was He alone, the Image of the Father, Who could recreate man made after the Image.

In order to effect this re-creation, however, He had first to do away with death and corruption. Therefore He assumed a human body, in order that in it death might once for all be destroyed, and that men might be renewed according to the Image. The Image of the Father only was sufficient for this need. Here is an illustration to prove it.

You know what happens when a portrait that has been painted on a panel becomes obliterated through external stains. The artist does not throw away the panel, but the subject of the portrait has to come and sit for it again, and then the likeness is re-drawn on the same material. Even so was it with the All-holy Son of God. He, the Image of the Father, came and dwelt in our midst, in order that He might renew mankind made after Himself, and seek out His lost sheep, even as He says in the Gospel: "I came to seek and to save that which was lost." This also explains His saying to the Jews: "Except a man be born anew . . ." He was not referring to a man's natural birth from his mother, as they thought, but to the re-birth and re-creation of the soul in the Image of God.[24]

FOR REFLECTION AND DISCUSSION

1. Athanasius never saw final victory for the cause he championed. What does that imply about how long it takes for God's truth to be established in great controversies? Or for the struggles in which you are now involved?

---

[24]Athanasius *On the Incarnation*, p. 25.

2. Why was the incarnation necessary? How does Athanasius's answer to this question help answer challenges from Jews and Muslims?

3. Why was Arius convinced the incarnation could not have happened?

4. How did Athanasius defeat the arguments of the Arians?

5. Why did Athanasius say that the Father is not all that is God?

6. How did Athanasius explain the passages that depict Jesus as suffering, ignorant and weak?

7. What can we learn from Athanasius's courage?

8. If you are in a group, have every member share one thing about Athanasius that will be difficult to forget.

FOR FURTHER READING

Athanasius, *On the Incarnation: The Treatise "De Incarnatione Verbi Dei."* Translated and edited by "A Religious of C.S.M.V." Crestwood, N.Y.: St. Vladimir's Seminary Press, 1996.

———. *Athanasius: The Life of Antony* and *The Letter to Marcellinus.* Translated by Robert C. Gregg. New York: Paulist Press, 1980.

Weinandy, Thomas G. *Athanasius: A Theological Introduction.* Burlington, Vt.: Ashgate, 2007.

4

Augustine

The Most Influential Theologian Ever

Augustine (354-430) was a thirty-two-year-old North African professor of rhetoric in the summer of A.D. 386. He had battled the demon of sexual lust for years. He knew in his heart of hearts that Christ was the Truth and that sexual abstinence was right, but Augustine was also afraid that life without sex would be unlivable. Some years before this he had prayed, "God give me chastity, but not yet!"

But the torment was excruciating. Augustine described it as "my sickness and my torture."[1] He said his mind was "lifted up by the truth" but was also "weighed down by habit." The result was a "madness with myself." He was angry at his inability to embrace what he knew to be the truth, and distressed that he was out of God's will.[2]

In this "bitter agony of heart" he was sitting one day in his garden in Milan, where he had gone to advance his career and seek better students. Suddenly he heard a voice from a nearby house—the voice of a child—chanting over and over again, "Take and read, take and read."

He stopped his weeping momentarily, stood up and remembered hearing that St. Antony had been converted by hearing a gospel reading at church, "Go sell all you have, give to the poor, and come follow me." Instantly he thought God might speak to him in a similar way. So he ran back to the table where he had been sitting and picked up the book on

---

[1]Augustine, *Confessions*, trans. Henry Chadwick (New York: Oxford University Press, 1991), p. 150.
[2]Ibid., p. 148.

the table. It was a collection of Paul's letters.

Augustine opened the book at random and started reading the first passage his eyes lit upon: "Not in riots and drunken parties, not in eroticism and indecencies, not in strife and rivalry, but put on the Lord Jesus Christ and make no provision for the flesh in its lusts" (Rom 13:13-14).

The young professor was stunned. "At once, with the last words of this sentence, it was as if a light of relief from all anxiety flooded into my heart. All the shadows of doubt were dispelled."

AUGUSTINE AND THE HISTORY OF CHRISTIANITY

This mystical moment proved to be the beginning of a new life for Augustine, and a new chapter in the history of Christianity.[3] Augustine plunged headfirst into a life of discipleship that resulted in his being ordained as a priest and then consecrated as a bishop, and starting a career as a theologian who transformed the thinking of Christians for the next sixteen hundred years.

Augustine probably has had greater influence on Christian thinking than anyone besides Jesus and Paul. He was a central shaper of the Catholic Church's understanding of original sin, ministry, sacraments, the Trinity and the church. But he also had a huge influence on Protestants through his understanding of salvation by grace, not works, and the authority of Scripture for knowing what is good and true. Luther learned from Augustine as he developed his powerful doctrine of justification by grace through faith. Calvin is well known for his doctrines of both sanctification and predestination, both of which were influenced by Augustine's writings. Calvin's doctrine of God's accommodation to finite human capacities in Scripture (that is, his representing divine realities in human terms that we can understand) was probably a development of Augustine's thought on this subject, such as his comment in his massive *City of God* that God had to "stoop" in his "descen[t]" to the level of human beings when inspiring the authors of Scripture.[4] Calvin uses the same idea about God stooping

---

[3]Augustine is not usually considered a mystic, and the mysticism that obliterates distinctions between the soul and God has been condemned by the church. But I use the word *mystical* in the generic and orthodox sense as referring to direct communion or contact with God. In this sense, Augustine's profound experience in which he heard the Word of God speaking to him personally and directly was mystical.

[4]Augustine *The City of God*, trans. Marcus Dods (New York: Modern Library, 1950), p. 515.

down in Scripture to make himself understandable to finite minds.[5]
The great medievalist Bernard McGinn says of Augustine:

> Alfred North Whitehead once described the history of Western philosophy
> as a series of footnotes to Plato. It would be no less true an exaggeration to
> say that the history of Western Christian theology is a series of footnotes to
> Augustine. Augustine wrote on every aspect of Christian belief, and he did
> so with such originality and skill that he must be ranked among the most
> influential of all the doctors of the church.[6]

AUGUSTINE'S CONTROVERSIES

Let me first give a thumbnail sketch of Augustine's theological emphases,
and then in the rest of this chapter I will focus on one that has had particular impact on the history of Christianity.

Augustine's thinking generally was shaped by a series of debates with
four opponents.[7] In his earlier period he was first a disciple of Manichae-
anism (a school of thought based on the teachings of Mani) and then a
fierce opponent of it. Mani was a Persian Gnostic of the third century who
liked Paul's letters but was disgusted by the physical world, especially the
human reproductive system.[8] The "elect" members of his sect were celi-
bate, and the "hearers" were married but tried not to procreate. Everyone
was vegetarian and avoided alcohol. Mani denied the historical reality of
the crucifixion of Jesus, and was appalled that the Catholic Church used
in its worship services readings about "Moses the murderer, David the
adulterer, and Joseph the state monopolist."[9] For the young Augustine the

---

Stoop is the same word Calvin uses in his doctrine of God's accommodation to human capacities in Scripture.
[5]See, for example, John Calvin *Institutes of the Christian Religion* 1.13.1.
[6]Bernard McGinn, *The Doctors of the Church: Thirty-Three Men and Women Who Shaped Christianity* (New York: Crossroad, 1999), p. 66. McGinn emphasizes Western Christianity because,
as Michael McClymond has remarked, there is an "Augustine blackout" zone in certain parts of
the Eastern Church. He tells the story of a European theological conference, where an Eastern
Orthodox bishop-theologian said after a few sessions, "I keep hearing this name again and
again, but I don't know who this is—someone named 'Augustine.'"
[7]This is how McGinn sees the outline of Augustine's career (see McGinn, *Doctors of the Church*,
pp. 66-69).
[8]Gnostics believed *gnosis* (Greek for "knowledge") would save them; therefore Jesus' death and
resurrection were either untrue or unnecessary. They also believed matter and this world were
created by the evil Old Testament God.
[9]Henry Chadwick, introduction to Augustine's *Confessions*, p. xiv.

most important doctrine of the Manichees was their answer to the problem of evil. They taught that there are two opposing realms, the Kingdom of Light and the Kingdom of Darkness. Each is roughly equal in power, so the god of the Kingdom of Light is good but not strong enough to defeat the Kingdom of Darkness. Evil comes from the Kingdom of Darkness, which is just as strong as God.

Augustine's response to the Manichees was to argue for the goodness of this created world (Mani had said it was the product of the Kingdom of Darkness), and to say that evil was not a thing or power but the absence of good. Evil is produced, argued Augustine (using Paul as his guide), by our sinful abuse of the good gift of freedom. Because we are all intimately related to Adam, his sin has infected us. The result is original sin—an inherited proclivity in all of us to self-will and self-obsession. (More on this subject in a bit.) God is all-powerful but permits evil because he uses it for his mysterious purposes.

Augustine's second series of debates was with the Donatists. They were Christians opposed to letting repentant bishops rejoin the ministry after having compromising their faith during the great Roman persecutions. The Donatists said the true church is a pure church. They refused to accept as bishop anyone thought to have been consecrated by *traditores*—those who had surrendered Bibles to the authorities to be burned. The Donatists taught that sacraments administered by priests or bishops who were connected with *traditores* were invalid. They were convinced that only those who were free of serious sin could faithfully administer the sacraments.

Augustine, in response, argued that the church is never holy in itself but is always a mixed body full of wheat and tares this side of the final judgment. A sinful minister or priest of Christ can still connect the believer to Christ (by the Holy Spirit's work through his administration of the sacraments) because the true minister in a sacrament is Christ himself, not the human minister. The church is not a group of perfected people but a community of ailing sinners engaged in a long convalescence that will be finished only on the day of resurrection.

Unfortunately for the later history of Christianity, Augustine developed a theology of persecution after the failure of the church's efforts to conciliate the Donatists. The bishop argued, using Luke 14:23, that the Donaists were to be "compelled to come in." The results were military occupation of Donatist regions and occasional executions, over Augustine's protests, of Donatists "convicted of mutilating priests or destroying churches." Later Christians used Augustine's argument to justify violent persecution of other heretics.

In Augustine's defense it should be said that he was convinced from his view of the Fall that fallen human beings need more than spiritual pressure alone to keep themselves from evil, and that God uses the state to help provide restraint. In that light he viewed the state's action against Donatism to be a "genuinely corrective treatment: it was a brusque way of winning over 'hardened' rivals, rather than an attempt to stamp out a small minority."[10]

Augustine's third battle was with Pelagius, a fourth- and early fifth-century British monk who was appalled by the sexual immorality among people claiming to be Christians, and insisted that one would be saved only by rigorous discipleship. Grace, he said, was simply free will. Salvation was a reward granted to those who used their gift of freedom in a way that proved they were faithful followers of Jesus. At birth there is no inherent evil tendency in humans; that idea, he thought, would make God the author of evil. That is, he thought all people are born innocent—just like Adam and Eve before their fall into sin.

Augustine replied that Pelagius held an unrealistic and unbiblical view of human nature. In real life, and from the very beginning of life, humans display a universal tendency to selfishness. Salvation comes, he said, not through self-effort but by grace through faith, which is a mysterious gift. Salvation then is finally a gift of God, not a human achievement.

Augustine's final duel was with pagans who had blamed the fall of Rome in 410 on Christian "atheism." By this charge they meant that Christians had failed to worship the pagan gods, and so the gods in anger had withdrawn their support for the "Eternal City." Pagans also said that Rome, which had become Christian, fell because its new Christian god was weak.

In his monumental *City of God*, written over a period of thirteen years, Augustine "secularized" history. Against those who wanted to make the history of the new Rome a Christian history, with its successes regarded as

---

[10]Peter Brown, *Augustine of Hippo: A Biography* (Berkeley: University of California Press, 1969), pp. 241, 240.

rewards for its Christian leaders and citizens, Augustine said true history is not a matter of Christian empires versus secular empires but an internal secret history between the City of God and the City of Man. The two cities coexist within both Christian and non-Christian empires. Rome fell because of internal moral corruption and idolatry. Bad things happen to both Christian empires and good Christians, and are because of God's secret purposes operating within both.

HUMAN NATURE

Many have observed that Augustine is one of those rare theologians who is open about himself, both the fascinating details of his life and his inner failings. In the *Confessions*, for example, we read that as a teenager he boasted to his friends of imaginary sexual exploits, lest he be thought less guilty than they. He confesses that even in church he had lusted after a "girl and start[ed] an affair." We learn that he deceived his mother, was in and out of depression, and even as a committed Christian had dreams in his sleep of sexual acts that would "arouse pleasure [and] even elicit consent." Every day, he wrote when he was in his mid-forties, he still struggled "against uncontrolled desire in eating and drinking." (Most of our great theologians, by the way, enjoyed God's gifts of food and drink. John Calvin, who was not known for self-indulgence, had the biggest wine cellar in Geneva; Jonathan Edwards, who was abstemious in his eating and drinking, knew enough about different wines to prescribe particular varieties to his children when they were sick. He also enjoyed brandy and rum from the West Indies, and he and his family were crazy about chocolate.)

In the *Confessions* Augustine expresses remorse that "the woman with whom I habitually slept was torn away from my side because she was a hindrance to my marriage."[11] He refers to the time in Milan, after being promoted to a prestigious position, when his common-law wife of nine years, with whom he had a son, was sent home to Africa. It had been arranged for Augustine to "marry up" by getting engaged to the ten-year-old daughter of a wealthy family (and procuring for him a mistress in the meantime). Augustine speaks of his own "sharp pain" (was she the love of his life?), but we can also imagine this African woman's pain after being

---

[11]Augustine *Confessions*, p. 109.

ripped from the man she loved and the son she would never see again.[12]

In the *City of God*, written in his sixties and early seventies, he writes of lust stirring in the mind but not the body, and body parts acting as "independent autocrat[s]."[13]

This profound self-portrait, perhaps the first genuine autobiography in the history of the West, has resonated with millions of readers over the last sixteen centuries. We see ourselves in it. Many have been struck by the psychological realism of Augustine's story of stealing pears with a gang of friends. He says he really didn't want the pears themselves, because they weren't good to look at or eat, and the gang wound up throwing them to some pigs. What he really wanted, he admits, was simply the "excitement of thieving and the doing of what was wrong."[14]

What stands out in this story, that has struck readers for centuries with a kind of self-recognition, is that sin is irrational and self-destructive, and yet we love it anyway. As Augustine puts it so starkly,

> I had no motive for my wickedness except wickedness itself. It was foul, and I loved it. I loved the self-destruction, I loved my fall, not the object for which I had fallen but my fall itself. . . . I was seeking not to gain anything by shameful means, but shame for its own sake.[15]

Augustine's composite portrait of human nature is of a good thing gone bad. The good God had made humanity good, but by its own perverse choices humanity has become corrupted.

The result is "rotten health." It starts at birth or even before. Augustine writes that he saw it even in a baby: "He could not yet speak[, yet,] pale with jealousy and bitterness, glared at his brother sharing his mother's milk."

Because of our being made in God's image, we have one will—from heaven, as it were—which shows us the good and tells us we ought to live according to it. But we find within ourselves another will that keeps us "bound to the earth." So in our one self we find two conflicting wills that keep us in "discord" and prevent us from concentrating on the good and true and beautiful. We find ourselves to be both willing and unwilling. In Augustine's words it is the "struggle of myself against myself." This inner

---

[12]Ibid.
[13]Ibid., pp. 27, 37, 81, 90, 203, 207; Augustine *City of God*, p. 465.
[14]Augustine *Confessions*, p. 29.
[15]Ibid.

war is both "sickness" and "torture."[16] Martin Luther and Jonathan Edwards were to write in very similar ways about our "unfree freedom"—our freedom to sin in a myriad of ways but our powerlessness (apart from Christ) to break our bondage to self-interest and self-obsession.

This is true even in people we consider good and exemplary. The problem with virtue is that it draws praise from others, and after hearing that for a bit we come to love it. Pretty soon we do virtue *in order* to receive praise. Augustine pointed to Roman civilization, which in many ways was the finest achievement of the ancient world. Romans sought glory from doing noble things, such as dying for liberty. This was good, Augustine wrote, but it also brought sinful pride. And once Rome achieved a measure of liberty (at least for the aristocracy), it then sought "domination" over others.[17]

Since self-obsession and lust and pride are so deeply rooted in human nature, salvation cannot come from anything within us. It must come from Someone *beyond* us. The rhetoric professor's description of his own salvation portrays, with rhetorical beauty, how God did for him what he could not do for himself.

> You called and cried out loud and shattered my deafness. You were radiant and resplendent, you put to flight my blindness. You were fragrant, and I drew in my breath and now pant after you. I tasted you, and I feel but hunger and thirst for you. You touched me, and I am set on fire to attain the peace which is yours.[18]

ADAM AND ORIGINAL SIN

Like all Christians who become aware of the power of sin, Augustine wondered why we are this way, and whether this means God is partially responsible for our sin. After all, he made us. If we all have a nature that continually produces evil, and God created our nature, is God responsible for evil? Could then God himself be evil?

Augustine's first response was that no evil is ever from God. Everything God created is good, and God created everything. God created the human race with free will, which was good. It was the human race in Adam that corrupted that good will and made it wicked. In Augustine's

---

[16]Ibid., pp. 35, 9, 140, 148, 152, 150.
[17]Augustine *City of God*, pp. 164, 160.
[18]Augustine *Confessions*, p. 201.

words, "We all were *in* that one man, since we all *were* that one man who fell into sin."[19] At this point in time, the whole human race was concentrated in Adam and Eve. Our futures were at stake. By a kind of virtual reality we were present in the first couple. What they were about to do would affect all of us as their descendants. Augustine concedes that you and I as individuals did not exist at that time, "but already the seminal nature was there from which we were to be propagated; and this being vitiated by sin, and bound by the chain of death, and justly condemned, man could not be born of man in any other state."[20]

In other words, there is only one human nature. It was given to Adam and Eve in a pure state, and they corrupted it for all their descendants, who now are made from that same human nature. The implication seems to be that we would have done the same thing that Adam did. Even if we think we would not have fallen, we are left with the question why we willingly cooperate with sin today. Every time we sin we imply that we agree with Adam's decision.

You may recall (the comic-strip character) Pogo's famous discovery, "We have met the enemy and he is us." Well, Pogo was right. The source of evil is not God or even Adam in complete isolation from us. Adam is the father of the human race and therefore human nature, and so his sin involved all his future descendants. We as individuals were not self-consciously choosing the forbidden fruit at that moment in the garden, but the human nature in Adam that became our human nature made that fateful choice.

Now some may ask, What about Satan, disguised as the serpent in the Genesis story of the Fall? Augustine said the serpent did indeed tempt Adam (and, I would add, continues to tempt us), but that Adam had already perversely turned to evil before the serpent's temptation. That was the only reason why the serpent's temptation was successful.[21]

Nothing made the will evil, he went on, but the will itself. It desired things inferior to the perfect being, God, and as a result made itself inferior to what it had been. "By craving to be more, man becomes less." No one or thing is evil by nature, since every thing and person was created by God, who is good and creates only good. God made human beings "upright and

---

[19]Augustine *City of God*, p. 422.
[20]Ibid., pp. 422-23.
[21]Ibid., p. 460.

consequently with a good will." If any being is evil, it is so because of its own vice. To insist on any other cause for evil—beyond the will's own perversity—is to insist on "see[ing] darkness or hear[ing] silence."[22]

Therefore original sin started with Adam *and* us. We inherit Adam's corrupted will because Adam's act involved all his future descendants. This is very difficult for us moderns to accept, since we have been raised from our mother's milk with the Enlightenment-inspired notion that we are all separate individuals, disconnected at the level of being from every other being. But let me suggest a way to think of this. Do you have any of the same sinful tendencies as your parents? If so (and I suspect this is true for all of us), can we say honestly that we do not also sometimes go along with these tendencies? I would suggest that our going along is a kind of voluntary agreement. We may dislike these tendencies in ourselves, but we nevertheless make choices from time to time to indulge these tendencies. At those moments we are silently saying yes to the sins of our parents. To take this one step further, at those moments we are participating with our parents in their sins.

Now this may still not make sense to you. But please understand that this made a lot of sense to most believers through most of Christian history—until the Enlightenment. It still makes sense to millions of believers in traditional societies where the principle of solidarity is still understood.

One last word on Augustine's view of human nature. It was not limited to sin! He is also noted for his view of the human person as a being unified by its affections. By this he meant that every part of the human being is affected by the fundamental inclination of the heart, either love for God or love for the self and world. This means that religion involves every part of us, not just our "spirit" or "soul." It also means that what finally determines the character of a person, and that person's final state, is the object of his or her love. We will see this same stress on the affections as the root of all life and religion in Schleiermacher and Edwards.

WHEN BAD THINGS HAPPEN TO GOOD PEOPLE

Augustine and his parishioners struggled, much as we do, over why bad things happen to good people. Especially when the good people are God's

---

[22]Ibid., pp. 386, 461, 448, 457, 386.

people—Christians.[23] He said most of the time God's reasons and ways are mysterious and hidden. But he also gave a number of intriguing answers to this question—answers that may strike us as unsentimental at best and unfeeling at worst. Yet it may be that, as C. S. Lewis put it, this is one area in which we need the "clean sea breeze of the centuries blowing through our minds" in order for us to get a broader understanding of why God permits his people to suffer.[24]

Plenty of bad things were happening to good people when Augustine was writing the *City of God*. The Goths had sacked Rome, which contained many Christians and many who did not embrace the faith. Christians had been tortured, raped and taken into captivity. As Augustine lay dying, reading the psalms and weeping over his sins, barbarian Vandals were besieging his own city in North Africa.

Christians were asking, Where is God amidst these horrors? Why did the same torments befall Christian and non-Christian alike? Why does God seem to not discriminate in giving power to both good and bad leaders?

Augustine was willing (some would say foolishly) to answer each of these questions. Barbarians tortured Christians in order to force the Christians to disclose where they had hidden their treasures. Augustine said God may have wanted to teach them the emptiness of temporal possessions, and to show them that the only possession worth clinging to is eternal life. He may also have wanted to develop in them a love for himself that was not "mercenary" but wanted God simply for himself.[25]

What then of rape? Augustine surmised that some of these women may have been burdened by sinful pride that would threaten their entrance to the kingdom of God. The humiliation of rape could have been used to kill the beast that would have poisoned their souls.

To many of us this sounds horrific—bad pastoral counsel and a cruel view of God. But try to think of what was behind this counsel. Augustine believed, with plenty of biblical support, that pride is the greatest of sins because it, more than any other sin, keeps us from God who is true life. He

---

[23]Of course Augustine would say that none of us is truly good. We all deserve hell, and so any distinction between good and bad people is relative, and based on God's mysterious grace.

[24]C. S. Lewis, introduction to Athanasius *On the Incarnation: The Treatise "De Incarnatione Verbi Dei,"* trans. and ed. "A Religious of C.S.M.V." (Crestwood, N.Y.: St. Vladimir's Seminary Press, 1996), pp. 8-9.

[25]Augustine *City of God*, pp. 13-15.

was also convinced that God is superabundant love. So the same One who permitted women to be raped is the tender Lover who wanted these women to spend eternity swimming in his infinite love.

Some wondered how God could have permitted so many Christians to be led away as captives. Augustine said this was nothing new: "The three youths [who were thrown into Nebuchadnezzar's fiery furnace] were captives; Daniel was a captive; so were other prophets: and God, the comforter, did not fail them." Nor did he abandon the prophet who was a captive in the belly of the whale.[26]

But why, it was asked, did the same tragedies strike the good and the wicked alike? Because, said the African theologian, God uses the same suffering in different ways for different people. For the wicked it might have been a punishment and perhaps a goad to repentance. But for believers it was for their moral and spiritual improvement. Those who were despoiled of property might have liked this life too much, failing to see that their eyes should have been focused on the kingdom of God. The same thing can be said for death: It "is good to the good and evil to the evil."[27]

There was also the question of why God, who gives as he pleases, gave power to both good and wicked men. Augustine said one reason is that if God gave it only to good people, then his saints might grow to like the kingdoms of this world too much and fail to yearn for the City of God. There are other reasons, but God keeps them hidden. Of one thing we may be sure, however—all God's reasons are just.[28]

Finally, Augustine proposed an aesthetic reason—one based on the concept of beauty. He said that without evil, beauty would not be as clear and full. The world is more beautiful because of its juxtaposition of sin with virtue, sinners with saints. He compared this to the beauty of a painting: "For as the beauty of a picture is increased by well-managed shadows, so, to the eye that has skill to discern it, the universe is beautified even by sinners, though, considered by themselves, their deformity is a sad blemish."[29]

Where then was God in this world of beauty and ugliness, sin and vir-

---

[26]Ibid., pp. 33-34, 19.
[27]Ibid., pp. 13, 418.
[28]Ibid., pp. 140-42.
[29]Ibid., p. 367.

tue, good and evil? Everywhere. He was punishing wickedness, proving our virtue, correcting our vices and rewarding the endurance of the saints.

> Our God is everywhere present, wholly everywhere; not confined to any place. He can be present unperceived, and be absent without moving; when He exposes us to adversities, it is either to prove our perfections or correct our imperfections; and in return for our patient endurance of the sufferings of time, He reserves for us an everlasting reward.[30]

LESSONS FROM AUGUSTINE

There are far more lessons to learn from this giant than can even be mentioned, let alone elaborated, in this tiny space. I will focus only on what we can gain from his writings on human nature and evil.

1. It is unrealistic and un-Christian to imagine that human nature after the Fall is basically good. It is a shallow conception of humanity to jump from the observation of the many good things people do, to the conclusion that human nature is naturally altruistic. Any deeper look into the human condition will follow lines traced by Augustine to the realization that while God has made us in his image and we have many noble ideals, we do not have the ability to carry them out. Instead we seem to be handicapped by inherent self-obsession. If it were indeed true that we have the ability to perfect ourselves and become righteous, then there was no need for Christ to die for us. The Passion would have been superfluous.

2. Augustine reminds us that the kingdom of God is for the sick not the healthy, for the sinners not the perfected. This is good news for those of us who realize how sinful we are. If the kingdom were really only for the righteous, the discerning among us would be in despair.

3. Augustine is often blamed for introducing an unhealthy self-hatred to the Christian church because of his pessimistic view of human nature, especially its moral inability to choose the good apart from God's supporting grace. He is also said to have made God into a cruel Being who created people who were sinful from the get-go and so never had a chance. But Augustine actually provides a way for us to see that God is good and created *only* good things. He created Adam (and us in Adam) as wholly good.

---

[30]Ibid., pp. 34-35.

It was Adam, and we in him, who turned what was good into something bad. This means that we can hold to the Christian doctrine of original sin *and* God's goodness at the same time. God not only created us good, but he also took infinite pains to rescue us from our self-inflicted badness.

4. Augustine also helps us to see that we should not look for the kingdom of God on earth, or for a pure church. Any political program that promises the end of evil and suffering should stimulate some healthy skepticism in us. We should also not be surprised or disillusioned if we encounter sin and evil in the church. It is the nature of the church to be a mixed company of wheat and tares. What's more, the devil is real and will attack inside the church more than outside it, for he knows who his real enemies are. This realization will protect us from being seduced by both utopianism and fanaticism.

A SELECTION FROM AUGUSTINE'S WORKS

Accordingly, two cities have been formed by two loves: the earthly by the love of self, even to the contempt of God; the heavenly by the love of God, even to the contempt of self. The former, in a word, glories in itself, the latter in the Lord. For the one seeks glory from men; but the greatest glory of the other is God, the witness of conscience. The one lifts up its head in its own glory; the other says to its God, "Thou art my glory, and the lifter up of mine head." In the one, the princes and the nations it subdues are ruled by the love of ruling; in the other, the princes and the subjects serve one another in love, the latter obeying, while the former take thought for all. The one delights in its own strength, represented in the persons of its rulers; the other says to its God, "I will love Thee, O Lord, my strength." And therefore the wise men of the one city, living according to man, have sought for profit to their own bodies or souls, or both, and those who have known God "glorified Him not as God, neither were thankful, but became vain in their imaginations, and their foolish heart was darkened; professing themselves to be wise"—that is, glorying in their own wisdom, and being possessed by pride—"they became fools, and changed the glory of the incorruptible God into an image made like to corruptible man, and to birds, and four-footed beasts, and creeping things." For they were either leaders or followers of the people in adoring images, "and worshipped and served the creature more than the Creator, who is blessed for ever." But in the other city there is no human wisdom, but only godliness, which offers due worship to the true God, and looks for its reward in the society of the saints, of holy angels as well as holy men, "that God may be all in all."[31]

FOR REFLECTION AND DISCUSSION

1. Is it encouraging to know that the church's greatest theologian was plagued with recurrent lust over a period of many years?

2. How does Augustine's analysis of human nature help us see the immensity of salvation?

3. How did Augustine connect Adam's sin to ours?

4. What were some of the reasons Augustine gave for why God permits bad things to happen to his people? Do any of them resonate with you?

5. What light does Augustine's idea of the two cities shed on politics today?

6. If you are in a group, let each member share something from this chapter that is particularly insightful or interesting.

FOR FURTHER READING

Augustine. *The City of God*. Translated by Marcus Dods. New York: Modern Library, 1950.

———. *Confessions*. Translated by Henry Chadwick. New York: Oxford University Press, 1991. This is the best translation.

Brown, Peter. *Augustine of Hippo*. Berkeley: University of California Press, 1967.

Kenney, John Peter. *The Mysticism of Saint Augustine: Rereading the Confessions*. New York: Routledge, 2005.

---

[31]Augustine *City of God*, p. 477.

5

Thomas Aquinas

The Teacher of the Catholic Church

Thomas Aquinas (1225-1274) was an Italian philosopher and theologian. He was born near Aquino, Italy (hence the name), and inducted into a Benedictine monastery at age five. At some later date his family transferred him to the secular University of Naples, where he joined the Dominicans. He and his family apparently knew he would be better at study and teaching than meditation—the Benedictines emphasized prayer and manual labor, while the Dominicans were committed to study, teaching and preaching. Besides, Thomas added, "It is a greater thing to give light than to simply have light, to pass on to others what you have contemplated than just to contemplate."[1]

But the Dominicans (whom some slyly called the *Domini canes*, "dogs of the Lord") were considered new upstarts by Thomas's blueblood family. According to one story passed on by G. K. Chesterton, the brothers kidnapped Thomas and locked him in a tower. They tried every argument they could think of to get him to leave the Dominicans, but nothing worked. So at last they decided to blacken his reputation, which would cause the new order of teachers to refuse him. They paid a fetching prostitute to come to the room where Thomas was held.

Thomas immediately grabbed a burning brand from the fire and pointed

---

[1]This and the following stories are indebted largely to Brian Davies, "The Shape of a Saint," in *The Thought of Thomas Aquinas* (Oxford: Clarendon, 1992). For this chapter I also consulted Timothy McDermott, *Aquinas: Selected Philosophical Writings* (New York: Oxford University Press, 1993); G. K. Chesterton, *Saint Thomas Aquinas: The Dumb Ox* (New York: Image Books, 1974), and Aquinas's *Summa Theologica* and *Summa Contra Gentiles.*

it at the woman, who shrieked in terror and ran from the room. Thomas slammed the door shut and seared into the back of the door the sign of the cross.[2] I tell this story to demonstrate that every theologian has a personal life, and this one in particular had to fight to protect his chastity and reputation—apart from which the dense tomes of his *Summas* would not have been possible.

At about the age of twenty Thomas began studies under Alfred the Great, in Paris. Immediately he showed his love for the books. When asked if he would like to be lord of Paris, the young scholar replied, "I wouldn't know what to do with the city. No, I'd rather have the [lost] homilies of St. John Chrysostom on the gospel of Matthew."

But Thomas was unusually quiet among his fellow students, who nicknamed their tall and bulky companion "The Dumb Ox." Alfred knew better, famously rebuking and prophesying at the same time, "You call him a Dumb Ox: I tell you this Dumb Ox shall bellow so loud that his bellowings will fill the world."

A BEAUTIFUL MIND

Thomas had a phenomenal mind. Chesterton reports that when Thomas was asked for what he thanked God most, he answered simply, "I have understood every page I ever read."[3] Often he would dictate to more than one secretary at the same time, on different subjects. One tradition insists he composed in his sleep. He was known for his prodigious ability to concentrate, but also for its occasionally unsociable effects. In 1269, at a meal with King Louis IX of France, Thomas was thinking about the false teaching of the Manichees (see chap. 4 on Augustine). Although he was in the midst of guests chattering with the king, Thomas suddenly struck the table and exclaimed, "That settles the Manichees!" He called out for his secretary to come over and take dictation. As soon as he completed the dictation, he turned to the king and profusely apologized: "I am so sorry, I thought I was at my desk."

In 1248 he and Albert started a school at Cologne (now in Germany). Four years later he was called to teach at the University of Paris, where for the rest of his life he split his time with the papal courts in Rome, until his

---

[2]Chesterton, *Saint Thomas Aquinas*, chap. 2.
[3]Ibid., p. 3.

final two years teaching in a Dominican house in Naples.

Thomas was canonized as a Catholic saint in 1326. Though normally the Church requires two miracles for the canonization of a saint, Pope John XXII is said to have explained that every question Thomas answered was a miracle. Thomas was known for his love for the Catholic mass, and his commitment to poverty and austerity.

Thomas was made "Doctor" (teacher) of the Catholic Church in 1567, and commended for study by Pope Leo XIII in 1879. The Church knew he was not as eloquent as Augustine, the former professor of rhetoric, but its leaders prized his extraordinary clarity. His greatest works are his *Summa Theologica* (a systematic presentation of Christian doctrine using Scripture, tradition, philosophy and theology) and *Summa Contra Gentiles*, an apologetic work that he intended to be used by missionaries to Muslims.

FAITH AND REASON

Aquinas (he is known by both this name and "Thomas") is especially known for his masterful Christianization of the man called "the" philosopher in the Middle Ages—Aristotle. Thomas accepted from Aristotle what he thought was in accord with Christian doctrine, rejected what he thought was not (and explained why), and used some of Aristotle's categories to help teach Christian faith.

One of Aquinas's most important achievements was to clarify the relationship between faith and reason. About this relationship he wrote both sophisticated works accessible only to philosophers and theologians, and also popular works such as the *Summa Contra Gentiles* that can be understood by nonscholars as well (see the selection at the end of this chapter). On this subject he drew an important distinction that has guided Christian thinkers ever since—the difference between what we can know by reason about God and what can be known about God only by revelation in the Bible. From reason alone, according to Aquinas, we can know ideas about God such as the following—that God exists, that God is perfect, that God is good, and that God is changeless, everywhere, eternal and one. He argued this was some of what Paul meant when he said of all human beings,

> What can be *known* about God is plain to them, because God has *shown* it
> to them. For his invisible attributes, namely, his eternal power and divine
> nature, have been *clearly perceived*, ever since the creation of the world, in

the things that have been made. So they are without excuse. For although they *knew* God, they did not honor him as God or give thanks to him. (Rom 1:19-21, italics added)

Thomas is famous for his "five ways" or proofs of the existence of God. He argued, first, that there must be something which causes change or motion in things without itself being changed or moved by anything. Then he says that causes arranged in a series (A caused B which in turn caused C) must have a first member: "We never observe, nor ever could, something causing itself, for this would mean it preceded itself, and this is not possible." Finally, he turns to things with varying degrees of perfection, and argues that perfections in things imply a source of perfections. The movement toward goals by things which lack intelligence (such as animals seeking food and planets pursuing perfect orbits) suggests they are governed by something that is intelligent.[4]

Aquinas's five ways are often misunderstood. Some have ridiculed Thomas for thinking they prove the Christian God. But while Thomas said they prove what "everyone understands to be God," he makes clear they are meant only to show a first cause, not the Christian God per se. The five ways themselves are only meant to "get the ball rolling, not to bring the [proofs] to an end."[5] They are the beginning of a long argument that stretches out over thirty-five more double-columned pages (questions 2-11) in the Dominican Fathers' edition of his *Summa Theologica*. It is also frequently assumed that Thomas believed these proofs would convince any unbeliever of God's existence. But Thomas knew that sin prevents unbelievers from thinking objectively, and wrote these brief summaries more to confirm the faith of theological students than to convince village skeptics. Thomas also made it clear that reason cannot show the distinctively Christian truths about God—such as his being Triune and Savior through Christ. These truths, he said, can be known only by revelation in Scripture.

THE *SUMMA THEOLOGICA* AND ARISTOTLE

It was not only the substance of what Aquinas said about faith and reason that was so helpful, but the way in which he did it was remarkable. Only a

---

[4]Thomas Aquinas *Summa Theologica* 1a.2.3.
[5]Brain Davies, *The Thought of Thomas Aquinas* (New York: Oxford University Press, 1992), p. 26.

reader of the *Summa Theologica* can appreciate the intricacy, fairness and clarity of this work. Each part of this *Summa* is divided into questions, and the questions into articles. In each case Thomas lays out the opposite of what he takes to be the case ("It would seem that . . ."), using arguments from the church fathers, Scripture, Aristotle and others to support a proposition he considers wrong. Then he uses the same sorts of authorities to mount his own argument against what was proposed, and proceeds to defeat every one of the subarguments used to support the main proposition. By forcing himself to consider in detail every argument used for positions he opposed, he set a standard for critical thinking that has seldom been equaled. *Scholastic* is a word often used pejoratively for overly subtle and hairsplitting argumentation in medieval schools, but Thomas's careful and patient deliberations over great and small questions is an unrivaled intellectual achievement.

I mentioned Thomas's use of Aristotle, which seems unremarkable today. But in Thomas's day there were church leaders and thinkers who thought Aristotle was dangerous. For example, Bishop Étienne Tempier of Paris condemned a long list of Aristotelian propositions in 1274, the year of Thomas's death. Among these were the ideas argued by radical Aristotelians at the University of Paris, that the soul is not immortal and that the world is eternal and not created at a point in time. For this and other reasons, Plato and the Platonists had been preferred by theologians up until Thomas's day.

Furthermore, Aristotle was a philosopher, but his work dealt with biology, astronomy, geology, economics politics, art theory and other disciplines as well. So when Thomas decided to use Aristotle in his Christian theology (but by chewing the meat and spitting out the bones, so to speak), he was not only picking the brain of the "rocket scientist" of that era and challenging the way theology had been done until then, but also forging a new synthesis of science and theology. His was a bold and original thought experiment, but one that also strove to remain within the confines of orthodoxy.

Although Aristotle was a very important dialogue partner for Thomas, Pseudo-Dionysius, a sixth-century mystical theologian in the Neo-Platonist tradition, may have been almost as influential. Recent scholars have noticed in Thomas's *Summa* a pattern of *exitus* and *reditus*—the outflowing of all things from God and the return of things to God. This is a pattern that was taught by Pseudo-Dionysius, and Thomas cites him frequently in the *Summa*. This motif also runs through the theology of Origen, Augustine and Jonathan Edwards.

NATURE AND GRACE

Thomas is also well known for his articulation of the relation between nature and grace. Here he used Aristotle for help. The Greek philosopher showed the Christian theologian not simply that "grace perfects nature" (as it is commonly reported), but that grace uses nature as its tool. As the Aquinas scholar Timothy McDermott (no relation) has put it, "Nature is a tool of grace, used to do something beyond its own powers, but only because it has its own powers to contribute." The natural world is still at work within God's providential ordering of the world. "Every natural doing and every chance doing in the world and every free doing of man is a tool of the doing of God."[6]

This helps us understand how things and events can be interpreted both from a *natural* point of view as simply human phenomena, and from a *revealed* point of view as instances of God at work. McDermott offers two examples: sacraments and language. He says that for Thomas the Christian sacraments are not simply mysterious medicines (we saw this in Athanasius, and Augustine thought similarly) that act merely by God's will, but *also* "ritual religious performances akin to those of natural religion but now become tools of God." In other words, they are similar to the rituals of some other religions, and so can be studied legitimately on that level by historians of liturgy and the religions. Their scholarly comparisons take nothing away from what they are on another level—the action of God in the world to mediate to us his presence and grace.

Biblical language illustrates the same principle. The religious language of the Old Testament is "both an example of the languages men use to address and express their gods *and* God's exploiting of that example to speak about himself." Words with their roots in nonbiblical cultures bear new and richer flowers when they are taken up and planted afresh in a redemptive context. Each word is born again, as it were, when it is used in the new context.[7]

---

[6]Timothy McDermott, *Aquinas: Selected Philosophical Writings* (New York: Oxford University Press, 1993), pp. xxvii, xxx.
[7]Ibid., p. xxvii.

In both cases—sacraments and language—the same phenomenon has both a natural and revealed face. Nature is real, is created by God and is the tool through which God not only shows that nature is real and good, but also reveals that there is something beyond it.

One more thing about grace. For Thomas, grace is God's action in us that leads us to union with him. Therefore it is "participation in the divine nature" (2 Pet 1:4). (Notice how important this verse has become for Christian theology. We have seen it in Origen and Athanasius, and now Thomas. We will see this idea of participation again in Edwards.) Grace for Thomas is not merely God's being well disposed toward us (which you could say is God's *attitude* of love for us), but it is also God's love *working* in us to actually make us better. Here God's love is almost a substance or thing that is actually put within us, as Paul suggests in Romans 5:4: "Hope does not put us to shame, because God's love has been poured into our hearts through the Holy Spirit which has been given to us" (my translation). We gradually *become* more lovable as God pours more and more of his love into us.

JUSTIFICATION

This is important for Aquinas's doctrine of justification (how we are accepted by God in the process of salvation). For it is at this point that he ran afoul, three centuries later, of Martin Luther and the Reformation. For Thomas, God in justification makes a difference *in* people (which, by the way, is what Athanasius and Augustine also taught). Justification is not just the beginning of the Christian life (as Luther described it most often) but its continuation and ultimate perfection. It is a change of inner nature, not just legal status (from being an enemy of God to becoming a friend of God). For Thomas, there is no distinction—as there is for Luther—between justification (God's declaration that he accepts us) and sanctification (our inner renewal).

So there are differences on justification and salvation between Thomas and Luther, whose doctrine of justification we will look at in chapter six. But we shouldn't exaggerate the differences. Like Luther (and Calvin, for that matter), Thomas believed justification is a gift of God procured by Jesus' life, death and resurrection, not a reward for human accomplishment. People can do nothing on their own to guarantee it or prepare for it.

Thomas was insistent that no one ever "merits the first grace," which means no one ever deserves to have God come the first time with the grace that causes the heart and mind to begin their journey back to him. Thomas talks about merit in the Christian life, but it is merit that is given to believers only because the grace of Christ is working in them to produce righteous works. So there is a principle of grace that runs through even Thomas's discussion of merit. Another point of similarity between Thomas and Luther, who are often presented as being violently opposed, is that Luther also saw justification as having an inner effect (see chap. 6).

NATURAL LAW

Another major achievement of Thomas's is his development of what is called natural law. This was his idea that reason can tell us certain moral absolutes that are true for all times and places. This idea has a long history going back to Aristotle, Cicero and Augustine. But Thomas developed it with his customary precision, so that it has had a major impact ever since.

Some examples of what Thomas thought reason can show all human beings by natural law are (1) "The first command of law, 'that good is to be sought and done, evil is to be avoided' "; (2) that, generally considered, it is a good thing to preserve ourselves; (3) therefore procreation and the education of the young are goods; (4) human beings should learn what can be learned about the meaning of reality (for Aquinas this meant God) and living in society—namely, that people should shun ignorance, not offend others needlessly, and live in civility with others.[8]

Thomas did not mean for natural law to be a list of detailed instructions or rules for every situation. Instead it was meant to be a framework to be supplemented by sound practical thinking, conscience and civil law intended to promote the common good and geared for a particular society. When civil laws agree with natural law, they could be said to participate in God's eternal law. But when they violate natural law, they are "unjust." They "are acts of violence rather than laws," and "such laws do not bind in conscience." The implication is, as Martin Luther King Jr. famously observed in his "Letter from Birmingham Jail," that the Christian is free or perhaps even obligated to engage in civil disobedience. You

---

[8]Aquinas *Summa Theologica* 1a2ae.94.2.

can see why Aquinas's articulation of natural law has been appreciated not only by legal theorists and moral theologians but also by human rights activists to this day.

THE SACRAMENTS

Now that we have gotten a snapshot of what Thomas was best known for, we will focus on one area of his thinking that has had great influence on later Christianity—his analysis of the sacraments. We focus on the sacraments for the following reasons:

1. The Catholic Church believes the primary way we get to God, and God reaches us, is through the church's sacraments.

2. More than any other theologian, Thomas Aquinas laid the theoretical foundation for the Catholic understanding of sacraments.

3. Low church Protestants (those who do not use a formal liturgy and reject the idea of sacraments as means of special grace) can best understand Catholicism by seeing Thomas's sacramental theory.[9]

4. High church Protestants (those who use a liturgy and believe in sacraments as means of special grace) and Catholics will better understand their own practices.

Augustine had taught that a sacrament is always a *signum* (sign) of some *res* (sacred thing). The *signum* is an image or reflection of the sacred thing that is itself invisible. So a sacrament, said Augustine, is a sacred sign. It shows forth and brings about what cannot be seen—cleansing from sin. Baptism by immersion brings about and shows forth burial with Christ and being raised with him to new life. So sacraments are some of the means by which the purpose of the incarnation (the salvation of human beings) is made real in the lives of believers. They are the work of Christ himself, independent of the worthiness of the minister serving them.

Thomas Aquinas adopted this view pretty much wholesale. In the beginning of his question on what is a sacrament (his *Summa Theologica* is

---

[9]Low church Protestants typically see baptism as simply the believer's way of telling the world that he or she has accepted Jesus, and the Lord's Supper as a reminder of what happened two thousand years ago. In neither case is special grace imparted. High churches, on the other hand, see baptism as imparting a special grace, and Communion as participation in the body and blood of Christ.

arranged as a series of answers to questions), Thomas quotes Augustine's *Confessions:* "The visible sacrament is the sacrament, that is, the sacred sign, of the invisible sacrament [Christ's redemptive work and person]." Thomas went on to say that the sacraments are the ways that people who live after Christ can become Christ's contemporaries. They are the means by which the "newness of life" achieved by Christ in his resurrection are disseminated and intensified. They are God's ways of making faith and doctrine real and existential. They are the means by which faith, hope and love are perfected.

But Thomas went further, to reflect on why we have sacraments at all. He observed first that our natural path to knowing things is through our senses. All our knowledge originates in sense perception. He also observed that the first way human beings came to know God in history was through their consciences. But then, he noted, sin clouded the conscience.

So God had to do something to clarify his truth to his human creatures, who had now become confused by sin ("their senseless hearts were darkened" [Rom 1:21, my translation]). He also had to make it more explicit that it is only the grace of Christ that makes people holy. For these two reasons he sent Christ in bodily form, which clarified truth and showed that holiness comes only from Christ.

But according to Thomas, now that Christ is no longer with us bodily, sacraments are the perfect vehicles through which Christ gives his grace to us. They are perfect because we are sensory creatures, and the sacraments use the senses to show us what they mean. They are well-suited to us for another reason—we tend to like external (rather than sheerly mental) activities because we are created bodies with connections to other bodies and things external to us, and they are external means of receiving Christ's grace.

Thomas's definition of sacrament is similar to Augustine's—a sign in action. He thought of the sacraments as a series of reenactments of Christ's passion and resurrection, the journey Jesus took in order to salvage the Father's creation. These reenactments are meant not merely to repeat or recall the journey, but to *apply* it to us, draw us into the journey, and to pass on its effects as if we ourselves had suffered and died. Through them we put on the grace of Christ, and Christ continues the work of salvaging the fallen creation.

Finally, Thomas said that sacraments not only signify divine realities but also cause them to happen. (At this point those in Baptist and other nonsacramental churches will disagree, saying that baptism and the Lord's Supper merely proclaim and recall the person and work of Christ.) For Thomas they are visible historical gestures of Christ in this present world. Just as humans use their material bodies to kiss and embrace in order to communicate love, Christ uses his body (ministers and helpers) and matter (bread, wine and water) to communicate love to his family and friends.

BAPTISM

Let us descend from the world of theory to something more concrete, and take a look at how Thomas handles the sacrament of Christian initiation— baptism. He says the grace of baptism is a moment-of-birth grace, the moment when a person is first joined to the death of Christ. At that moment we also become part of Christ's body: "As many of you as were baptized into Christ have put on Christ" (Gal 3:27).

Now those of us who are not Catholics or high-church Protestants may balk at this point and say, Baptism doesn't automatically make you a member of the body of Christ! Look at Simon in Acts 8, who was baptized but had "neither part nor lot in the matter" of Christ (Acts 8:21). But we might agree that baptism confers a spiritual seed, as it were, that requires faith to germinate and grow, so that salvation is linked not indissolubly to the rite of baptism alone but to persevering faith instead. In that case, baptism is still a means of grace that connects a person to the body of Christ, but the nature and future of that connection depend on a faith that grows.

Thomas said there are three elements in baptism: (1) the sign, (2) the reality it signifies (the internal grace of new life), and (3) the character imprinted. By "sign" Thomas meant water. He cited Titus 3:5: "He saved us, not by works of righteousness which we performed. But according to his mercy, through a *washing* of new birth and renewal by the Holy Spirit" (my translation). Thomas liked what Augustine said about this: baptism "touches the body and cleans the heart."[10]

Which mode of baptism is best? Thomas said immersion is better than sprinkling because it symbolizes Christ's burial and is the more common

---

[10]This citation and much of the material on baptism is based on Davies, "Signs and Wonders," *Thought of Thomas Aquinas.*

one in the New Testament. But he also said we should not think there is magic in the water. The sacrament is not in the water itself but in the *action* of applying water to the person.

What reality is signified? Or what really happens? According to Thomas, baptism removes our liability for our sins and disposes our souls to worship God in and through the church. Every baptized person shares in the suffering of Christ, as if that person him- or herself had suffered and died. Thus the person is freed from all punishment for sins. Since he or she is now a member of Christ's body, it is as if the person had suffered that penalty. This is why Thomas said baptism should not be repeated: we are born only once. So we are baptized into the death of Christ once, just as Christ himself died only once.

By "character" Thomas meant two things. First, a badge or token. In ancient times, enlisted soldiers were tattooed, and this tattoo was called a "character." The sacraments, Thomas said, imprint a spiritual tattoo or character. It is invisibly imprinted on the soul, but it can be known when people see a person washed with the water of baptism. We have to remember that most people in the ancient world lived in small towns and villages, where everyone knew everyone, or in densely packed neighborhoods in big cities where all neighbors were well known. When someone was baptized, it was known by all, just as a tattoo today is often quite visible.

Second, "character" is a kind of special ability to take part in the worship of God. The sacramental character is a special imprint of Christ's priesthood, whereby he shares his priesthood with us as we are motivated to give thanks and praise to God.

Yet Thomas believed we can lose our salvation, and thus the use of this character. Since the soul is subject to alteration by free will, so too can grace be. It can come and go—if we decide to turn away from Jesus Christ.[11]

Finally, a few other interesting points about Thomas and baptism.

1. Aquinas said baptism is the most necessary sacrament, and so infants have no other way of salvation. This is why Catholics and even some high-church Protestants have been anxious to baptize a baby in danger of death. Without baptism, people cannot receive full forgiveness of both sin and its punishment.

---

[11]Aquinas *Summa Theologica* 1a.24.

2. Lest Thomas's view seems cruel in cases where baptism is impossible to procure, he taught a "baptism of desire," arising from faith working through love (Gal 5:6). The will for salvation counts for the deed.

3. Thomas said there are conditions that should be met for baptism, such as repentance. Adults who convert, he said, should not be given baptism immediately. They must *intend* to receive what is given, since God justifies not those who come by force but those who come willingly. (Thomas might have been thinking of those who converted under compulsion in war or from terror of hell alone.) True faith is also a prerequisite, since grace cannot be received without it.

4. Yet there are times when the baptismal character can be imparted without faith, since infants for example do not have faith. In this case the character is there but without its full effects. The tattoo is imprinted but it hasn't taken its full effect, since it requires faith and acts of the will to make it fully real. A person can have the tattoo marking membership in a club, but he or she must voluntarily participate in the club to receive the benefits of membership.

5. Infants are in the womb of the Church, so to speak, and so receive salvation not by their own act but by the Church's, by the actions of those who offer them for baptism. Similarly, Thomas said, the Church believes and repents for the insane.

Aquinas's treatise on the sacraments was the last thing he ever wrote. On the morning of December 6, 1273, while celebrating mass, he fell into a trance. From that moment, and without explanation, he stopped writing and spoke little. According to his secretary, persistent questioning drew the reply that in comparison to what God had now revealed to him, all he had written seemed like chaff. Some moderns might say he had a stroke, but that is pathologizing what this great Doctor (teacher) said was a spiritual experience. Less than three months later, while riding a mule to the Council of Lyons, he ran into the branch of a tree and was injured. Within two weeks, at the age of forty-nine, he was dead.

WHAT CAN WE LEARN FROM THOMAS?

1. Thomas gives us an elegant portrayal of the Christian life. By his account, the life of Christ set up a road for us to follow—a road to Jerusalem, carrying a cross, through death and resurrection, through the veil of God's

hiddenness, coming from the Father originally and going now back to the Father. (Recall the pattern of *exitus* and *reditus*.) It is the last act in the drama of salvaging God's creation, undoing the damage we have done to ourselves and the creation, but an undoing in which God asks us to cooperate with him. We don't cooperate in salvaging ourselves from sin and sowing the seed of new life in ourselves. Those things are done by God alone. But we do cooperate in our actualization of this new life—nurturing that seed, earning and reaping its eternal harvest.[12] The sacraments are the ways for us to actualize the new life.

2. There is a certain power in Thomas's presentation of baptism as something whose character can be received without its benefits—but that faith and repentance are necessary for the benefits to be received. We could use several analogies: a minister declares a man and woman to be husband and wife, but they must sign the register and consummate their union sexually for marriage to become real. An inheritance can be deeded by a father to his son, but the son must claim the inheritance in order to enjoy its possession. Queen Elizabeth inherited the throne on her father's death, but her reign did not actually begin until she claimed it and the country's officials confirmed it. So too baptism confers a status that must be adopted; it conveys an inheritance that must be claimed; its outward validity is complete, but its spiritual efficacy is conditional.

A SELECTION FROM THOMAS AQUINAS'S WORKS

There is a twofold mode of truth in what we profess about God. Some truths about God exceed all the ability of the human reason. Such is the truth that God is triune. But there are some truths which the natural reason also is able to reach. Such are that God exists, that He is one, and the like. In fact, such truths about God have been proved demonstratively by the philosophers, guided by the light of the natural reason.

That there are certain truths about God that totally surpass man's ability appears with the greatest evidence. Since, indeed, the principle of all knowledge that the reason perceives about something is the understanding of the very substance of that being (for according to Aristotle "what a thing is" is the principle of demonstration) it is necessary that the way in which we understand the sub-

---

[12]When Aquinas used *earning* he had in mind the many biblical references to rewards, whereby God rewards our obedience that has been inspired and empowered by grace.

stance of a thing determines the way in which we know what belongs to it. Hence, if the human intellect comprehends the substance of some thing, for example, that of a stone or of a triangle, no intelligible characteristic belonging to that thing surpasses the grasp of human reason. But this does not happen to us in the case of God. For the human intellect is not able to reach a comprehension of the divine substance through its natural power. For, according to its manner of knowing in the present life, the intellect depends on the sense for the origin of knowledge; and so those things that do not fall under the senses cannot be grasped by the human intellect except in so far as the knowledge of them is gathered from sensible things. Now, sensible things cannot lead the human intellect to the point of seeing in them the nature of the divine substance; for sensible things are effects that fall short of the power of their cause. Yet, beginning with sensible things, our intellect is led to the point of knowing about God that He exists, and other such characteristics that must be attributed to the First Principle. There are, consequently, some intelligible truths about God that are open to the human reason; but there are others that absolutely surpass its power.[13]

FOR REFLECTION AND DISCUSSION

1. Do you agree with Thomas that reason can show us that God exists?

2. Can you think of an example where we can see Thomas's principle that in all things both nature and God are interpenetrating and at work simultaneously?

3. How did Luther and Thomas differ on justification? How did they agree?

4. Thomas said the sacraments enable us to become Christ's contemporaries, living together in the same time. What did he mean by this?

5. According to Thomas, how is sacramental "character" like a tattoo?

6. Did Thomas believe one can rely on infant baptism by itself to save, without any response from the baby as it grows? Why?

7. Does Thomas's image of the Christian life as a journey help you to understand your own walk of faith?

---

[13]Thomas Aquinas *On the Truth of the Catholic Faith: Summa Contra Gentiles* 1.3.2-3, trans. Anton C. Pegis (New York: Image Books, 1955), pp. 63-64.

FOR FURTHER READING

Thomas Aquinas. *Introduction to Thomas Aquinas.* Edited by Anton Pegis.
New York: Modern Library, 1964.

―――. *Summa Theologica.* 5 vols. Translated by the Fathers of the English
Dominican Province. Allen, Tex.: Benziger, 1981.

Chesterton, G. K. *Saint Thomas Aquinas: The Dumb Ox.* New York: Image, 1974.

McInerny, Ralph M. *Saint Thomas Aquinas.* Notre Dame, Ind.: University
of Notre Dame Press, 1982.

6

Martin Luther

The Monk Who Rose Up Against Heaven and Earth

The great Luther scholar Paul Althaus once referred to Luther as an "ocean."[1] This word can be used both for Luther's enormous literary output (over one hundred folio volumes—each more than one foot high—in the German edition of his Works) and his originality. Only a handful of theologians in the history of Christian thought approach his stature—perhaps Augustine, Thomas Aquinas, Edwards and Barth.

A MINI-PORTRAIT

Eyewitnesses recounted that whoever spoke to Luther was riveted by the intensity of his eyes. After his interview with Luther in August 1518, Cardinal Cajetan spoke of the monk with the strange eyes. A Swiss student in Wittenberg described Luther's eyes as "deep, black, blinking, and glittering like a star."[2]

Luther was of medium build and had a good sense of humor—often crude, always robust. For instance, at the end of his life he promised, "When I get home to Wittenberg again, I will lie down in my coffin and give the worms a fat doctor to feast on."[3] But he wasn't always fat. When

---

[1]Paul Althaus, *The Theology of Martin Luther* (Philadelphia: Fortress, 1966), cited by Timothy George, *The Theology of the Reformers* (Nashville: Broadman, 1988), p. 51. The subtitle of this chapter comes from Heiko Oberman, who says that Luther "rose up against these powers of Heaven and Earth: he stood alone with only God and his omnipresent adversary, the Devil" (Heiko Oberman, *Luther: Man Between God and the Devil* [New Haven, Conn.: Yale University Press, 1989], p. xix).
[2]Oberman, *Luther*, p. 325.
[3]Martin Luther, cited in ibid., p. 5.

he left the monastery in his mid-thirties, he had fought the flesh so long that a friend said he was "haggard from worrying and studying, so that one can almost count his bones through the skin."[4]

Luther was an emotional man. He had a temperament like a volcano that could explode at any moment. Yet a contemporary said he had a clear and articulate voice, and was usually courteous, even cheerful. But "he criticizes a bit too caustically and aggressively."[5] While his tendency to criticize was not unusual for his age, it reflects a huge personality who was completely down to earth—at the same time full of humor and occasionally foul-mouthed. Those who think theology makes for dull reading have not read Luther. Try his *Table Talk* (notes made by his theological students on his remarks over meals) for starters.[6] Here's a typical statement by this "hearty" theologian: "If our God makes excellent large pike and good Rhine wine, I may very well venture to eat and drink [them]! You may enjoy every pleasure in the world that is not sinful; your God doesn't forbid it, but rather wills it. And it pleases God whenever you laugh from the bottom of your heart."[7]

Luther was rarely at a loss for confidence. While scholars often wrote *ni fallor* ("if I am not mistaken"), Luther wrote *immo* ("certainly!").[8] Perhaps because of this self-confidence, he wrote so much that sometimes scholars complain we can find anything we want in his writings, and occasionally differing opinions on the same subject. Of this intellectual restlessness Luther said about himself, "They are trying to make of me a fixed star. I am not—I am a wandering planet." The result is that in his gargantuan writings, there is plenty of nearly everything, which means that reading Luther can be like panning for gold—there are dross and waste, but also precious nuggets of pure gold.

The German Reformer loved nature. Throughout the great Leipzig disputation he was wearing a silver ring, with an amulet against evil, and holding a flower, occasionally smelling it. He loved to relax in a garden,

---

[4]Oberman, *Luther*, p. 326.
[5]Ibid.
[6]"The Table Talk of Martin Luther," Center for Reformed Theology and Apologetics <www .reformed.org/table_talk/table_talk.html>.
[7]Martin Luther, quoted in Augustus Hopkins Strong, *Systematic Theology* (Philadelphia: American Baptist Publication Society, 1907), 1:364. I have modernized the translation a bit. Thanks to Michael McClymond for the citation.
[8]Oberman, *Luther*, p. 299.

and "in defiance of the devil" delighted in flowers, especially roses, as God's gift.[9]

THE LEGEND

Who and what was Luther? It depends on whom you ask. For some centuries following the Reformation, Catholic historians portrayed him as

> a mad monk, a psychotic demoniac pulling down the pillars of Mother Church. To orthodox Protestants Luther was the godly knight, a Moses, a Samson (pulling down the temple of the Philistines!), an Elijah, even the Fifth Evangelist and the Angel of the Lord. . . . The German nationalists hailed him as a folk hero and 'father of his country'; the Nazi theologians hailed him as a proto-Aryan and precursor of the Führer.[10]

Luther said he never wanted to start a new church.

> In the first place, I ask that men make no reference to my name; let them call themselves Christians not Lutherans. What is Luther? The teaching is not mine. Neither was I crucified for anyone. . . . How then should I—poor stinking maggot-fodder that I am—come to have men call the children of Christ by my wretched name?[11]

Nor did Luther claim to have started the Reformation.

> I simply taught, preached, wrote God's Word; otherwise, I did nothing. And then, while I slept, or drank Wittenberg beer with my Philip and my Amsdorf, the Word so greatly weakened the papacy that never a prince or emperor did such damage to it. I did nothing. The Word did it all.[12]

We are not surprised to learn, however, that he and the Roman Church separated, after reading the sorts of things he said about the pope of his day. He referred to Pope Paul III as "His Hellishness," and the Roman hierarchy as the "whore-church of the devil." He was asked, "Are not the pope and his associates members of the Body of Christ?" Yes, Luther replied, "as much as spit, snot, pus, feces, urine, stench, scab, smallpox, ul-

---

[9]Ibid., pp. 326-27.
[10]George, *Theology of the Reformers*, p. 53.
[11]Martin Luther, "A Sincere Admonition from Martin Luther to All Christians" (1522), in *Luther's Works* 45, ed. Walther I. Brandt (Philadelphia: Muhlenberg Press, 1962), p. 70.
[12]Martin Luther, Second Wittenberg sermon, in *Works of Martin Luther* (Philadelphia: Muhlenberg, 1915), 2:399-400.

cers and syphilis are members of the human body."[13]

Luther often complained about Rome's failure to preach the Word, and insisted faith comes from hearing the Word. In fact, he taught, the chief function of a Christian is to hear the Word of God.

> For if you ask a Christian what the work is by which he becomes worthy of the name "Christian," he would be able to give absolutely no other answer that that it is the hearing of the Word of God, that is, faith. Therefore the ears alone are the organs of a Christian man.[14]

By *hearing*, Luther did not mean merely letting sounds strike the ear. He said we must hear and receive them personally. It is never enough, he preached, to know simply that Christ died, or even why he died. He would quote James 2:19: "The devils believe the same and tremble," and insist that saving faith must break through to personal appropriation. The good news cannot be grasped in abstraction but only from the depths of experience. "A person who wants to be saved should act as though the Bible was written for him alone, and there was no one else on earth."[15]

JUSTIFICATION BY GRACE THROUGH FAITH ALONE

Luther's cardinal insight was justification by grace through faith alone. He called it "the summary of all Christian doctrine." As a Catholic monk the phrase in the Latin version of Romans 1:17 ("in the gospel the *righteousness* of God is revealed") struck terror into his soul. He thought "righteousness" (*iustitia* was the word in Luther's Latin Bible) meant God's active punishment of sin (what we would call justice) and feared that his attempts to avoid that punishment were not enough. He had prayed for hours on end, fasted until he looked emaciated, kept vigils and performed good works—but he still had a guilty conscience. His mood swung from despair over his own failures to a simmering rage at God: "I did not love, yes, I hated, the righteous God who punishes sinners, and secretly, if not blasphemously, certainly murmuring greatly, I was angry with God."[16]

---

[13]Luther, cited in George, *Theology of the Reformers*, p. 88.

[14]Martin Luther, *Lectures on Hebrews, Luther's Works* 29, ed. Jaroslav Pelikan (St Louis: Concordia, 1968), p. 224.

[15] Luther, cited in George, *Theology of the Reformers*, pp. 59-60.

[16]Martin Luther, preface to the complete edition of Luther's Latin writings (1545), in *Luther's Works* 34, ed. Lewis Spitz (Philadelphia: Muhlenberg, 1960), pp. 336-37.

But Luther kept reading Paul, desperate for relief and guidance. He says he meditated on Paul night and day, until finally he saw the light.

> I began to understand that the righteousness of God is that by which the righteous live by a gift of God, namely by faith. And this is the meaning: the righteousness of God is revealed by the gospel, namely, the passive righteousness with which merciful *[sic]* God justifies us by faith, as it is written: "He who through faith is just shall live" [Hab 2:4]. Here I felt that I was altogether born again and had entered paradise itself through open gates.[17]

The year was 1519. Luther was thirty-five.

What had driven Luther to such torment? Why was he, an Augustinian monk, unable to see the grace of God which Augustine had taught?

There were three reasons.

1. The first problem was the doctrine of divinization, which we have seen in Athanasius and Augustine. Athanasius said God was made human so that humans could become god. Augustine said we share this divine nature by participating in the sacraments. The implication, as this doctrine became hardened in the Middle Ages, was that we are accepted as righteous (in Luther's Latin translation, "just") by God only after we have *become* righteous by the infusion of God's nature. The question that tormented Luther was, What if I don't sense this divine nature within me? Am I perhaps trusting an idol?

2. The Fourth Lateran Council (1215) had pronounced that only sins confessed to a priest could be forgiven. This drove a conscientious soul like Luther absolutely frantic. He was obsessed with the fear that he might have overlooked one sin. He would spend hours in the confessional with his spiritual director Johann von Staupitz, walk away, and then come rushing back because he had remembered another little foible.

> Staupitz was exasperated. "Look here, brother Martin. If you're going to confess so much, why don't you go do something worth confessing? Kill your mother or father! Commit adultery! Quit coming in here with such peccadillos!"[18]

Then Luther had another doubt. Was he really sorry for his sin or just

---

[17]Ibid., p. 337.
[18]Johann von Staupitz, quoted in Roland Bainton, *Here I Stand: A Life of Martin Luther* (Nashville: Abingdon, 1950), p. 41.

afraid of hell? At this point he was driven to the depths of despair, so that he wished he had never been born. He turned from hating himself to hating God for making him and for making justification seem impossible.

2. The fifteenth-century German theologian Gabriel Biel had taught that God gives grace only to those who try their best. This was much like our American saying today, "God helps those who help themselves." The assumption was that God's grace is based on what we do. He gives it only to those who are trying their hardest. But again, Luther, with his sensitive conscience, always wondered if he was doing his best. How could he know, since he also knew that the human heart is "devious above all else" (Jer 17:9)? Maybe he *thought* he was trying his best but his heart actually was tricking him, camouflaging his half-heartedness. How could he know for sure?

The breakthrough came when he saw, from Paul's epistles and Paul's own life story, that what precedes grace is not great effort but in fact active rebellion. As Paul put it in Romans 5:6, "Christ died for the *ungodly*"— not the godly. Paul didn't find grace while trying his hardest to serve Christ. Quite the opposite: he found grace when trying to *kill* Christ! He was on his way to Damascus to arrest Christians and deliver them over to punishment and possible death. And Jesus said that since he was trying to kill Christians, he was really after Christ himself: "I am Jesus, whom you are persecuting" (Acts 9:5).

Luther felt liberated. He felt like he had been born again. God is not looking for religious and moral perfection before he would bestow grace. Instead he joins people to Christ when they are even fighting against him—and not *because* of their goodness but *in spite of* their badness. The only stipulation is that they believe that it is Christ's works and not their own that brings them to God.

IMPUTATION

Luther moved from the language of medicine, which we saw in the previous chapters on Athanasius and Augustine, to the language of the law court. Rather than seeing grace as a new substance *infused* into a sick body, he thought of justification in terms of a judge absolving a prisoner of guilt and declaring him free from any more accusations. The judge *imputes* innocence to the prisoner because his guilt and penalty have been taken by someone else. Luther saw that God accepts the righteousness of Christ, which is alien to our nature, as our own. Although our sins are not actually removed in justification, they cease to be counted against us.

His famous term for this is the *joyous* or *happy* exchange by which we give Christ our sins and condemnation, and he gives us his righteousness and eternal life: "Is this not a joyous exchange—the rich, noble, pious bridegroom Christ takes this poor, despised wicked little whore in marriage, redeems her of all evil, and adorns her with all his goods?"[19]

While Augustine and his medieval theological disciples had interpreted Paul as saying that in justification we are *made* righteous, Luther said the essential thing in justification is that we are *declared* righteous. He never rejected the notion of being made righteous, but came to the conclusion that justification is based finally not on a gradual curing in the sinner but on what Christ did on the cross. The sinner just has to accept and receive this great news. Christ will indeed begin to transform him, but he must look to Christ's work first, not what might be happening in his own heart.[20]

Many Lutherans and evangelicals in the past century have said that what distinguishes Luther's (and therefore the Protestant) view of justification from the Catholic view is imputation versus infusion: Luther taught imputation (that God only *declares* us righteous in justification) while Aquinas and Catholics teach infusion (that God *makes* us righteous in justification). But Luther did not restrict justification to a legal transaction in the sky, removed from the real life of the new believer. "In the joyous exchange Christ really makes the ungodly his own, and really breathes his Spirit to awaken faith in her, so that there is a union of Christ and the believing sinner on the basis of which the verdict of justification is pronounced."[21] Here are Luther's own words:

> Therefore faith justifies because it takes hold of and possesses this treasure, the present Christ. . . . Where the confidence of the heart is present, there-

---

[19]Martin Luther, quoted by Oberman, *Luther*, p. 78.

[20]For more on Luther's belief that justification begins the process of changing the sinner's inner nature, see Gerald R. McDermott, "Jonathan Edwards on Justification by Faith: More Protestant or Catholic?" *Pro Ecclesia* 17, no. 1 (2008): 97-104.

[21]Personal note from Luther scholar Paul Hinlicky to me, July 26, 2008.

fore, *there Christ is present*, in that very cloud and faith. This is the formal righteousness on account of which a man is justified. . . . Therefore *the Christ* who is grasped by faith and who *lives in the heart* is the true Christian righteousness, on account of which God counts us righteous and grants us eternal life.[22]

Therefore for Luther imputation is not a legal fiction whereby God justifies us on the basis of something that happens outside us, declaring righteous a person who is no different after faith than he or she was before faith. Quite the contrary—faith brings union with Christ and "God's love . . . poured into our hearts through the Holy Spirit" (Rom 5:5). It is on this basis that the legal verdict of justification is pronounced.[23]

FAITH ALONE

Luther taught that faith alone, without works, is what joins us to Christ our Savior. By *faith* he meant the Latin *fiducia*, which means personal trust, reliance, a grasping or taking hold of Christ *pro me* (for myself). Medieval theology had emphasized Aquinas's stress on faith being "formed by love." For Luther, this created insuperable problems. It implied that the work of love—which is what I do—is also necessary for me to be joined to Christ. Thus I become something of a cosavior, helping Christ save me. This, for Luther, was not only unbiblical but also, as he had found in his own experience, psychologically impossible. Often he seemed incapable of real love. And besides, how would we ever know we have enough love or the right kind of love? It would suggest that Christ died not for the *un*-godly but for the godly.

Luther also recognized that his emphasis on faith could be misinterpreted as the idea that *my* faith saves me. Then faith would be a work, a way of thinking that I am saving myself. So Luther kept insisting that faith itself does not justify. It only *receives* the gift of justification. It does not cause grace to come but becomes conscious of grace already in existence. Besides, Paul said faith is "not your own doing; it is the gift of God" (Eph 2:8). It is not self-generated but a gift of the Holy Spirit.

---

[22]Martin Luther, *Lectures on Galatians 1535, Chapters 1-4*, in *Luther's Works* 26, ed. Jaroslav Pelikan (Saint Louis: Concordia, 1963), p. 130, italics added.

[23]This has been noted by a new generation of Luther research among Finnish scholars. See Tuomo Mannermaa, *Christ Present in Man: Luther's View of Justification* (Minneapolis: Fortress, 2005).

AT THE SAME TIME RIGHTEOUS AND A SINNER

Lest believers become so impressed with their new life and start to imagine it is their appropriation of this new life that caused God to favor them, Luther also taught *simul iustus et peccator*—the believer is at the same time righteous and also a sinner.

It depends on the perspective we use to look at our new lives. From the perspective of our first birth, we are truly and totally sinners. But from the perspective of our second (new) birth, Christ has been given to us so that now, in him, we are totally holy and righteous. So from different perspectives, we are both righteous and sinners at the same time.

Luther therefore said that for the believer there is no sin at all (since God sees the righteousness of Christ, to whom we are joined), and that in the believer everything is sin (our sinful nature is still very much with us in this life). There are both hell and heaven in us at the same time.

MISREPRESENTATIONS

A new generation of Luther scholars is now arguing that twentieth-century writing about Luther has misrepresented his theology by putting human experience at the center of his doctrine of justification. Instead, they insist, trinitarian Christology was his center, and justification was an expression of that Christology.[24] The result of twentieth-century stress on the human subject of justification is that generations of scholars have portrayed Luther's doctrine of justification as an existential (centered in human experience) answer to human anxiety about meaning and forgiveness—completely separated from the person of Christ and the rest of Christian theology. All that matters, some of these writers have implied, is that you know that you are forgiven. It doesn't matter who you think Jesus is, whether the Trinity is true or even whether Jesus rose from the dead. It might not even matter how you live your life.

But in his Smalcald Articles (1537) Luther wrote, "The first and chief article is this, *that Jesus Christ, our God and Lord, died for our sins*, and was raised again for our justification." For Luther, the work of Christ could not be separated from the person of Christ. Justification could not be separated from the deity of Christ and the Trinity. Justification therefore was

---

[24]See, for example, Dennis Bielfeldt, Mickey L. Mattox and Paul Hinlicky, *The Substance of the Faith: Luther's Doctrinal Theology for Today* (Minneapolis: Fortress, 2008).

not primarily an experience in which we feel let off the hook, but the way the trinitarian God reconciles a sinful world to himself. Justification is one part of a much larger story, so that justification and Luther's theology are distorted if that larger story is not put front and center.

Another mistake has been the traditional Protestant interpretation that Luther's "evangelical breakthrough" was a decisive break with Catholic teaching, making the rise of a new church (Protestantism) inevitable. Scholars are now questioning this. They have found that the driving question in his early theology was not How can I find a gracious God? but Where can I find the *real* God? In other words, he was concerned not with assurance of salvation but discernment—How can I be sure that I am not worshiping a false God, an idol? He was deeply impressed by Augustine's idea that God's grace so transforms us that it breaks our self-obsession and makes us love God not for our own sake but for his. Luther thought the theology of his day (including the indulgence practices of the church) downplayed the radical nature of this transformation, reducing grace to something you can buy and store up for a better transaction after death. In that case it was no longer the grace of the true God but a so-called benefit promised by a false god. The sign of the true God's grace was the cross: he brings to the believer trouble and suffering. Luther was saying, "If you are trusting the real God, you will know it when he tortures and crucifies you as he did to Jesus Christ." Luther found this comforting. The important point for this new generation of scholars is that Luther turned in this early theology of the cross not *away from* Catholic theology to resolve his fundamental dilemma but to a preeminent Catholic theologian, Augustine.

If Luther's initial dilemma was more discernment and idolatry than assurance, later on when he wrestled with the question of assurance, he turned again not to some existential discovery but to traditional Catholic theology of the sacraments. This is another conclusion by recent scholarship. According to David Yeago, "From 1518 on, it is the particularity and concreteness of God's presence that now foreclose idolatry; the true God, who by definition cannot be used, is the God who makes Himself available as He chooses, in the flesh born of Mary and the Church's sacramental practice, not in our religious speculation and self-interest."[25] Now, say

---

[25]David Yeago, "The Catholic Luther," *First Things* 61 (1996): 40.

Yeago and a new generation of Finnish scholars of Luther, the Reformer said the Christian must turn to the church's sacraments for assurance. Believers must trust that when the minister says, "This is the body and blood of Christ," Christ himself is offering grace and forgiveness. They must believe in the sacrament of penance that Christ gave his ministers authority to "loose on earth" (Mt 16:19), and therefore their sins are absolved in heaven. To doubt those declarations of the church is to "make Christ a liar."[26]

Therefore, says Yeago and others, the split between Catholic and Protestant churches in the sixteenth century was theologically unnecessary. Luther was reacting to Catholic excesses of his day, but drew from the Catholic tradition to correct those excesses. His reteaching of the gospel used what he learned from the Catholic Augustine. As Paul Hinlicky puts it, "Luther's argument had never been with Catholicism, but with the papacy. . . . [He] sought ever and again to establish the catholic credentials of [his] teaching."[27] These scholars conclude that the Reformation split the Western church because of the unwillingness of Roman authorities to use the best of their tradition, the unfortunate influence of financial politics on doctrine, Luther's impatience and his rash claim that the papacy itself was antichrist.

THEOLOGY OF THE CROSS

One result of Luther's doctrine of justification is his "theology of the cross." It has had a major impact on twentieth-century theology, best seen in Jürgen Moltmann's 1974 book, *The Crucified God*. Luther's theology of the cross is clearly expressed in his Heidelberg Disputation (1518), where he distinguished between theologians of glory, who base their views of God on created things that can be seen, and theologians of the cross, who say God best reveals himself through "the passion and the cross."[28] Only in Christ's passion and death do we gain true knowledge of God and ourselves. A theology of glory views our works as things that please God and

---

[26]Ibid., p. 39. See also Carl Braaten and Robert Jenson, eds., *Union with Christ: The New Finnish Interpretation of Luther* (Grand Rapids: Eerdmans, 1998).

[27]Paul R. Hinlicky, *Luther and the Beloved Community: Resources for Theology After Christendom* (Grand Rapids: Eerdmans, forthcoming), chap. 7.

[28]"Disputation Held at Heidelberg," in *Luther's Works* 31, ed. Harold J. Grimm and Helmut T. Lehmann (Philadelphia: Muhlenberg, 1957), pp. 39-58.

therefore justify us. But the theology of the cross teaches that all of our works are condemned on the cross, and that only God's work at the cross, in his "weakness" and "foolishness" (in the world's eyes), justifies us.

In his book *Luther's Theology of the Cross*, Alister McGrath argues that the theology of the cross is necessary for us to interpret our experience properly.[29] On Good Friday the disciples probably concluded that Jesus had failed and perhaps wasn't the Messiah after all. They may have even doubted God's love for them, since he seemed to have let them down. God seemed to be absent. If they had used their experience as a rule, they would have concluded that Jesus was not who he said he was, and God had abandoned them.

But Easter Sunday morning brought new realizations—that Jesus is Messiah after all, God had honored his promises to love and save his people, and God had been present after all on Good Friday. The point is that knowing the resurrection helps us make sense of our experience—not only Good Friday but all the other times when God seems to be absent. A theology of the cross, which emphasizes that the true God cannot be known apart from the cross and his resurrection, helps us interpret our experience when God seems absent.

THE REACTION

This renewed understanding of justification and the cross "fell like a bombshell on the theological landscape of medieval Catholicism. It shattered the entire theology of merits and indeed the sacramental-penitential basis of the church itself." Jacob Hochstraten, a Dominican at Cologne, said it was blasphemy to describe the union of the soul to Christ as a spiritual marriage based on faith alone. How could Christ be joined to a sinner? That would make the soul a prostitute and an adulteress, and Christ himself a pimp and a cowardly patron of her disgrace.[30]

Timothy George remarks that this was indeed shocking, but no more shocking than Paul's own declaration that God justifies the ungodly. Or Jesus' story of the loving father who hugs and kisses his sorrowful son after

---

[29]Alister McGrath, *Luther's Theology of the Cross: Martin Luther's Theological Breakthrough* (Oxford: Blackwell, 1985).
[30]Jacob Hochstraten, quoted in George, *Theology of the Reformers*, p. 72.

squandering his dad's money and falling in with prostitutes.[31]

It seemed to many that Luther was eliminating the need for good works in the Christian life. Duke George of Saxony was caustic: "Luther's doctrine is good for the dying, but no good for the living." Erasmus was more cutting: "Lutherans seek only two things—wealth and wives. . . . [T]o them the gospel means the right to live as they please."[32]

But for Luther, good works are essential as *evidence* of true faith. He believed that his understanding of justification, as faith active in love, actually frees us to love our neighbor not for our own sake but for the neighbor's. Whereas when I believed my works would get me justified, I would love my neighbor *in order to* win God's approval, now that I know God bestows his approval on the ungodly and gives them faith, I can love my neighbor in gratitude for God's gift to me. I don't serve my neighbor in order to win Brownie points with God, which is a subtle way of *using* my neighbor for my own religious purposes. Instead, I thank God for his unmerited grace, and turn to my neighbor in love for his or her own sake.[33]

RECENT CRITICISMS

Since World War II and the Holocaust, some historians have blamed the rise of Nazism on Luther's theology. In his *Rise and Fall of the Third Reich* (1960), for example, William L. Shirer tried to draw a straight line from Luther to Hitler, arguing that Luther's "ferocious [belief] in absolute political authority" rendered Germans passive during Hitler's rise to power. The problem with this assertion is that Luther advocated "an almost foolhardy opposition against all governmental injustice" and provided his followers with precise directives on how to remove tyrants from power.[34] It is true that Luther counseled submission to the authorities during the Peasants Revolt (1524-1526) because he feared it could undo his reform efforts. But he also wrote repeatedly to political leaders about how to think rightly about church and state.

Many others have traced Nazi anti-Semitism back to Luther's violent

---

[31]George, *Theology of the Reformers*, p. 72.
[32]Ibid., pp. 72-73.
[33]For a wonderful presentation of Luther's ethics, see George W. Forell, *Faith Active in Love: An Investigation of the Principles Underlying Luther's Social Ethics* (Minneapolis: Augsburg, 1954).
[34]Uwe Siemon-Netto, *The Fabricated Luther: Refuting Nazi Connections and Other Modern Myths* (St. Louis: Concordia, 2007), p. 24.

invective against Jews late in his career. This is bad historiography, for two reasons. First, Luther's denunciations were based on Jewish religion and religious practice, not race. Second, the truly racial anti-Semitism that became the source of Nazi hatred goes back not to Luther but to the so-called scientific anti-Semitism stemming from eighteenth-century deists in England, whose anti-Jewish thinking was popularized by the French philosophes. Voltaire, for example, learned from the deists when he was in London and came to call Jews "execrable." Once he wrote that a Jew is someone who should have engraved on his forehead, "Fit to be hanged."[35]

Luther himself showed deep appreciation for the Jewish tradition. His own scholarly specialty was the Hebrew Bible, his close colleague Philip Melanchthon was a Hebrew scholar and friendly with rabbis, and Luther wrote a number of philo-Semitic essays including "That Jesus Christ Was Born a Jew" (1523).

But Luther did say nasty things about Jews late in life. Because of their refusal to accept Jesus as Messiah, and in an effort to "save some from the flames and embers . . . their synagogues should be set on fire . . . [Jewish homes] be broken down or destroyed . . . [and Jews themselves be] put under one roof, or in a stable, like Gypsies, in order that they may realize that they are not masters in our land."[36]

Some Luther scholars have recently concluded that these frightening words were motivated by Luther's apocalypticism—his belief that the world would end in his lifetime and that all enemies of the gospel were driven by the devil. Luther demonized not only the Jews but also the Turks, the peasants who started revolts in 1524-1526 and the papacy. He seems to have forgotten, for a time, that the devil is a dog on God's leash. We should beware of similar end-times prophets today who would demonize all non-Christians and suggest that the devil is a second God.

SO HOW DO WE FIND THE TRUE GOD?

If we are now in the position Luther was when he was thirty-five, and we too seem unable to find the real God, Luther's teachings can help. If we

---

[35]For more on this deist connection to European anti-Semitism, see Frank Manuel, *The Broken Staff: Judaism Through Christian Eyes* (Cambridge, Mass.: Harvard University Press, 1992).

[36]Martin Luther, "On the Jews and Their Lies" (1543), quoted in Bielfeldt, Mattox and Hinlicky, *Substance of the Faith*, p. 176.

have been consciously or unconsciously trying to please God with our moral or religious lives, and hoping that would save us, but have now realized that those efforts will never bring peace to a sensitive soul, we must see the following:

1. Salvation is by *grace* (which means a free and unearned gift) through faith. It is not by works—or at least, not ours. Salvation *does* come by the works of Christ, in *his* perfect life, death and resurrection. Our good efforts contribute nothing to our salvation. Instead, as we may have already realized, our sins of indifference and stubbornness vastly outweigh whatever good we can offer God. And if we are even more aware, we recognize that even our few good works are tainted by self-interest and pride.

2. Our faith should be in what Christ did on the cross, not in our inner holiness. Our own holiness is puny and invariably mixed with sinful motives. But Christ died for just that purpose, to take our sins to hell where they belong and to give us his own righteousness as a gift. Now we need not worry that our righteousness is not enough (it never will be!), but thank God that by faith he has joined us to Christ and therefore to Christ's righteousness. And it is *Christ's* righteousness that is joined to us and saves us.

3. True faith is trust and a matter of the heart. It is not merely intellectual assent to the idea that Christ died for sins, but the heart's reliance on Christ's work for our forgiveness and salvation from God's wrath. This trust is nourished by worship with other believers. So we will want to join a church where this gospel is preached. There alone, in a community of believers, will we be able to walk the journey of faith, and grow in our knowledge of God.

4. Then, Luther says, we will be freed from the agony of trying to earn our salvation by being good people. We will be freed to love our neighbors, thinking of their needs and not just our own. Only when we are freed from trying to be good, and find that Christ alone is good, will we become good.

A SELECTION FROM MARTIN LUTHER'S WORKS

The third incomparable benefit of faith is that it unites the soul with Christ as a bride is united with her bridegroom. By this mystery, as the Apostle teaches, Christ and the soul become one flesh [Eph. 5:31-32]. And if they are one flesh and there is between them a true marriage—indeed the most perfect of all marriages, since human marriages are but poor examples of this one true marriage—it fol-

lows that everything they have they hold in common, the good as well as the evil. Accordingly the believing soul can boast of and glory in whatever Christ has as though it were its own, and whatever the soul has Christ claims as his own. Let us compare these and we shall see inestimable benefits. Christ is full of grace, life, and salvation. The soul is full of sins, death, and damnation. Now let faith come between them and sins, death, and damnation will be Christ's, while grace, life, and salvation will be the soul's; for if Christ is a bridegroom, he must take upon himself the things which are his bride's and bestow upon her the things that are his. If he gives her his body and very self, how shall he not give her all that is his? And if he takes the body of the bride, how shall he not take all that is hers?

Here we have a most pleasing vision not only of communion but of a blessed struggle and victory and salvation and redemption. Christ is God and man in one person. He has neither sinned nor died, and is not condemned, and he cannot sin, die, or be condemned; his righteousness, life, and salvation are unconquerable, eternal, omnipotent. By the wedding ring of faith he shares in the sins, death, and pains of hell which are his bride's. As a matter of fact, he makes them his own and acts as if they were his own and as if he himself had sinned; he suffered, died, and descended into hell that he might overcome them all. Now since it was such a one who did all this, and death and hell could not swallow him up, these were necessarily swallowed up by him in a mighty duel; for his righteousness is greater than the sins of all men, his life stronger than death, his salvation more invincible than hell. Thus the believing soul by means of the pledge of its faith is free in Christ, its bridegroom, free from all sins, secure against death and hell, and is endowed with the eternal righteousness, life, and salvation of Christ its bridegroom. So he takes to himself a glorious bride, "without spot or wrinkle, cleansing her by the washing of water with the word" [cf. Eph. 5:26-27] of life, that is, by faith in the Word of life, righteousness, and salvation. In this way he marries her in faith, steadfast love, and in mercies, righteousness, and justice, as Hos. 2[:19-20] says.

Who then can fully appreciate what this royal marriage means? Who can understand the riches of the glory of this grace? Here this rich and divine bridegroom Christ marries this poor, wicked harlot, redeems her from all her evil, and adorns her with all his goodness. Her sins cannot now destroy her, since they are laid upon Christ and swallowed up by him. And she has that righteousness in Christ, her husband, of which she may boast as of her own and which she can confidently display alongside her sins in the face of death and hell and say, "If I have sinned, yet my Christ, in whom I believe, has not sinned, and all his is mine and all mine is his," as the bride in the Song of Solomon [2:16] says, "My beloved is mine and I am his." This is what Paul means when he says in I Cor. 15[:57], "Thanks be to God, who gives us the victory through our Lord Jesus Christ," that is, the victory over sin and death, as he also says there, "The sting of death is sin, and the power of sin is the law" [1 Cor. 15:56].[37]

FOR REFLECTION AND DISCUSSION

1. What kept Luther as a monk from seeing the grace of God? Are some of these false beliefs still prevalent in churches?

2. What finally opened the door for Luther? Can that still help us today?

3. Did Luther's view of imputation separate him from historic Catholicism? Should it have?

4. Why did Luther say that his faith did *not* justify him?

5. Is Luther's teaching of *simul iustus et peccator* reassuring? Why?

6. How does the theology of the cross help us through dark times?

7. Was Luther truly anti-Semitic?

8. If you are in a group, have each person share something particularly significant from this chapter.

FOR FURTHER READING

Luther, Martin. *Luther's Works*. Edited by Jaroslav Pelikan and Helmut Lehmann, 55 vols. St. Louis: Concordia; Philadelphia: Muhlenberg, 1955- .

———. *Martin Luther's Basic Theological Writings*. Edited by Timothy F. Lull. Minneapolis: Fortress, 1989.

Althaus, Paul. *The Theology of Martin Luther*. Translated by Robert Schultz. Philadelphia: Fortress, 1966.

Bainton, Roland. *Here I Stand: A Life of Martin Luther*. Nashville: Abingdon, 1950.

Plass, Ewald M., ed. *What Luther Says*. St. Louis: Concordia, 2006.

---

[37]Martin Luther, *Christian Liberty* (Minneapolis: Fortress, 1957).

7

John Calvin

Greatest Theologian of the Reformed Tradition

Timothy George reports that the greatest theologian of the twentieth century, Karl Barth, was overwhelmed by John Calvin (1509-1564).[1] Barth was mesmerized by Calvin's knowledge of God, which was so unlike the liberal philosophy and theology in which Barth had been trained.

Barth said,

> Calvin is a cataract, a primeval forest, a demonic power, something directly down from Himalaya, absolutely Chinese, strange, mythological. I lack completely the means, the suction cups, even to assimilate this phenomenon, not to speak of presenting it adequately. What I receive is only a thin little stream, and what I can give out again is only a yet thinner extract of this little stream. I could gladly and profitably set myself down and spend the rest of my life just with Calvin.[2]

Barth was so taken by Calvin that in one period of his career he studied the Reformer's writings incessantly, searching for Calvin's meaning until the wee hours of the night. "More than once, what I presented at seven AM was not ready until 3-5 AM." One time Barth dismissed class because he did not feel prepared. Out of these struggles grew a rebirth of Calvin scholarship and a new recognition that biblical revelation must be the source of all true theology.[3]

---

[1]Timothy George, *Theology of the Reformers* (Nashville: Broadman, 1988), p. 163.
[2]Karl Barth, *Revolutionary Theology in the Making*, trans. James D. Smart (Richmond: John Knox Press, 1964), p. 101, quoted in Eberhard Busch, *Karl Barth: His Life from Letters and Autobiographical Texts*, trans. John Bowden (Grand Rapids: Eerdmans, 1994), p. 138.
[3]George, *Theology of the Reformers*, pp. 164-65.

Although Luther was the first great Reformer, Calvin took Reformation insights (such as salvation by the grace of God in Christ and through faith not by works, and the final authority of Scripture) and organized them in a systematic but accessible way. Luther published more theology and commentary than any human in history, but Calvin produced the Reformation's only systematic theology—the *Institutes of the Christian Religion*. Because this great work was written in clear Latin (the universal language of theology in that day), and because Calvin trained pastors from many European countries in his own church at Geneva, it made a huge impression on the new churches and societies of England, Poland, Hungary, Holland, Scotland and New England. This is why the French historian Émile Léonard called Calvin the "founder of a civilization."[4]

One reason for Calvin's influence on Western civilization is that Geneva became a model for Reformers and would-be reformers from all across Europe. They came to visit, and often wrote Calvin for advice. John Knox, the Reformer of Scotland who had stayed in Geneva to learn from Calvin, famously called Geneva the "most perfect school of Christ" since the days of the apostles. The Marian exiles, English Christians who had fled England during the reign of the Catholic Queen "Bloody" Mary (1553-1558), took refuge in Geneva and returned after Mary's death to lay the foundations for Puritanism. Their theology sowed the seeds for the thinking of Jonathan Edwards, "America's theologian," whom we will encounter in a few chapters.

THE SHY REFORMER

Calvin was a true scholar who loved the isolation of his study. We might call him a bookworm. Luther was made for his part in the Reformation drama—a veritable volcano of personality exploding at the Diet of Worms: "Here I stand, I can do no other, so help me God!"[5] Calvin, on the other hand, was shy, almost unsociable. He would not do well with small talk at a party today.

His mother died when he was five or six, and his father sent him to live

---

[4]Émile G. Léonard, *History of Protestantism* (London: Nelson, 1965). This is the title of the last chapter.
[5]Martin Luther, quoted in Roland Bainton, *Here I Stand: A Life of Martin Luther* (Nashville: Abingdon, 1978), p. 144.

with another family shortly after. It's no wonder that he never spoke warmly of his father, but preached often of the gospel bringing comfort to those who feel homeless, alienated and dispossessed. Most of his career was spent in exile in Geneva, away from the France he loved, because Catholic France was persecuting Protestants like himself.[6]

Trained as a lawyer, Calvin had to be pulled, kicking and screaming as it were, into the ranks of the Reformers. When as a twenty-six-year-old man he was passing through Geneva, he was accosted by Gillaume Farel, Geneva's head pastor, who had just led the Genevans to embrace the Reformation. Farel begged Calvin to stay and help. When Calvin declined, saying he preferred to study, Farel warned that his study might be cursed because he had refused to assist the work of the kingdom. The young theologian reluctantly stayed.

Calvin was not gregarious, but he did like good company. And he enjoyed God's good gifts. Food, he wrote in the *Institutes*, was created by God not only because we need it but also for our "delight and good cheer." Wine is not only "very healthy" but is given to us to make us "merry."[7] He owned the biggest wine cellar in Geneva.

But if Calvin's childhood was full of sorrow, so was his later life. His only son died in infancy, and his wife ("the best companion of my life") died after only nine years of marriage, when Calvin was forty-three. He then cared for her two children by a previous marriage (she had been a widow), sharing his home with his brother and his eight children, not to mention other friends. It is hard to believe that amid all these children and adults, with the inevitable commotion, he wrote treatises and Bible commentaries that now fill fifty-nine volumes in the Latin edition of his collected works.

Despite his enormous reputation as a theologian, Calvin seems to have considered his preaching to have been more important than his formal theological works. He preached, on average, 170 sermons per year, which is more than three a week. When he was recollecting his accomplishments on his deathbed, he mentioned his sermons ahead of his theological works.[8]

[6]William Bouwsma, *John Calvin: A Sixteenth Century Portrait* (New York: Oxford, 1988), pp. 9-11, 16.
[7]Ibid., pp. 52, 136. See also John Calvin, *Institutes of the Christian Religion*, ed. John T. McNeill, trans. Ford Lewis Battles (Philadelphia: Westminster Press, 1960), pp. 720-21.
[8]John Calvin, cited in Bouwsma, *John Calvin*, p. 29.

Parish ministry was not easy for Calvin. He was often at odds with members and leaders of the Geneva church. In one letter to Martin Bucer, a Reformer in Strasbourg, Calvin complained, "I am entangled in so many troublesome affairs that I am almost beside myself." To the Lutheran Reformer Philip Melanchthon he wrote, "There is almost no day on which some new pain or anxiety does not come." His weariness made him feel close to the apostle Paul, who, he said, had seen "how weak many, indeed all of his people were" and "by what varied devices Satan disordered everything." The lot of ministers is especially vexed, for "none are more exposed to slanders and insults than ministers; wicked men find many occasions to blame them; they never avoid a thousand criticisms; as soon as any charge is made against ministers of the word it is believed as surely and firmly as if it had already been proved." As a result, "God's servants can only tremble and suffer great anguish, all the more since they must swallow many things in silence for the peace of the churches."[9]

PREDESTINATION

Calvin broke new ground in theology, but not without citing his debt to the theological tradition. He often praised the fourth-century preacher John Chrysostom (though not uncritically), and called Augustine "the best and most reliable witness of all antiquity" to whom "the godly by common consent justly attribute the greatest authority." He thought Augustine was the only one among all the fathers who had the right view of the human will (that it was not free when it comes to finding and following God). Although he thought Luther "insufficiently careful" with facts and style, he agreed with him that the gospel is scandalous in the world's eyes because it "glorified not the magnificent and sublime but the harsh and lowly." Calvin adopted Luther's view of justification; like Luther, he said it is "the sum of all piety." Using a Lutheran argument, he even criticized Augustine for confusing justification and sanctification.[10]

Often it is said that Calvin's new ground was predestination. Many claim predestination was the center of his theology. Neither is true. Luther also believed in double predestination (that God predestines both the elect

---

[9]Calvin, quoted in Bouwsma, *John Calvin*, p. 26.

[10]Calvin, quoted in Bouwsma, *John Calvin*, pp. 119, 83; Calvin, *Institutes*, pp. 259-60; Bouwsma, *John Calvin*, pp. 119, 161; Calvin, *Institutes*, pp. 794, 746.

and the damned), but wrote of it little.[11] Calvin was distressed by it, calling it a "dreadful" doctrine that must be treated with "great soberness," but
wrote of it more than Luther because he believed good theology is an exposition of the teaching of Scripture, and Scripture teaches election often.
The whole Bible, he taught, is structured around it: God chose Israel, and
he also chooses individuals after Christ has come. As Jesus said, "Many
are called, but few are chosen" (Mt 22:14). Calvin seemed distressed by
what appears to be injustice in God choosing some but not others. But he
reminded his readers that it has its own "equity," which is "unknown, indeed, to us but very sure." He said he agreed with Augustine that "they
who measure divine justice by the standard of human justice are acting
perversely."[12]

Two more points on predestination. In his final editions of the *Institutes*, Calvin put his discussion of it in the third of four books, which explains salvation, or "how we receive the grace of Christ." In other words,
predestination was not to be considered by those outside the faith, and
certainly not as the beginning or first principle of theology—as if the first
thing to know about God is that he decides from the beginning to save
some and damn others. Instead the doctrine is to be considered by those
already saved as a way to understand their own salvation. They are to understand from this doctrine that they were not saved because they were
better than others—in fact, they deserve hell—but simply because of God's
mercy. Therefore the doctrine was to inspire "humility."[13]

Thus predestination (which Calvin more commonly calls "election")
falls under Calvin's explication of "God the Redeemer" (as opposed to
"God the Creator"). Calvin means this quite literally—that God is our
redeemer because Jesus Christ, whom we typically think of as our redeemer, reveals the true God to us. God is sovereign will, and this is a
central theme for Calvin's theology, but even deeper is Calvin's repeated
assertion that God is Redeemer and Savior. In fact, this is the purpose of
his sovereignty—to redeem. God takes total control of his creation so that

---

[11]See Luther's discussion of predestination in *The Bondage of the Will*, trans. J. I. Packer and
O. R. Johnston (Westwood, N.J.: Fleming Revell, 1957), pp. 84, 202, 209, 215-16, 234. For
more on this subject, see Paul R. Hinlicky, *Luther and the Beloved Community: Resources for
Theology After Christendom* (Grand Rapids: Eerdmans, forthcoming 2010), chap. 5.
[12]Calvin, *Institutes*, pp. 955, 924, 957, 987.
[13]Ibid., p. 921.

he might redeem it. Predestination shows both God's sovereignty and God's deep desire to redeem. The question of why God also sends or permits some to go to hell is for Calvin "inscrutable," "inexplicable" and "improper." Yes, they too have chosen to separate themselves from God, but the question of why God permitted that is "incomprehensible."[14]

It was also to inspire "confidence" and "comfort." The great Reformation historian Heiko Oberman once explained that Calvin's doctrine of predestination can best be understood if we remember that Calvin taught it in his church at Geneva, which was made up largely of refugees from Catholic France.[15] They were afraid that if they once more fell into the hands of Catholic French persecutors, they would be tortured and might renounce their Protestant faith because of the duress. In that case, they believed (wrongly, in my opinion) they would be damned and sent to hell for apostasy. The doctrine of election (another name for predestination) persuaded them that they would never lose their faith, even if tortured: "Let [us not] abandon a quiet reliance upon the Lord's promise, where he declares that all by whom he is received in true faith have been given to him by the Father, no one of whom, since he is their guardian and shepherd, will perish."[16] This was a source of great comfort to those living in regular danger of persecution. For Calvin and his parishioners, then, predestination was a sign not of God's unfairness but of God's love.

BIBLICAL THEOLOGY

Calvin was innovative in a number of respects. Although Luther was the first Reformer to declare so systematically the need for Scripture to be primary in theology, Calvin saw even more thoroughly the need for theology to be an exposition of the meaning of Scripture and an application of that meaning to the questions of culture. That's why Luther scholar George Forell told my Calvin seminar at the University of Iowa that Luther was more of a systematic theologian than Calvin, in his incessantly relating all of theology to Christ's person and work on the cross—this despite the fact that Calvin wrote a systematic theology and Luther didn't. Calvin, on the other hand, saw theology's task to be the patient and careful

---

[14]Ibid., pp. 952-53, 955, 931.
[15]Heiko Oberman, unpublished paper at a conference in the late 1980s.
[16]Calvin, *Institutes*, p. 973.

exploration of Scripture and its relevance for all of life—even if that exploration was not able to relate every part of revelation to one or more overall
themes. So even if Scripture taught things not directly related to the
cross—such as in Proverbs and Ecclesiastes—these things were to be explored and mined for answers not only to salvation but also to more ordinary matters of everyday life—such as how to handle money.[17] Perhaps
this is why Luther delivered lectures or sermonic commentaries on less
than half the books of the Bible, but Calvin wrote a commentary on every
book of the Bible except Revelation.[18]

It may still be a stretch to call Luther more systematic than Calvin, given
the careful and exquisitely organized execution of the *Institutes*. Perhaps a
better way to put it is that Luther was more Christocentric that Calvin, since
for Luther the definition of true theology is *Was Christus treiben* (whatever
promotes or urges Christ). In comparison, Calvin was more consistently
trinitarian by giving fuller attention to the other two Persons.

Yet both Luther and Calvin were emphatic that good theology is reflection on the meaning of Scripture, first and foremost. We will see in later
chapters that Jonathan Edwards also was insistent on Scripture as the
ground of all good theology, and that Karl Barth boldly insisted on this
after generations of theologians had slighted Scripture during the heyday
of Protestant liberalism.

Calvin is better known for his notion of God's "accommodation" in
Scripture to our human capacities. Some of the church fathers thought in
a similar way, but Calvin gave this idea more explicit and frequent development. The gist of it is this: the reason why the Bible often speaks of God
in human terms, even attributing physical characteristics such as a mouth,
eyes, ears, hands and feet to God, is because God is descending from infinity to speak to us finite creatures who can better understand him if he
uses such terms:

---

[17]At the same time, Calvin knew that God accommodated his message to differing cultures,
and that the form, for example, of worship and law which God prescribed for Israel was not
often applicable for sixteenth-century Geneva. Calvin consistently sought to discern the underlying spiritual principle while regarding the cultural form as suited for only some historical
contexts.

[18]Luther also wrote on certain biblical fragments, such as the Sermon on the Mount and the
last words of David. But the difference with Calvin reflects a difference perhaps in method—
Luther felt theology should be more systematically related to the preaching of the cross, while
Calvin saw it more as a faithful exposition of Scripture, from start to (nearly) finish.

For who even of slight intelligence does not understand that, as nurses commonly do with infants, God is wont in a measure to "lisp" in speaking to us? Thus such forms of speaking do not so much express clearly what God is like as accommodate the knowledge of him to our slight capacity.[19]

For example, when the Bible says "God repented" (e.g., Gen 6:6), God represents himself "not as he is in himself, but as he seems to us." When human beings repent, Calvin explains, they correct their thinking and action. When the Bible says that God repents, it only means that God changes in response to human changes. If they suddenly repent after persisting in sin, God will "repent" his earlier attitude of judgment and now show mercy to them. God did not really change his mind, for he knew "from eternity" that those humans would sin for a while and therefore merit judgment, and that they would repent and thus invite mercy.[20]

The same principle applies to differences in what God requires between the Old and New Testaments. God adjusted the shape of his commandments—not their underlying meaning—to the various cultures he encountered. God "accommodated different forms to different ages, as he knew would be expedient to each." So a sacrifice of an animal was required of Jews in Old Testament times, but when the perfect sacrifice was offered by Christ in the New Testament, a sacrifice—of thanksgiving—was now demanded.[21]

Of course there is another reason for God's accommodation—he created us in his image. When he represents himself in human terms, those terms are not so unlike God. They may not be literal replicas, but there must be some similarity. For example, when the Bible says "the mouth of the Lord has spoken" (Is 1:20), we know God doesn't have a physical mouth, but that his capacity for speech is the original "speech organ" of which our mouths are copies. Therefore Calvin's doctrine of accommodation reminds us that there is already an analogy between our Creator and us, and that's why God represents himself in the Bible in our terms.[22]

Calvin is also famous for a number of other teachings about the Bible—that its authenticity cannot be proven by reason but is self-authenticating

---

[19]Calvin, *Institutes*, p. 121.
[20]Ibid., p. 227.
[21]Ibid., pp. 462-63.
[22]Thanks to an anonymous reader for this insight.

by the "inward witness" of the Holy Spirit; that Word and Spirit always belong together, so that we cannot understand the Word without the Spirit, and we cannot know what the Spirit is saying without the Word; and his helpful image of the Scriptures as "spectacles" that bring clarity to our vision of reality. His point here was that we can know something of God through nature and conscience (this is knowledge of God the Creator), but this knowledge falls far short of what we need to know for salvation. Scripture shows us Christ and how to find Christ for salvation (knowledge of God the Redeemer), and it provides clarity for what is otherwise a fuzzy and confused view of the world.[23]

SANCTIFICATION

When Augustine was new in the faith, he imagined that maturity in the faith meant total victory over sin. Not just the breaking of bad habits but reaching the point where temptation was no longer alluring. You may remember that Augustine was beset with sexual temptation. By the time Augustine was an old man, however, he concluded that the battle between flesh and spirit, God and Satan, in the soul of a Christian was not only a contest for the young Christian but a never-ending struggle as long as the Christian lives on this planet. Augustine concluded that the struggle depicted in Romans 7 ("I do not do the good I want, but the evil I do not want is what I do") was a picture not of Paul's pre-Christian experience, but his (and our) normal Christian life.

Calvin reached the same conclusion, but much earlier in his Christian life. Perhaps he was defeated earlier and more often. His besetting sin was not sexual lust but anger—his "ferocious beast."[24] It may have been anger more than anything else that drove him to support the execution of Servetus (c. 1511-1553), the antitrinitarian heretic. Servetus was obnoxious in his heresy, the kind of person who went out of his way to publicly tweak Calvin's nose by hurling scurrilous charges at Calvin. Servetus was a physician who had attacked the doctrine of the Trinity, saying among other things that the term itself is unbiblical. He also said God was essentially unknowable and that the Word existed only as long as the earthly life of Jesus. He was imprisoned by the Inquisition (the Catholic tribunal to de-

---

[23]Calvin, *Institutes*, pp. 78-92, 95, 70; Bouwsma, *John Calvin*, p. 100.
[24]Bouwsma, *John Calvin*, p. 51.

tect and prosecute heresy) but then escaped to Geneva, where he also argued against the use of force to defend Christian truth.

Besides being fearful of Servetus's effect on the Geneva church (possibly leading them into heresy and unbelief), Calvin was personally enraged that Servetus would slander him before his very own flock. In Calvin's defense it must be said that he pleaded with the Geneva city council that Servetus not be burned but given a less painful form of execution. The council refused Calvin's humanitarian request. As a result, Calvin's humanist friends lost respect for him, and his reputation has been smeared by Servetus's execution ever since.

Calvin showed his anger in other ways. He was often snooty and condescending to his opponents, calling them "dogs" and "curs" and "mongrels." In the *Institutes* he calls the ancient materialist Lucretius a "filthy dog."[25] He seemed to have fallen into the trap of thinking that those who disagreed with him were defying the truth plainly seen, and therefore they were wicked. Perhaps this is the reason for the legend that his schoolmates gave him the nickname "the accusative case."[26] It may also be why Calvin, in one of his precious few comments on his own conversion, recalled that God "brought my mind (already more rigid than suited my age) to submission."[27] People who are given to anger can be rigid and need the grace of God to teach them to submit to his will.

So Calvin, like Augustine, argued that the Christian life is a neverending struggle against the world, the flesh and the devil. But he said the greatest enemy is the human self with all of its vices. Christians are never fully purified of their sinful nature in this life. The power of sin was broken by Christ's cross, to which we are joined by faith and the Spirit. Yet the Christian heart remains a "smoldering cinder of evil" that contains an "obstinacy that must be beaten down with hammers."[28]

That doesn't mean, for Calvin, that the new birth makes no difference. It does indeed! It causes the *reign* of sin to cease, by the power of Christ's cross. But sin continues to dwell in the believer.

---

[25]Calvin, *Institutes*, p. 58.

[26]George says this is not true, but that Calvin was censorious toward his friends (*Theology of the Reformers*, p. 170).

[27]This is in Calvin's preface to his commentary on the Psalms, in *Calvin: Commentaries*, Library of Christian Classics, ed. Joseph Haroutunian (Philadelphia: Westminster Press, 1958), p. 52.

[28]Calvin, *Institutes*, p. 599.

Why, asked Calvin rhetorically, doesn't God clean up the whole mess in us at once? His own answer was that God wants to humble us. We need to be reminded of our own evil nature because we are so tempted by pride, and pride would destroy us if it were left unchecked.

So while nonbelievers barely notice their sins and in fact are often proud of them, believers are reminded of them and by that very reminder stay humble, seeking the grace of Christ.

Christians struggle—unlike unbelievers, who think they are just fine spiritually. True believers keep on struggling until the end. This is what Calvin called the "perseverance of the saints." He lambasted the Anabaptists and Jesuits for their "giddy spirit which brings forth such fruits that it limits to a paltry few days a repentance that for the Christian man ought to extend throughout his life." Even more than Luther, Calvin stresses the necessity for continual—even daily—repentance, gradual growth in grace (sanctification), and the gospel promise that God's saints will keep on keeping on until the end.[29]

CREATION

Calvin stressed redemption, but was also a theologian of creation. He called the world "the theater of the glory of God." He said one cannot look anywhere in the world "without seeing some sparks of His glory."[30] More than Luther, Calvin emphasized the creation itself as a gift of grace and area for God's self-manifestation. This set a precedent for Puritan theology and for Jonathan Edwards, who was inclined all his life to find God in nature. For that purpose he kept a notebook in which he recorded the "images" and "shadows" of God's truth he saw there.[31] Barth, curiously, was also strongly influenced by Calvin but insisted we cannot see the glory of God in nature. (We will discuss this more when we come to the chapter on Barth.)

THE SOVEREIGNTY OF GOD

We have looked at many important themes in Calvin, and we have said that none—least of all, predestination or election—can be called the cen-

---

[29]Calvin, *Institutes*, pp. 971-78.
[30]Ibid., 1.6.2; 1.14.20; 2.6.1; 3.9.2.
[31]Jonathan Edwards, "Images of Divine Things," in *Typological Writings*, ed. Wallace E. Anderson and Mason I. Lowance Jr. (New Haven, Conn.: Yale University Press, 1993).

ter of this theology. But there is one theme I have saved for last because it is a predominant theme that runs through all of Calvin's writings, and it is not stressed quite so forthrightly and repeatedly in the theologians we have studied so far. This is the sovereignty of God, which means God's complete control over all things and events. It is related to predestination, but the latter is a smaller subset of the former. (Luther said creatures are but the "masks of God" because God works through them. But he did not highlight absolute sovereignty as starkly and consistently as Calvin.)

Calvin usually preferred to call God's sovereignty his "providence." By it he meant God's absolute control of everything that happens, so that "not one drop of rain falls without God's sure command." Even the devil "can do nothing unless God wills and assents to it." This includes sin, for "the blinding of unbelievers is God's work, although he [in Scripture] had [also] called it the activity of Satan." Therefore there is no such thing as chance or "fortune and fortuitous happenings." Calvin calls all this "providence" because through his control of everything that happens God provides what is perfect for his people. "God has destined all things for our good and salvation."[32]

The result is a bit of a paradox, however. For the most part, God's intentions and purposes in sovereignty are hidden from us. God's "wonderful method of governing the universe is rightly called an abyss [in Scripture]." In these times when we cannot understand why God permits what he does, "we ought reverently to adore" and "hold in reverence." But at the same time, God's purposes are sometimes evident, such as when a cruel kingdom is toppled. That clearly is the judgment of God.[33]

God's whys and wherefores are usually hidden from us, but the fact that he is in control seemed clear to Calvin. He appealed to both history and Scripture. Wars, he claimed, are often decided not by superior arms or money or strength but by God. This is why "inferior or cowardly troops sometimes win, while those more skillful or better equipped struggle in vain." Those relatively unskilled often get the better of people more capable, because of what is called luck or chance.[34]

Scripture makes this even more apparent. Religious leaders "intended

---

[32]Calvin, *Institutes*, pp. 204, 175, 176, 198, 181.
[33]Ibid., pp. 213, 212.
[34]John Calvin, commentary on Daniel 8:20-25, cited in Bouwsma, *John Calvin*, p. 169.

to destroy Christ; Pilate and his soldiers complied with their mad desire; yet in solemn prayer the disciples confess that all the impious ones had done nothing except what 'the hand and plan' of God had decreed." Calvin also pointed to Scripture declaring that Absalom's "detestable crime" of incest was God's own work (2 Sam 12:12). Jeremiah said "every cruelty the Chaldeans exercised against Judah was God's work." Nebuchadnezzar is called God's servant. God says "in many places" that he is the one who rouses nations to war. He calls the Assyrians the "rod of his anger," and the ruin of Jerusalem and its temple "his own work." David confesses that the curses of Shimei proceeded from God's command. "We very often find in the Sacred History that whatever happens proceeds from the Lord, as for instance the defection of the ten tribes, the death of Eli's sons, and very many examples of this sort."[35]

Calvin believed knowledge of God's sovereignty can be of great benefit pastorally. "Gratitude of mind for the favorable outcome of things, patience in adversity, and also incredible freedom from worry about the future all necessarily follow upon this knowledge." In other words, if I know that a tragic event in my life was permitted by God, I can be assured that God meant it for good. I might not understand why this thing was permitted, but at least I will have the comfort of knowing that in the long run things will be better because of it. I may still suffer because of the tragedy, but at least I won't add to the suffering the frustration that comes from thinking that it was a random event that could have been prevented. Or the bitterness that comes from thinking I am a victim without hope. The faith that God works everything for the good of his people will add comfort to my sorrow and enable me to look to the future with confidence. That is why Calvin said "ignorance of providence is the ultimate of all miseries; the highest blessedness lies in the knowledge of it."[36]

Faith in God's sovereignty can not only prevent unnecessary pain over the past but also prevent undue worry about the future. If I worry about the future, I can assuage that worry with the knowledge that God will not permit anything to come my way, even evil things, without making sure those things work for my good. Calvin was a man given to anxiety himself, and it is clear that when he said "incredible freedom from worry" will

---

[35]Calvin, *Institutes*, pp. 230-31.
[36]Ibid., pp. 219, 225.

come from knowledge of God's sovereignty, he was speaking from personal experience.[37]

WHAT WE CAN TAKE FROM CALVIN

Let's sum up what we can learn from this great Christian mind and heart.

1. *The importance of preaching.* Luther also called attention to the role of the preached Word in bringing God's truth to people. But Calvin by both precept and practice demonstrated his conviction that the primary job of the minister is to bring God's Word to his people. He urged ministers to study hard and carefully to be sure they are presenting biblical truths and not just their own ideas. And like Luther, he believed that when the minister preaches biblical truth, God himself speaks through that minister in a special way.

2. *Predestination.* Calvin shows us that predestination is a doctrine that should bring comfort and humility, not terror. He reminds us that Jesus never casts out anyone who comes to him (Jn 6:37), and that election is part of the doctrine of salvation. In other words, it is best viewed retrospectively, not prospectively. It tells us how to look *back* and see why we were chosen (simply because of God's gracious love, not because we were better than others), and is not a way to think about the "time" before creation and look *ahead* to speculate why God decided as he did. It should also help us face the future, knowing that God will give us the grace we need to stay in the faith.

3. *Biblical theology.* Calvin taught the church that all theology should be rooted in the biblical story, and that whenever theology wanders away from that story and vision, it wanders into error. Theology, in short, is a way of using the Bible to assess the claims made by rival religions and worldviews. And it is only the Scriptures, finally, that give us knowledge of God the Redeemer.

4. *Sanctification.* Luther started the Reformation with his emphasis on justification, or how to get saved. Calvin continued the Reformation by placing more emphasis on sanctification, which is the lifelong process of becoming holy. He teaches us that we will always have sin mixed with our

---

[37]Ibid., p. 219. See also "Calvin's Anxiety," in Bouwsma, *John Calvin.*

holiness, but that we must never stop trying to grow in holiness. He also insisted that holiness comes principally by regular repentance and dying to self. But these flow from a heart of love and reverence for God: "I call piety that love conjoined with reverence for God which the knowledge of his benefits induces."[38]

5. *The sovereignty of God.* Calvin was convinced that God is the mover of everything that moves, even Satan himself. God does not directly will sin and evil, but he superintends the historical process and even the little events of our lives so that they ultimately work toward our good and his glory. Calvin found from experience that this conviction brings a certain freedom and peace amidst the anxieties and confusion of our lives.

A SELECTION FROM JOHN CALVIN'S WORKS

Nearly all the wisdom we possess, that is to say, true and sound wisdom, consists of two parts: the knowledge of God and of ourselves. But, while joined by many bonds, which one precedes and brings forth the other, is not easy to discern. In the first place, no one can look upon himself without immediately turning his thoughts to the contemplation of God, in whom he "lives and moves" [Acts 17:28]. For, quite clearly, the mighty gifts with which we are endowed are hardly from ourselves; indeed, our very being is nothing but subsistence in the one God. Then, by these benefits shed like dew from heaven upon us, we are led as by rivulets to the spring itself. Indeed, our very poverty better discloses the infinitude of benefits reposing in God. The miserable ruin, into which the rebellion of the first man cast us, especially compels us to look upward. Thus, not only will we, in fasting and hungering, seek thence what we lack; but, in being aroused by fear, we shall learn humility. For, as a veritable world of miseries is to be found in mankind, and we are thereby despoiled of divine raiment, our shameful nakedness exposes a teeming horde of infamies. Each of us must, then, be so stung by the consciousness of his own unhappiness as to attain at least some knowledge of God. Thus, from the feeling of our own ignorance, vanity, poverty, infirmity, and—what is more— depravity and corruption, we recognize that the true light of wisdom, sound virtue, full abundance of every good, and purity of righteousness rest in the Lord alone. To this extent we are prompted by our own ills to contemplate the

---

[38]Calvin, *Institutes* 1.2.1.

good things of God; and we cannot seriously aspire to him before we begin to become displeased with ourselves. For what man in all the world would not gladly remain as he is—what man does not remain as he is—so long as he does not know himself, that is, while content with his own gifts, and either ignorant or unmindful of his own misery? Accordingly, the knowledge of ourselves not only arouses us to seek God, but also, as it were, leads us by the hand to find him.[39]

FOR REFLECTION AND DISCUSSION

1. How do you think Calvin's sad childhood and marriage might have influenced his theology and ministry?

2. Are you surprised by what this chapter says about the meaning and content of Calvin's teaching on predestination? How does it help you understand the doctrine?

3. What is Calvin's doctrine of "accommodation"? How does it help us understand the Bible? Give some examples.

4. Can you give an example of how the "inner witness of the Spirit" demonstrates the divine character of the Bible?

5. What part of Calvin's teaching on sanctification is most meaningful to you? Why?

6. Calvin found great pastoral comfort in the doctrine of God's sovereignty. Do you agree? Can you give an example from your own life?

7. Calvin believed that God speaks in a special way through preaching. Have you observed this happening?

8. If you are in a group, let each member share what he or she appreciates or disagrees with in this chapter.

FOR FURTHER READING

Calvin, John. *Calvin: Commentaries*. Library of Christian Classics. Translated by Joseph Haroutunian. Philadelphia: Westminster Press, 1958.

———. *Institutes of the Christian Religion*. Edited by John T. McNeill. Translated by Ford Lewis Battles. Philadelphia: Westminster Press, 1960.

---

[39]Calvin, *Institutes*, pp. 35-37.

McGrath, Alister. *A Life of John Calvin: A Study in the Shaping of Western Culture*. Oxford: Blackwell, 1990.

McKim, Donald K. ed. *Readings in Calvin's Theology*. Grand Rapids: Baker, 1984.

McNeill, John T. *The History and Character of Calvinism*. Oxford: Oxford University Press, 1954.

8

Jonathan Edwards

America's Theologian

Jonathan Edwards (1703-1758) has always provoked extreme reactions. People have found it impossible to be neutral or indifferent toward him. Harriet Beecher Stowe complained that Edwards's sermons on sin and suffering were "refined poetry of torture." After staying up one night reading Edwards's treatise on the will, Mark Twain reported that Edwards's God "shines red and hideous in the glow from the fires of hell, their only right and proper adornment. By God I was ashamed to be in such company."[1]

Generations of Americans have drawn similar conclusions after reading his "Sinners in the Hands of an Angry God" sermon in their high school and college literature classes. They would be surprised to learn that Edwards was obsessed by God's beauty, not wrath, and that, as historian Patrick Sherry recently argued, Edwards made beauty more central to theology than anyone else in the history of Christian thought, including Augustine and the twentieth-century Swiss Catholic Hans Urs von Balthasar.

They would also be surprised to learn that Edwards is widely regarded as America's greatest philosopher before the twentieth century, and arguably this continent's greatest theologian ever. One measure of his greatness is Yale University Press's critical edition of his works, which has twenty-six volumes—but even that represents only half of his written products. An-

---

[1]Mark Twain, *The Letters of Mark Twain, Volume 5, 1901-1906*, compiled by Albert Bigelow Paine (Project Gutenberg, 2006), e-book <http://infomotions.com/etexts/gutenberg/dirs/3/1/9/3197/3197.htm>.

other token of Edwards's importance is the three-volume *Encyclopedia of the American Religious Experience*, which contains far more references to Edwards than to any other single figure.

Although Edwards was revered for his piety and intellectual prowess in antebellum America, the Unitarians who gained cultural power after the Civil War dismissed Edwards as an anachronistic symbol of the Puritanism that allegedly slowed America's advance to modernity. There were demurrals: Edwards was the hero of H. Richard Niebuhr's *Kingdom of God in America* (1937), and Ola Elizabeth Winslow's biography of Edwards won the Pulitzer Prize in 1940. But intellectuals generally did not take Edwards seriously again until 1949, when Harvard historian Perry Miller published his acclaimed biography of the New England thinker, suggesting that only Edwards's unshrinking assessment of evil was capable of dispelling modernity's naive utopianism.

Since mid-century Edwards scholarship has exploded, with the number of dissertations on his work doubling every decade. The most prestigious university presses and journals have published hundreds of books and articles on his thought and influence.

Why such a profusion of interest? One reason is certainly, as William Sparkes Morris once put it, "because genius fascinates," but also because of the extraordinary range and depth of his thinking. For Miller, Edwards was a prophet of modernity. Miller said famously that Edwards stood so far above and ahead of his immediate culture that our own time is "barely catching up." Edwards's understanding of the human psyche was so advanced that "it would have taken him about an hour's reading in William James, and two hours in Freud, to catch up completely." Edwards scholars have concluded that Edwards's relationship to modernity was far more ambivalent, but Miller's comment shows the intrigue Edwards has excited in many thinkers outside the bounds of the Christian churches.

EDWARDS'S MANY HATS

Another reason for the breadth of Edwards's influence is the wide range of his work. Historians have studied Edwards's role as a pastor and the effect of his sermons and books on the Great Awakening, the American Revolution, the modern missionary movement (he has been called, with good reason, the grandfather of the modern Protestant missionary movement),[2] and the course of both American theology and philosophy. Theologians appreciate his insights into the history of salvation (he relates sacred to secular history in his *Work of Redemption*), the Trinity (more than others in the West, he emphasized the Trinity as a divine community), the relationship between divine sovereignty and human freedom (some say he did as well as anyone showing how the two are compatible), original sin (he linked our sin with Adam's but not without showing our complicity in Adam's), typology (Edwards believed all the world was filled with divinely implanted pointers to Christ and his kingdom), and spiritual discernment. Ethicists profit from his writings on true virtue and Christian morality, as well as his attack on Enlightenment ethics. Literary critics are fascinated by his masterly employment of imagery and other literary strategies; students of aesthetics point out that he related God to beauty more than anyone else in the history of Christian thought; historians of American philosophy argue that he was America's premier philosopher before the great flowering of American philosophy at the turn of the twentieth century (his treatises on the will and original sin not only defended doctrinal Calvinism but also set the agenda for philosophers in the nineteenth century). Some scholars even suggest that Edwards offered the eighteenth century's most penetrating critique of the Enlightenment and has something to teach us about how Christians should think about non-Christian religions!

Perhaps most important for serious readers of religion and theology, Edwards is widely recognized as America's greatest theologian. Nearly twenty years ago Robert Jenson, the great American Lutheran theologian, published a monograph titled *America's Theologian*. The nearest competitor to Edwards for that moniker, H. Richard Niebuhr, confessed he was greatly indebted to Edwards and saw himself as extending the Edwardsian vision. Nineteenth-century American theologians at Andover, Princeton and Yale nearly universally claimed his mantle. But it wasn't only the theologians who were impressed: in large sections of antebellum America many homes contained two books—the Bible and a collection of Edwards writings.

---

[2]Edwards wrote about the central place of missions in the history of redemption, published the life and diary of David Brainerd (which became a bestseller in the nineteenth century and continues in print and missionary influence to this day), and set a personal example by going to Stockbridge, Massachusetts, to be a missionary to Native Americans.

Those antebellum Americans were drawn to Edwards for some of the same reasons he attracts legions of followers today outside of academia. Many are captivated by what prolific pastor-writer John Piper calls Edwards's "God-entranced vision of all things." Others desire personal renewal or corporate revival for their communities, and find in Edwards a singular guide to spiritual renovation. J. I. Packer, the Oxford-trained theologian who has written enormously popular books for the nonacademic Christian reader, thinks Edwards's theology of revival is the most important contribution Edwards makes to today's church. Others have considered his *Religious Affections* to be the most penetrating guide to spiritual discernment ever written. Still others are drawn to his rigorous pattern of spiritual discipline, his logical and compelling sermons, and the way he includes God's holiness and wrath in the larger picture of divine beauty.

EDWARDS'S THEOLOGY

Edwards's theological project was gargantuan, addressing hosts of issues both parochial and perennial. Because his thought is so complex and multidimensional, a brief description such as this can easily distort. But we can say that much of his work was related to his lifelong battle with deism, the early modern rationalist movement that identified religion with morality, and judged all religious expressions by what its thinkers deemed to be "common sense"—which was by no means common even to those in its own era.

Deists claimed that ordinary reason can determine what is true religion, so that the problem with bad religion and human relations generally was a failure to use reason properly. Edwards responded that this analysis of the human condition was too superficial. There is no such thing as "ordinary" or "naked" reason because the mind is darkened and disabled by indwelling sin. Hence reason is not neutral but conditioned by self-interest. It is no wonder, he remarked more than once, that intelligent people are responsible for great evil.

Deists assumed that all human action proceeded from good or bad thinking. But Edwards insisted that the springs of human motivation lie much deeper than the thoughts of the mind. In his famous formulation, he asserted that all human feeling, thinking and acting are rooted in the "affections," the underlying loves and dispositions that incline us toward or away from things. (These are not the emotions, as many scholars have erroneously reported, but something akin to what earlier traditions called the "soul," from which emotions arise.) This is the source of true religion as well as all other human perception and behavior. Hence true religion, Edwards wrote, must influence and spring from these deepest levels of the human psyche. The Scriptures, he said, confirm this. They place the heart of religion in the affections: fear, joy, hope, love, hatred, desire, sorrow, gratitude, compassion and zeal.

On the one hand, then, Edwards defended the religion of the heart against the critics of revival who condemned emotionalism to the point that they were left with a religion of the head only. But Edwards also denounced religion that was merely emotion, devoid of cognitive understanding of basic Christian truth. In a manner unmatched by most other spiritual theologians, Edwards linked head and heart, experience and understanding. As we will see toward the end of this chapter, Edwards believed that heart and head were inseparably connected, and that all true religion involves proper thinking. For the human self in its basic inclination toward reality includes both an affective (feeling) and cognitive (thinking) dimension.

Because true religion comes from sources much deeper than human thinking, Edwards insisted that we need a "divine and supernatural light." The Spirit must penetrate beneath the surface convictions of human reason to awaken a "sense of the heart" focused on the glory of the divine nature and the beauty of Jesus Christ.

Therefore the essence of true religious experience is to be overwhelmed by a glimpse of the beauty of God, to be drawn to the glory of his perfections and to sense his irresistible love. George Marsden once wrote that it is something like being overwhelmed by the beauty of a great work of art or music. We can become so enthralled by the beauty that we lose consciousness of self and self-interest, and become absorbed by the magnificent object. So also we can become drawn out of self-absorption by the power of the beauty of a truly loveable person. Our hearts are changed by an irresistible power. But this power gently lures; it does not coerce. Edwards taught that our eyes are opened when we are captivated by the beautiful love and glory of God in Christ, when we see this love most powerfully demonstrated in Christ's sacrificial love for the undeserving. Then we feel forced to abandon love for self as the central principle of our lives and turn to the love of God.

Edwards describes our side of this experience as like being given a sixth sense: a sense of the beauty, glory and love of God. He observes, "The Bible speaks of giving eyes to see, ears to hear, unstopping the ears of the deaf, and opening the eyes of them that were born blind, and turning from darkness to light." Therefore the spiritual knowledge gained in true conversion is a kind of "sensible" knowledge—as different from intellectual knowledge as the taste of honey is different from the mere intellectual understanding that honey is sweet.

True Christian experience, then, is sensible and affective. The Christian, says Edwards, does not

> merely rationally believe that God is glorious, but he has a sense of the gloriousness of God in his heart. . . . For as God is infinitely the Greatest Being, so He is allowed to be infinitely the most beautiful and excellent: and all the beauty to be found throughout the whole creation is but the reflection of the diffused beams of that Being who hath an infinite fullness of brightness and glory; God . . . is the foundation and fountain of all being and all beauty.[3]

This emphasis on beauty as the center of one's vision of God was not unique to Edwards, for Augustine and Balthasar (see chap. 13) also used the aesthetic as a major theological category. But as Patrick Sherry argued in *Spirit and Beauty*, no one made beauty as central to the vision of God as Edwards.[4] Athanasius, for example, would have appreciated Edwards's description of God's redemption as a thing of beauty, for Athanasius himself said "everything about [Christ's work] is marvelous, and wherever a man turns his gaze he sees the Godhead of the Word and is smitten with awe."[5] But Athanasius did very little with the concept of beauty per se. For Amer-

---

[3]Jonathan Edwards, "A Divine and Supernatural Light," in *A Jonathan Edwards Reader*, ed. John E. Smith, Harry S. Stout and Kenneth P. Minkema (New Haven, Conn.: Yale University Press, 1995), p. 111; Jonathan Edwards, "The Nature of True Virtue," in *Works of Jonathan Edwards*, vol. 8, *Ethical Writings*, ed. Paul Ramsey (New Haven, Conn.: Yale University Press, 1989), pp. 550-51.

[4]Patrick Sherry, *Spirit and Beauty: A History of Theological Aesthetics* (New York: Oxford University Press, 1992).

[5]Athanasius, *On the Incarnation*, trans. and ed. "A Religious of C.S.M.V." (Crestwood, N.Y.: St. Vladimir's Seminary Press, 1996), p. 93.

ica's theologian, on the other hand, beauty was absolutely integral to his view of God and redemption, so that no part of theology is complete without consideration of God's beauty and what that means for human understanding.

If Edwards challenged the religion of the Enlightenment (deism), he also took on Enlightenment ethics and cosmology. When nearly all eighteenth-century moralists were constructing ethical systems based on self-interest, presuming that human nature naturally seeks the good, Edwards countered that the affections are fallen. Therefore true virtue can come only from a heart spiritually transformed so that it sees God's glory, and seeks his will and the public good rather than private interest.

Deists in the eighteenth century were also disconnecting the world from God's immediate control, positing a clockwork cosmos that runs on its own. The result was to objectify the universe, separating nature from the human and its feelings so that it could be used for technological purposes. But Edwards was relentlessly God-centered. He taught a kind of panentheism in which no part of the creation is ever independent of God, but all is sustained by God, moment by throbbing moment, by God's direct action.

Yet Edwards was no pantheist. God is not the same as the universe. Just as a sunbeam is sustained by the sun but is different from the sun, so the world is sustained by God as his emanation, but is different from God. So while Enlightenment theorists said that the universe is a great machine that operates autonomously, Edwards said God sustains it nanosecond by nanosecond. In fact, God's power is literally the binding force of atoms: the universe would collapse and disappear unless God upheld its existence from moment to moment ("In him all things hold together" [Col 1:17]). As Avihu Zakai has recently put it, Edwards reenchanted a cosmos that had been stripped of the divine.[6]

This is one of the many ways in which Edwards was ahead of his time. He anticipated post-Newtonian physics, in which all matter is ultimately seen in terms of interacting fields of energy, with every part dependent on every other part, and the forces governing these rather mysterious. Physicists have been concluding for almost a century what Edwards declared

---

[6]Avihu Zakai, *Jonathan Edwards's Philosophy of History: The Reenchantment of the World in the Age of Enlightenment* (Princeton, N.J.: Princeton University Press, 2003).

two-and-a-half centuries ago: there are no independent substances that can subsist on their own.

SEEING THE BEAUTY OF HOLINESS

Since Edwards did more to connect God and beauty than any other Christian theologian, I will use this last part of this chapter to describe in more detail what this meant for Edwards and what it can mean for us.

Edwards said that what distinguishes the regenerate from the unregenerate is that the former see the beauty of holiness. The latter see only God's holiness. This is why the devils in hell see that God is holy, but remain in hell. The regenerate love that holiness because they see its beauty. So it is aesthetic vision that separates the saved from the unsaved.

Let me give an example. Sojourner Truth (1797-1883) was drawn to God by the beauty of the holiness of Jesus. Born a slave in New York, she was the property of a wealthy Dutch landowner until her emancipation in 1827. Then she traveled to America as a powerful preacher for Christ and against slavery. In her autobiography she wrote that when she first drew near to God, a sense of her own sinfulness kept her at a distance. She felt that she needed someone to stand between her and God and plead on her behalf. Suddenly, she said, she saw "a friend" standing between her and God.

"Who are you?" the woman asked.

The figure then "brightened into a form distinct, *beaming with the beauty of holiness*, and radiant with love." She strained body and soul to see who it was. An answer came, "saying distinctly, 'It is Jesus.' "

Until this time, Sojourner explained, she had thought of Jesus as simply an eminent man, like Washington or Lafayette. But now it was different. He appeared to be "so mild, so good, and so every way lovely." She was overjoyed that God was not an avenging judge and that her friend was Jesus, who was "altogether lovely."

Now that she could see the beauty of Jesus' holiness, all the world looked different. "The world was clad in new beauty, the very air sparkled as with diamonds, and was redolent of heaven."

NOT JUST THE SUPERSTARS

You might say Sojourner Truth was a superstar of the faith, because she is now one of the most famous nineteenth-century Christians in America. But it's not just the superstars who are drawn to the beauty of holiness in Jesus. Harold Payne, a dear friend of mine who spent many years in prison, was an ordinary saint who was also drawn to Christ because of his beauty. The beauty of Christ's love won Harold's heart. After twenty years of "doing things my way" Harold was dumbfounded to discover that Jesus was willing to wipe his slate clean. "I couldn't believe it that this Jesus, who had suffered so horribly for me, was also willing to forgive me in an instant for all those years when I was stubborn and hardhearted," Harold told me. "All I can say is that he is a God so beautiful, that I can never praise him enough."

Let's now try to understand what Edwards meant by the beauty of holiness. Although holiness involves more than morality, it will help us to examine its moral dimension. But even when we think about moral beauty, we are *not* talking about mere outward behavior. Through the ages many have led lives that were outwardly moral but, like some of the Pharisees, have not known the inward sanctifying power of the Holy Spirit.[7] It is one thing to follow the letter of the law, but quite another to love God for the beauty of his moral excellence.

MORAL GOODNESS VERSUS NATURAL GOODNESS

To fully understand what Edwards meant by the beauty of holiness, which is God's moral goodness, we must see the difference between moral and natural goodness. Moral goodness encompasses character traits that have moral significance, such as telling the truth and remaining faithful to your promises. Natural goodness, on the other hand, is not related to morality. Pleasure, strength and knowledge, for example, are all natural goods. It is easy to see that they are not moral goods. Knowledge of how to build a house is neither moral nor immoral. It is amoral—that is, it has nothing to do with morals (unless, of course, one purposely builds the house in such a way that it collapses after the owner moves in!). We consider it "good" that a person knows how to build a house, but that knowledge does not make him or her a morally good person.

Just as natural goodness is distinguished from moral goodness in human beings, Edwards distinguished between the moral and natural perfections of God. God's "natural perfections" are attributes that, when con-

---

[7]Some Pharisees supported Jesus and presumably came to experience the Holy Spirit (Lk 7:36; 14:1; see also Mt 23:3).

sidered by themselves, have no moral significance: omnipotence, omniscience, omnipresence and eternity. These perfections represent various kinds of power (the power to do all things, know all things, be everywhere and be outside of time). Until they are used in specific ways, they have no moral significance. God's moral perfections, on the other hand, are moral in and of themselves. By their very definition they involve moral considerations. Edwards referred here to God's righteousness, truthfulness, goodness, kindness, mercy, longsuffering, compassion, justice and faithfulness. Each attribute points to a moral quality: righteousness means adherence to what is morally right, truthfulness is refusal to tell a lie, goodness is the determination to do what is morally right and loving, and so on.[8]

Edwards distinguished natural from moral goodness because God's goodness has to do with the latter, not the former. In short, holiness involves (among other things) moral goodness.[9] The beauty of God's holiness is the splendor and excellence of his moral character. So when Edwards talked about holiness, he was not talking about power or infinite greatness. Neither was he talking about a goodness that is only external or a matter of appearance. He referred instead to an intrinsic moral goodness. In God it is *absolute* moral perfection, the shining radiance of perfect love. God's moral goodness is absolutely perfect, shining with absolute purity. God *never* acts in any way that is inconsistent with perfect love and justice.[10] He *always* does the right thing, the loving thing, the just thing—even when it brings him infinite pain, as we saw on Calvary. This is part of what Edwards meant by the beauty of holiness.

A CUT ABOVE—INFINITELY SO

So far we have scratched only the surface of what Edwards meant by the beauty of holiness. To dig a little deeper, we need to look at the word *holy*. Its root goes back to a Hebrew word meaning "to cut or separate." It refers to things that are "a cut above" or "a cut apart" from the ordinary. Because

---

[8]Jonathan Edwards, *Works of Jonathan Edwards*, vol. 2, *Religious Affections*, ed. John E. Smith (New Haven, Conn.: Yale University Press, 1959), pp. 254-55.
[9]Such as the majesty and awesomeness of God.
[10]We must understand that love and justice are not some abstract qualities separate from God but simply words for different aspects of God's character. So God does not conform to anything outside himself; he is simply true to who he is.

this holiness is *God's*, and God is infinite, these things are *infinitely* above or separate from everything else. As Søren Kierkegaard expressed it, there is "an infinite qualitative difference" between God and everything human. In Rudolf Otto's words, God is "Wholly Other."[11]

God's moral goodness, then, is infinitely superior to any moral goodness we can imagine. God is not just a human shouting loudly. He is an infinite purity that is absolutely distinct from all creaturely purity, infinitely exalted above human goodness. Drawing on biblical metaphors, Calvin said that our goodness is so pathetic in comparison to God's that we are rottenness itself (Job 13:28), worms and dirt (Job 7:5; Ps 22:6). Because of God's infinite purity the cherubim must veil their faces in fear (Is 6:2), the sun has to blush, and the moon is confounded (Is 24:23).[12]

The beauty of God's holiness is particularly demonstrated in his love. Unlike human compassion, God's compassion never fails (Lam 3:22). The infinitely intelligent Being who created galaxies and sustains them moment by moment allows himself to hurt when we hurt (Is 63:9). This is the spectacular love in the heavens that reduces the angels to a reverent awe.

Edwards saw the beauty of God's holiness most clearly in Jesus Christ, especially in the ways that Jesus combines divine infinity with care for finite humanity. For instance, Jesus combines infinite greatness with infinite care. He has perfect wisdom, infinite power, infinite terrifying majesty and infinite knowledge, yet he graciously stoops to love unworthy sinful human beings. He goes even further, to become their friend and companion—and "yet lower for them, even to expose himself to shame and spitting; yea, to yield up himself to an ignominious death for them."[13]

Second, Jesus combines infinite justice and infinite mercy. He hates sin and yet forgives the greatest of sinners. And he did the latter by suffering a shameful and horrifyingly painful death: "the most ignominious and

---

[11]At the same time that God is Wholly Other, he makes human beings in his own image. Edwards appreciated this balancing truth and went back and forth, as any biblical theologian should, stressing on the one hand that God's holiness is infinitely above ours, and yet teaching on the other hand that Jesus was human like us and wants to share his divine holiness with us.

[12]John Calvin, *Institutes of the Christian Religion*, ed. John T. McNeill, trans. Ford Lewis Battles (Philadelphia: Westminster Press, 1960), p. 39.

[13]Jonathan Edwards, "The Excellency of Christ," in *The Sermons of Jonathan Edwards: A Reader*, ed. Wilson Kimnach, Kenneth Minkema and Douglas Sweeney (New Haven, Conn.: Yale University Press, 1999), p. 165.

tormenting, and every way the most terrible that men could inflict; yea, and greater sufferings than men could inflict, who could only torment the body, but also those sufferings in his soul, that were the more immediate fruits of the wrath of God against the sins of those he undertakes for."[14]

Finally, he combines infinite majesty with unparalleled meekness. Think of it! Scripture says he is the one "at whose presence the earth doth quake, and the hills do melt; . . . who rebukes the sea and maketh it dry, . . . [and] whose eyes are as a flame of fire." Yet he is meek and lowly of heart. He is strong enough to be meek. When insulted, he did not respond in kind. He forgave those who murdered him and tortured him. With meekness he stood "in the ring of soldiers, that were condemning and mocking him, when he was silent, and opened not his mouth, but went as a lamb to the slaughter. Thus is Christ a lion in majesty, and a lamb in meekness."[15]

WHAT MAKES DIVINE THINGS BEAUTIFUL

Previously we have seen how Athanasius, Origen, Augustine, Thomas, Luther and Calvin have shown in different ways how salvation means that God *gives* himself to us. His nature is to give. This is a stunningly common theme in the great theologians. Well, Edwards takes this one step further. He argued that it is this excellency of God's moral character—the infinitely pure, self-giving love so vividly seen in Jesus—that makes him beautiful and elicits the worship of his creatures. God's holiness overwhelmed the seraphim in Isaiah 6: "And one called to another and said: 'Holy, holy, holy is the LORD of hosts; the whole earth is full of his glory'" (v. 3).[16]

The four living creatures in John's vision (Rev 4) worshiped God for the

---

[14]Ibid., p. 166.

[15]Ibid., p. 168.

[16]This paragraph and the rest of the chapter are based on Edwards's descriptions of the "third distinguishing sign" of true saints in *Religious Affections*, esp. 258-66. Edwards did not have a zero-sum view of glory, thinking that God's glory would diminish if we share in it. Quite the contrary, God's glory increases when we share in it. In the *End for Which God Created the World*, he says in fact that both we and God grow as we share more and more of the glory of God. God, "from his goodness, as it were enlarges himself in a more excellent and divine manner . . . by flowing forth, and expressing himself in [his creatures], and making them to partake of him, and rejoicing in himself expressed in them, and communicated to them" (Edwards, *The End for Which God Created the World*, in *The Works of Jonathan Edwards*, ed. Paul Ramsey [New Haven, Conn.: Yale University Press, 1989], 8:433, 461-62).

same reason. Day and night they sing before God's throne, entranced by the beauty of God's holiness: "Holy, holy, holy, is the Lord God the Almighty, / who was and is and is to come" (v. 8). John also saw the martyrs who conquered the beast standing beside the sea of glass mixed with fire (Rev 15). With harps of God in their hands, they sang the song of Moses. More than anything else, they were struck by the holiness of God:

> Who will not fear, O Lord,
>   and glorify your name?
> For you alone are holy. (v. 4)

Centuries before, Hannah had been struck by the same. "There is none holy like the LORD," she prayed, "there is none besides you; / there is no rock like our God" (1 Sam 2:2).

Edwards said that what first and foremost impressed the New Testament saints about Jesus was his holiness. They called him the "Holy and Righteous One" (Acts 3:14), "your holy servant Jesus" (Acts 4:27) and "the holy one, the true one" (Rev 3:7). Its holiness is what makes God's word so precious. The psalmist writes, in lyrical language that exudes awe and reverence:

> The law of the LORD is perfect,
>   reviving the soul;
> the testimony of the LORD is sure.
>   making wise the simple;
> the precepts of the LORD are right,
>   rejoicing the heart;
> the commandment of the LORD is pure,
>   enlightening the eyes;
> the fear of the LORD is clean,
>   enduring forever;
> the rules of the LORD are true,
>   and righteous altogether.
> More to be desired are they than gold,
>   even much fine gold;
> sweeter also than honey,
>   and drippings of the honeycomb. (Ps 19:7-10)

According to America's theologian the same can be said for heaven: it is beautiful and wonderful because it is a place of holiness. Isaiah refers to it as God's "holy and beautiful habitation" (Is 63:15). In John's revelation heaven's holiness is its beauty, represented by precious stones and light:

> It has the glory of God and a radiance like a very rare jewel, like jasper, clear as crystal. . . . [E]ach of the gates is a single pearl, and the street of the city is pure gold, transparent as glass. . . . [T]he river of the water of life [is as] bright as crystal, flowing from the throne of God and of the Lamb. (Rev 21:11, 21; 22:1 NRSV)

The saints of Scripture frequently praise God because of his holiness. Edwards cites the psalmist:

> Let them praise your great and awesome name.
>   Holy is he! . . .
> Extol the LORD our God;
>   worship at his footstool!
>   Holy is he! . . .
> Exalt the LORD our God,
>   and worship at his holy mountain;
>   for the LORD our God is holy! (Ps 99:3, 5, 9)

Edwards suggests that this is why saints love the gospel—because, at least in part, of its holiness. The good news (the literal meaning of *gospel*) is that a holy God joins an unholy people to himself, confers on them Jesus' own holiness so that in the Father's eyes they are holy, and then gradually makes them *actually* holy by the power of his *Holy* Spirit. This is the mind-boggling happy news of the gospel.

WHAT THE SAINTS SENSE AND TASTE

In Edwards's great work on spiritual discernment, *Religious Affections* (1746), he argues that true Christians (whom he calls "saints") have a new sense and taste. They perceive divine things that the unregenerate miss because they do not have this special sense and taste. What the saints perceive with their new sense is the beauty of holiness. This is the sweetness that their new taste enjoys. This is why the psalmist could say that the Word is "sweeter also than honey, / and drippings of the honey-comb" (Ps 19:10). This is why Jesus could say after a long journey to Samaria (his starving disciples had gone to town to look for food) that he was satisfied without food: "I have food to eat that you do not know about. . . . My food is to do the will of him who sent me and to accomplish his work" (Jn 4:32, 34).[17]

Edwards wrote that to the saint, the holiness of God and his works are beautiful. Contemplating them provides both food and enjoyment to the soul. For Edwards they were a source of spiritual ecstasy.

> Holiness . . . appeared to me to be of a sweet, pleasant, charming, serene, calm nature. It seemed to me, it brought an inexpressible purity, brightness, peacefulness and ravishment to the soul. . . . Once, as I rode out into the woods for my health, anno 1737; and having lit from my horse in a retired place, as my manner commonly has been, to walk for divine contemplation and prayer; I had a view, that for me was extraordinary, of the glory of the Son of God; as mediator between God and man; and his wonderful, great, full, pure and sweet grace and love, and meek and gentle condescension. This grace, that appeared to me so calm and sweet, appeared great above the heavens. The person of Christ appeared ineffably excellent, with an excellency great enough to swallow up all thought and conception. Which continued, near as I can judge, about an hour; which kept me, the bigger part of the time, in a flood of tears, and weeping aloud.[18]

PASTOR AND REVIVALIST

It might be easy for us to get the impression that Edwards was merely a talking head who sat in his ivory tower concocting theories without real experience in the world and church. Quite the opposite was the case. Edwards was a pastor and then missionary for thirty-six years, delivering two to three sermons almost every week and caring for thousands of souls. He believed revivals were the engines that drive human history and that preaching is the principal method God uses to bring revival. Edwards was not only a leading preacher of the massive revival called the Great Awakening that swept up and down the American colonies in the 1730s and early 1740s, but he was also a foremost theologian of revival. His revival

---

[17]The new creation for Edwards was not simply a new spiritual vision to be enjoyed on earth and in some sort of dematerialized heaven. Edwards was a postmillennialist who looked forward to a literal new heaven and new earth. For more on this, see Edwards's *Apocalyptic Writings*, vol. 5, in *The Works of Jonathan Edwards*, ed. Stephen Stein (New Haven, Conn.: Yale University Press, 1977).

[18]Jonathan Edwards, "Personal Narrative," in *A Jonathan Edwards Reader*, ed. John E. Smith, Harry S. Stout and Kenneth P. Minkema (New Haven, Conn.: Yale University Press, 1995), pp. 287, 293.

treatises *(A Faithful Narrative of the Surprising Work of God; The Distinguishing Marks of a Work of the Spirit of God;* and *Some Thoughts Concerning the Revival)* defended the revivals against critics who denounced them as mere emotionalism.[19] One could say, in fact, that the "Little Awakening" in Edwards's church in 1734-1735 was the laboratory, so to speak, for his later thinking and writing on not only revival but spiritual experience in general. Just as with Augustine's youthful years in North Africa, Luther's experiences in the monastery and Calvin's labors to reform Geneva, Edwards's leadership of both the Little Awakening and the Great Awakening form the essential background for his theological achievements.

This experience as shepherd of souls, both in his own huge church at Northampton (thirteen hundred people) and for the countless others who came to him for spiritual counsel, eventuated in Edwards's great manual of spiritual discernment, *Religious Affections* (1746). Harvard historian Perry Miller called it the greatest work of religious psychology ever penned in the New World. Others have said it is the most acute work on the spiritual life in the history of Christian thought.

Edwards's objective in this work was to draw the fine line between true and false religion. He aimed to so describe the nature of genuine experience with God that both insiders and outsiders to Christian faith could distinguish between the Holy Spirit's work and its counterfeits. The book argues, first, that religious experience is centered in what he called the "affections." These lie at a deeper level of the human person than either thoughts or feelings, and in fact are the source and motivating power of thoughts and feelings. Indeed, he claimed they are at the root of all spiritual experience, both true and false. Holy affections are the source of all true religion, and other kinds of affections are at the root of false religion. My definition of what Edwards means by affections is strong inclinations of the soul that are manifested in thinking, feeling and acting. So the affections are not emotions but give rise to emotion; they are strong inclinations and so not simply preferences; and they involve mind, will and feeling at the same time. In fact, the thoughts of the mind are strongly affected by the affections. Holy inclinations will lead us to love God (feelings),

---

[19]These are available in abridged form in *Jonathan Edwards: On Revival* (Edinburgh: Banner of Truth, 1984), and in their critical edition, *The Great Awakening*, vol. 4, *The Works of Jonathan Edwards*, ed. C. C. Open (New Haven, Conn.: Yale University Press, 1972).

think rightly about God (thinking) and try to obey his commandments (acts of the will). Unholy affections will cause a person to feel distaste for faith and Christians (feelings), believe there are excellent reasons for rejecting faith (thinking) and refuse to pray or attend church or promote the influence of religion in society (actions).

The rest of the *Religious Affections* is divided between twelve "negative" or unreliable signs of true religion (criteria Christians typically use to determine the presence of true faith) and twelve "positive" or reliable signs of grace (criteria Edwards says Christians *ought* to use). For example, one of the negative signs is frequent and passionate praise for God. Edwards said that true believers will praise God often, but that the Israelites praised God just before worshiping the golden calf, and people praised Jesus as he rode into Jerusalem on his donkey but a few days later cried out, "Crucify him" (Mk 15:13). So the mere fact of passionate praise is not a reliable sign of true grace. Christian practice, on the other hand, *is* a reliable sign—in fact, the most reliable sign. The person who practices the principles of the kingdom of God shows most clearly the presence of true grace. This does not mean perfection but commitment over time to the lordship of Christ. What someone does in life is finally more illustrative of grace than what he or she says.[20]

HIS ACHILLES' HEEL

Because of this breathtaking vision of God's holiness and beauty, Edwards is now something of a theological hero for multiplied thousands of Christians. But it would do us well to note that he also had his flaws. One was that he was not a people person. He had a hard time with small talk. He was criticized for not regularly calling on his parishioners, as most pastors of that era did, but instead telling them he would come to their homes if they asked.

Edwards was also fearless in the pulpit. He seemed to have no compunction about offending people in the pews if he felt sins needed to be preached against. Repeatedly Edwards criticized business people who took advantage of market conditions to gain exorbitant profits from the poor. When the church elders decided to give the best seats in the new church

---

[20]I have rewritten the *Religious Affections* in simpler form and accessible language in *Seeing God: Jonathan Edwards and Spiritual Discernment* (Vancouver: Regent College Publishing, 2000).

building to the wealthy, he denounced them from his pulpit. His 1742 covenant requiring Northampton entrepreneurs not to cheat in business dealings was not appreciated by town merchants and probably created resentments that came home to roost in 1750, when Edwards, New England's best-known pastor, was dismissed by his own congregation in a vote led by the elite.

One factor might have been the flip side of one of his strengths. He held himself to lofty moral and spiritual standards, but found it difficult to empathize with ordinary folks. Not everyone wanted to be a spiritual hero. It wasn't every Christian who, when the occasion called for it, was ready to fall on the sword. Some were content to plod their way to heaven, often distracted, just as long as they got their nose over the finish line, so to speak. These Christians might have felt like they never measured up to Edwards's exacting standards. In this respect, Edwards was something like Calvin. Both were dedicated scholars with unusually high expectations for themselves, and both had difficult times with their congregations.

Among other things we notice today are his denunciation of charismatic gifts and fulminations against Catholicism. Of course, these were rather common for Reformed Protestants in his day. And sad to say, so was his acceptance of slavery.

Many Edwardsphiles would be surprised to know that Jonathan and Sarah always owned at least one slave. Two of their slaves were sold after his death to a Connecticut man for twenty-three British pounds. Some years before, when another pastor was criticized by his parishioners for owning African slaves, Edwards defended the pastor and the institution of slavery. He said the Bible allowed slavery. Even though God in the early stages of revelation "winked at" practices that were condemned at a later stage, such as polygamy, the New Testament, in his opinion, does not condemn slavery.[21]

In some respects, Edwards distanced himself from the racism so preva-

---

[21]Edwards was right that the New Testament nowhere explicitly condemns slavery, and the Old Testament appears to condone it. But the grand historical narrative of the Bible is about freedom from slavery to sin and the devil. Every time the Old Testament mentions slavery, it tries to mitigate its harshness. In the New Testament Jesus treats slaves as equals, and Paul counsels a slaveowner to stop treating his runaway "as a slave" but as "a beloved brother" (Philem 16). Besides, as the nineteenth-century abolitionists argued, the Golden Rule implicitly condemns the practice.

lent in his day. He said that blacks and Indians are not inherently inferior ("we are made of the same human race") and that in the millennial age "many of the Negroes and Indians will be divines." Blacks and Indians were spiritual equals to whites, he preached. His Northampton church admitted nine Africans to full membership during his years there. Though he defended the institution of slavery, Edwards nonetheless condemned the African slave trade, saying no nations "have any power or business to disenfranchise all the nations of Africa." His own son Jonathan Edwards Jr. and his foremost disciple Samuel Hopkins were early outspoken abolitionists.[22]

Nevertheless, Edwards's support for slavery as an institution, his own complicity in it by buying and owning slaves and his inability to see the implicit biblical argument against it, are all unsettling. As Sherard Burns has written, "To condemn the [slave] trade and at the same time to participate in the selling and buying of slaves was a glaring contradiction."[23]

In that each was a sinner and got things wrong, Edwards was no different from every other theologian. It is a good reminder to us not to treat any theologian as having it all together right, and to remember that we too are prone to error.

WHAT WE CAN TAKE FROM EDWARDS

1. Edwards can help us beware of theologies that reduce Christian faith to morals or diffuse experience. Christian discipleship is not simply a way of living that is morally superior, but a vision of the beauty of God in Christ. Nor is it merely an experience of feeling forgiven by God. Instead it is focused on the beauty of Jesus Christ who procured forgiveness by his sufferings on the cross.

2. Edwards can also show us, perhaps better than anyone else in the history of American Christianity, that true faith involves both mind and heart. Faith without engagement of the mind is mere sentimentalism. Religion that does not spring from commitment of the heart can be mere intellectualism. Edwards demonstrated a brilliant mind engaging the best

---

[22]For more on Edwards and slavery, see Kenneth Minkema, "Jonathan Edwards on Slavery and the Slave Trade," *William and Mary Quarterly* 54 (1997): 823-34; and George Marsden, *Jonathan Edwards: A Life* (New Haven, Conn.: Yale University Press, 2003), pp. 255-58.

[23]Sherard Burns, "Trusting the Theology of a Slave-Owner," in *A God-Entranced Vision of All Things: The Legacy of Jonathan Edwards*, ed. John Piper and Justin Taylor (Wheaton, Ill.: Crossway, 2004), p. 153.

minds in the West, from a heart that was on fire for God. In fact, he is a model for those wanting to do theology today. He used the best of what the Enlightenment had to offer to understand reality on its terms, while at the same time undermining key Enlightenment assumptions in ways that opened up new visions of reality.

3. Edwards's *Religious Affections* shows us that the presence of religious feeling does not prove that spirituality is true—that there are plenty of religious experiences that involve deep feeling but are nevertheless unholy. In that work Edwards also demonstrates that judgment in religion is often necessary, especially to distinguish true religion from false. His exposition of twelve unreliable signs of true religion and twelve reliable signs of genuine biblical faith provide for us an invaluable guide to competing theologies and spiritualities today.

4. Edwards is a veritable gold mine for thinking Christians today. Besides being one of the historic church's most penetrating practitioners of biblical theology (especially in his twelve hundred sermons), he has provided compelling answers to some of theology's most difficult questions: how God's sovereignty and human freedom can be reconciled (see his treatise *Freedom of the Will*); why God made the world, if he was already happy and self-sufficient in his triune self *(The End for Which God Created the World);* what difference there is between pagan and Christian virtue *(The Nature of True Virtue);* if and how we are blamed for Adam's sin *(Original Sin);* and what secular history has to do with salvation history *(History of the Work of Redemption).*

A SELECTION FROM JONATHAN EDWARDS'S WORKS

He that sees the beauty of holiness, or true moral good, sees the greatest and most important thing in the world, which is the fullness of all things, without which all the world is empty, no better than nothing, yea, worse than nothing. Unless this is seen, nothing is seen, that is worth the seeing: for there is no other true excellency or beauty. Unless this be understood, nothing is understood, that is worthy of the exercise of the noble faculty of understanding. This is the beauty of the Godhead, and the divinity of Divinity (if I may so speak), the good of the infinite Fountain of Good; without which God himself (if that were possible to be) would be an infinite evil: without which, we ourselves had better never have been; and without which there had better have been no be-

ing. He therefore in effect knows nothing, that knows not this: his knowledge is but the shadow of knowledge, or the form of knowledge, as the Apostle calls it. Well therefore may the Scripture represent those who are destitute of that spiritual sense, by which is perceived the beauty of holiness, as totally blind, deaf and senseless, yea dead. And well may regeneration, in which this divine sense is given by its Creator, be represented as opening the blind eyes, raising the dead, and bringing a person into a new world. For if what has been said be considered, it will be manifest, that when a person has this sense and knowledge given him, he will view nothing as he did before; though before he knew all things after the flesh, yet henceforth he will know them so no more; and he is become "a new creature, old things are passed away, behold all things are become new"; agreeable to II Cor. 5:16-17.[24]

FOR REFLECTION AND DISCUSSION

1. How has this chapter changed your view of Jonathan Edwards?

2. Why did Edwards feel Enlightenment deism was wrong in its view of reason? Do you agree?

3. In what ways did he relate beauty to God?

4. How did Edwards define holiness? Does this definition help you see God better?

5. Does his conviction of beauty as God's heart help you see the world and faith differently? How?

6. Does Edwards's involvement with slavery disappoint you? What does that teach us about theology? About ourselves?

FOR FURTHER READING

Edwards, Jonathan. *A Jonathan Edwards Reader.* Edited by John E. Smith, Harry S. Stout and Kenneth P. Minkema. New Haven, Conn.: Yale University Press, 1995.

Marsden, George. *A Short Life of Jonathan Edwards.* Grand Rapids: Eerdmans, 2008.

McDermott, Gerald R., ed. *Understanding Jonathan Edwards: Introducing America's Theologian.* New York: Oxford University Press, 2009.

---

[24]Edwards, *Religious Affections*, pp. 274-75.

9

Friedrich Schleiermacher

Father of Liberal Theology

Most Christians have never heard of Friedrich Schleiermacher (1768-1834), but his influence is hard to overestimate. He has been called the Kant of modern theology, which means that just as Immanuel Kant laid the foundation for modern philosophy, Schleiermacher is widely regarded as starting a whole new way of seeing God and theology in the modern age. For this reason Schleiermacher is usually called the father of liberal theology. He launched a "Copernican revolution" in theology by turning to the subject—Christian experience as interpreted by the Christian community—as the primary source for knowledge of God. Karl Barth rightly called this "*the* watershed" of modern theology.[1]

It's not surprising that Schleiermacher was so influential, for he was extraordinarily gifted and industrious. While a full-time pastor for nearly forty years at Holy Trinity Church in Berlin, he wrote enough to fill thirty volumes in his collected works, and at the same time was professor of theology at the University of Berlin, which he cofounded. There he lectured not only on theology but also on dialectics (a combination of metaphysics and logic), ethics, psychology, aesthetics, education, politics and the history of philosophy. He also found time to produce the classic translation of Plato into modern German and become the chief progenitor of modern hermeneutics, the discipline that thinks about how we interpret texts. In his spare time, he was a prolific writer and activist in national politics, trying to nudge the Prussian and German states toward the protection of the

---

[1] Karl Barth, *Protestant Thought from Rousseau to Ritschl* (New York: Clarion, 1969), pp. 306-54.

"rights of human beings." His influence is felt today even beyond the realm of theology, for "we are still living in a later phase of that Romantic Movement inaugurated by Schleiermacher and his circle at the beginning of the nineteenth century."[2]

A REMARKABLE LIFE

Schleiermacher was the son of a Reformed pastor who served as a chaplain in the Prussian army. He was educated by Pietists in Moravian schools,[3] where he said he learned "that mystic tendency . . . [which] has supported and carried me through all the storms of skepticism." But if he drank in Moravian mysticism with appreciation (later in life he said he had become "a Moravian again, only of a higher order"), he was also disillusioned by it.[4] For it was supposed to induce the experience of the risen Christ, but Schleiermacher never found it. This failure apparently caused him to doubt the necessity and morality of Christ's atoning sacrifice.

Schleiermacher transferred to the University of Halle, which was founded by Pietists but also employed some professors who explored the new rationalism emerging in Germany. Here Schleiermacher read Kant behind drawn curtains, with the excitement of a miser who has come upon a stash of gold. Here he also dove into Plato, Spinoza (the Jewish pantheist philosopher) and other German philosophers such as Fichte, Leibnitz and Schelling. Schleiermacher later came to criticize Kant for his neglect of history and individuality, but retained from Kant the key insight that shaped all of Schleiermacher's later theology—that knowledge of ultimate reality is limited to what can be known from human consciousness. Showing the influence of his education at Pietist schools, Schleiermacher also came to criticize the rationalism of the Enlightenment, which Kant did so much to foster, and the idea that religion is in its essence morality or metaphysics.

---

[2]James C. Livingston, *Modern Christian Thought*, 2nd ed. (Upper Saddle River, N.J.: Prentice Hall, 1997), 1:93.
[3]Pietists were Christians who emphasized Christian experience in reaction to what they thought to be dry rationalism in orthodox theology in the seventeenth century. The Moravians were a remnant of the Bohemian Brethren, led by Nicholas von Zinzendorf (1700-1760), who settled in a community at Herrnhut (Germany). They emphasized fellowship, missions and service more than creeds, and "religion of the heart"—a "felt" fellowship with the Savior.
[4]Friedrich Schleiermacher, *Letters*, trans. F. Rowan (London: Smith, Elder, 1860), 1:283; cited by Livingston, *Modern Christian Thought*, p. 94.

Schleiermacher's first major work was *On Religion: Speeches Addressed to Its Cultured Despisers* (1799). In this series of lectures Schleiermacher told the intellectual skeptics of his day that if they thought they were rejecting genuine religion when they rejected Christianity, they were wrong. In actuality, he said, they were rejecting simply dogma and morality—not true religion. For true religion, he argued, was a matter of inner feeling and was not connected directly with any particular set of doctrines or ethics.

Schleiermacher's most productive years were 1808 to 1834, when he held the chair of theology at the University of Berlin. Here he wrote his most famous work, *The Christian Faith* (1821-1822, rev. 1830). Schleiermacher's herculean productivity is all the more remarkable in view of his continual poor health and personal disappointments. Through his entire career he suffered from nearsightedness and recurring stomach problems, and took a long time to find love. In his mid-thirties he fell in love with the wife of a Berlin pastor, but she refused to leave her husband. It wasn't until he was forty that he married the young widow of a pastor who had two children of her own. With Friedrich she bore four more, but their only son died at age nine from scarlet fever.

THE FEELING OF ABSOLUTE DEPENDENCE

Schleiermacher is most famous for his definition of the essence of religion as the "feeling of absolute dependence." In order to understand this, we must see first what Schleiermacher was reacting against. He objected to two tendencies in that era of the Enlightenment—first, the assumption that religion is essentially morality, and second, the presumption that religion is instead a matter of believing certain things about God and the world. In other words, he rejected the idea that religion at its heart simply tells us either what to believe or how to live.

Rubbish, said Schleiermacher. "Piety cannot be an instinct craving for a mess of metaphysical and ethical crumbs." Religion in its essence does not consist of propositions or dogma or philosophy or morals. Instead, it is "the immediate feeling of the Infinite and Eternal."[5] By "immediate" Schleiermacher meant intuitive, and by "feeling" he meant an inner sense—not necessarily emotional—that is linked with thinking. The

---

[5]Friedrich Schleiermacher, *On Religion: Speeches to Its Cultured Despisers*, trans. John Oman (New York: Harper & Row, 1958), pp. 31, 16.

thought involved is the rational perception that somehow there is Something or Someone infinite holding up everything around me that is finite, and that this Something or Someone is beyond space and time.

This "immediate feeling" is an inner experience that is not entirely subjective or psychological, for it also feels the impact of the universe on it, and the universe is an objective entity. It is there whether I feel it or not. When I do feel it, I know it is outside of me and not simply a figment of my imagination. Therefore this inner feeling, which lies at the heart of all true religion, is more than just an emotion or psychological experience within my head. It is a perception of the ultimate reality that really lies beyond me and actually sustains my existence from moment to moment. This feeling or perception is actually "a co-existence of God in the self-consciousness." It is God telling me that I am in relation to him.[6]

Schleiermacher believed that this feeling of absolute dependence is common to all religions and genuine piety. In fact, he said, it is part of human nature. Today we would say it is hard-wired into the human mind and heart. This means that, for Schleiermacher, we seek God by nature: "An essential element of human nature . . . [is its] striving . . . towards Christianity."[7] So we naturally seek God. In our heart of hearts we want him, and it is only ignorance or the baser parts of our nature that deter us from our natural quest for him.

Schleiermacher's understanding of the essence of religion had implications for his conception of redemption. If religion itself is a feeling within us, then so is redemption. It is not an objective event that took place on the cross two thousand years ago but an experience that takes place continually within those of us who realize our dependence. In this way Christ communicates to us his God-consciousness and so God's redemptive power. This is what the grace of Christ means: an experience in ourselves whereby Jesus' perfect God-consciousness becomes, at least in part, our own.

This also changed his view of doctrine or *dogmatics* (from the Latin, "that which must be believed"). "Dogmatic propositions," he taught, "[arise] solely out of logically ordered reflection upon the immediate utterances of

---

[6]Friedrich Schleiermacher, *The Christian Faith*, ed. H. R. Mackintosh (Philadelphia: Fortress, 1976), p. 126.
[7]Ibid., pp. 26, 74.

the religious self-consciousness."[8] In other words, the source of what Christians believe is their own consciousness—their feeling of absolute dependence. Christian belief arises from the Christian community's drawing out the implications of that feeling, as they relate to God, self and world.

At the beginning of the nineteenth century, this was a remarkable accomplishment. After a century of critics had attacked the historical reliability, apologetic value and moral authority of the Bible, some Christian thinkers wondered how theology was possible anymore. Schleiermacher seemed to provide a new way forward by giving theology a new sense of self-authentication. Christians would no longer have to justify theology by appealing to science or ethics, as Enlightenment thinkers had insisted. In other words, they no longer had to be intimidated by Enlightenment skeptics who said the Christian faith contradicted science (as, for example, when it taught biblical miracles) or opposed Kantian ethics (as, for instance, when the Bible promised rewards for obedience).[9] Now they could say that the heart of true religion lies not in the Bible—which they thought was riddled with mistakes and faulty counsel stemming from provincial ancient cultures—but in the universal *a priori* experience of absolute dependence. Some Christians had rejected Calvin's and Edwards's insistence that the Bible authenticates itself by the witness of the Holy Spirit, and supposed that their new appeal to inner experience would provide the clarity that they felt the Bible lacked.

Schleiermacher also rejected the appeal to a universal religion of nature or "rational" religion that deists and others had proposed in their rejection of "positive" and historical religions such as Judaism and Christianity. Schleiermacher said there is no such thing as "religion in general," and that every religion genuinely founded on the feeling of absolute dependence had a history and set of beliefs that flow from that feeling. True religion, he said, is by nature concrete and historical. It is found in real communities and institutions. So Schleiermacher did not support the kind of individualistic spirituality where we are free to do our own thing, unrelated to a religious community. Humans are social by nature, he said, and therefore it should not surprise us that the church is the historical medium

---

[8]Ibid., p. 81.
[9]Kant said that if self-interest is any part of my motivation for an action, then my action is unethical.

in which people find redemption through Christ. People are inclined to share their religious experience with others, and God uses this social bond to communicate his life through Christ to human beings. The church's purpose is the care of souls—who usually cannot attain God-consciousness without it.[10]

Nor did Schleiermacher teach a religion of self-help. After all, his description of true religion is a feeling of absolute *dependence*. But even more important, he said redemption comes from outside the self, from Jesus Christ as Redeemer. Jesus is not simply an example to us but actively imparts to us by grace his own God-consciousness, which sets us free from a life of sensuality and meaninglessness. Redemption is a gift, not a human achievement. (Again we see this recurring theme, which has run through all the great theologians—that God is a giving God, and redemption is by a gift from God.)

The centrality of Christ runs through all of Schleiermacher's theology. He insisted that every dogma be related to the consciousness that Christ imparts to believers. No Christian belief could be properly understood, he argued, without its being related to Christ and his redemption.

EDWARDS AND SCHLEIERMACHER

Many students of the history of theology have noticed striking affinities between Schleiermacher and Edwards. They shared a similar view of human nature. Both saw that the deepest affections are at the base of the human person, controlling what we choose, think and feel. Therefore both of these theologians realized that religion's essence lies beyond mere thinking (doctrine) and doing (ethics), and both used a kind of critical empiricism (focusing on tangible experience, but not taking all experience at face value) in their theological work.

But the similarities stop there. As Barth and many others have pointed out, Schleiermacher's subject matter is less Christ and redemption than our own religious experience. He seems trapped within the anthropological horizon. He refuses to discuss the objectivity of God apart from human experience because of his conviction that we can only know God's

---

[10]Schleiermacher said "most men, following their nature, will belong to an existing form [some world religion], and there will be only a few whom none suffices." So not all have an absolute need for an institutional religion (see Livingston, *Modern Christian Thought*, p. 99).

relation to us, and only as that is felt by us in consciousness of our dependence. Our other great theologians have also said we cannot know God in
himself—in his essence—but they believed we can know something of
God outside of our experience because God has revealed himself, both in
history and in the words of Scripture. For Schleiermacher the words of
revelation are not given by God but invented by human beings as a series
of human reflections on religious experience. Theology, or the study of
God, runs the risk of becoming anthropology, or the study of humanity. It
is no wonder that Schleiermacher's theology departs from Edwards's orthodoxy: Schleiermacher ignored the Trinity, relegating it to an appendix
at the back of his biggest work, *the Christian Faith*, because he could not
find it within his idea of piety. For Schleiermacher there is no external
authority that takes precedence over the immediate experience of believers. Because he could not find these things within their immediate experience, he rejected the virgin birth and second coming of Christ, and had
trouble with miracles.

Edwards, on the other hand, looked to a norm outside experience—the
revelation of God in the Scriptures. He was more critical of religious experience than was Schleiermacher, evaluating it by the norm of Scripture,
but at the same time no less insistent than Schleiermacher on the importance of experience in religion. While Schleiermacher spoke in somewhat
abstract ways about "piety" and "the feeling of absolute dependence," Edwards was more of a clinical student of concrete religious experiences, fill-
ing treatises with actual accounts of diverse religious events and people.
Perhaps this is why some scholars think Edwards was more subtle and
probing in his evaluation of religious experience than Schleiermacher. For
example, Richard R. Niebuhr, perhaps the foremost American interpreter
of Schleiermacher, writes that Schleiermacher "falls below the standard
set by Jonathan Edwards in his sensitivity and perspicacity in the realm of
the Christian and religious affections."[11]

Another basic difference between Edwards and Schleiermacher is their
divergence on both human nature and epistemology (how one knows).
Schleiermacher believed God-consciousness was "already present in human nature," as an a priori of human existence. Regeneration is a matter of

---

[11]Richard R. Niebuhr, *Schleiermacher on Christ and Religion* (New York: Charles Scribner's,
1964), p. 17.

"the quiescent self-consciousness, looking at itself reflected in thought and finding a consciousness of God included there."[12]

For Edwards, on the other hand, regeneration is truly a new birth—a miracle whereby the Holy Spirit brings new life to a heart that was dead. So while for Schleiermacher there is only one epistemology (everyone can experience God by self-reflection), for Edwards there are two—that of the regenerate and that of the unregenerate. One comes by natural use of human reflection, and the other comes by a miraculous event. For the emerging Romantic movement, which included such figures as Ralph Waldo Emerson and Henry David Thoreau, Schleiermacher was right—every human being has access to a "deeper awareness" of reality. No special experience of divine grace is needed.

SCHLEIERMACHER'S THEOLOGICAL METHOD

Schleiermacher was revolutionary because he reversed the traditional method for doing theology, which had been to go first to God's revelation for knowledge of God. Schleiermacher went instead to religious consciousness as a new foundation for religious belief. It is no surprise that he starts his *Christian Faith* not with God but the church. Of course, beginning with church can be refreshing in this day when so many are rejecting "organized religion" for hyper-individualized spirituality. But when theology looks to the church's experience rather than objective revelation coming from outside the church for its primary source of truth, the church itself loses its ability to find enduring truth.

This new method explicitly rejected the old. To know God, Schleiermacher taught, we do not to go to Scripture or to "creeds which are naturally last in religious communication, to stimulate what should properly precede them."[13] Instead, he said, we must retreat into ourself and abandon external things, both intellectual and physical. This is what Schleiermacher meant by the mysticism that is at the heart of true piety: "From of old, all truly religious characters have had a mystical trait, and . . . all imaginative natures, which are too airy to occupy themselves with solid and rigid worldly affairs, have at least some stirrings of piety."[14] Schleier-

---

[12]Schleiermacher, *Christian Faith*, pp. 476, 478-79.
[13]Schleiermacher, *On Religion*, p. 161.
[14]Ibid., p. 133.

macher meant that true mysticism, which is the same thing as true religion, is abandonment of all ideas and written words and external things, to reflect upon one's inner religious sensibilities. One should not do it in isolation from other believers, for the church is corporate, but nonetheless true Christian thinking must think about what collective Christian experience *means*.

Theology, then, is confession of a person's inner state, a kind of self-analysis. "Theological thinking is, according to Schleiermacher, reflection upon and clarification of believing experience."[15] This means that anything the Christian church thinks about God is to come from thinking about its own experience. The church should not think anything about God that is not found within itself. Piety is more important than ideas, and feelings of piety should judge ideas. This is why Schleiermacher told the church it need no longer believe in the Trinity or the virgin birth or the second coming of Christ—none of these could be derived from the feeling of absolute dependence.

For Schleiermacher, then, there is no knowledge of God that is given directly through Scripture. For God, he decided, had not revealed himself directly in the Bible. If there was any revelation at all, it was only in the feeling of dependence. If the Bible contains truth, it is only when it corresponds to what our religious consciousness tells us is true. When the two disagree, the Bible is wrong. Therefore we cannot know God outside of our religious experience; we can know him only in relation to ourselves, in our own feeling of absolute dependence.

THE NEW METHOD'S RESULT

Barth was right: Schleiermacher placed himself "above Christianity" in such a way that neither the Bible nor church tradition could limit what he would say about God.[16] The result was a series of Schleiermachian beliefs about God, Jesus and the Bible that reject traditional Christian doctrine.

Christology. Schleiermacher rejected the orthodox teachings that Christ was preexistent before his incarnation and was a cocreator with the Father and the Spirit. He claimed that Christ "never maintained He was the only

---

[15]Niebuhr, *Schleiermacher on Christ*, p. 139.
[16]Barth, *Protestant Thought*, p. 325.

mediator, the only one in whom His idea actualized itself."[17] And most damaging to the future of Protestantism, Schleiermacher referred to Christ's divinity only in terms of having perfect God-consciousness. Christ, in his view, was a perfect human who attained more perfect God-consciousness than anyone else. But for Schleiermacher he was not, and is not, the second person of the Trinity who is fully equal in divine nature and being with the Father.

Therefore when Schleiermacher talked about Christ's redemption, he did not mean that on the cross Christ took our sins and gave us his righteousness. On the contrary, for Schleiermacher redemption means Christ being a "medium" for communication of his perfect God-consciousness. Jesus redeems us by implanting his God-consciousness in us as the dominant principle of our lives. This has the effect of our "gaining the victory over the sensuous impulses and ordering human consciousness in such a way that pain and melancholy give way to a new sense of equilibrium and joy, a new attunement of the soul in its relation to God and the world."[18]

Schleiermacher also rejected the church's historic teaching that some would be damned. At the end of *The Christian Faith* he wrote, "Through the power of redemption there will one day be a universal restoration of all souls."[19] Schleiermacher decided that Christ never taught the doctrine of damnation: "Such testimony is wholly lacking."[20] How could he dismiss the frequent reference by Jesus in the Gospels to a place of "fire" and "torment" and "gnashing of teeth" (see, e.g., Mt 5:21-22, 29-30; 8:12; 10:28; 23:15, 33; Mk 9:45-48; Lk 16: 23-24)?

God. Not surprisingly, Schleiermacher's doctrine of God was equally unorthodox. He called into question traditional ideas of God's eternity and omnipresence by relating them solely to the idea of dependence. God's eternity, he said, means simply that God is the timeless cause of everything and even of time itself. This begs the question of whether God was before time and thus never had a beginning. When Schleiermacher treats omnipresence, he says it means God is the spaceless cause of all space. But then is God

---

[17]Schleiermacher, *On Religion*, p. 248.
[18]Livingston, *Modern Christian Thought*, p. 103.
[19]Schleiermacher, *Christian Faith*, p. 722.
[20]Ibid.

separate from all space? One is not sure from Schleiermacher's theology.

We should not be surprised that Schleiermacher runs into such difficulties with orthodox doctrine, for he limits himself to saying only what can be derived from what he thinks is common to Christian experience. Even the word *God* itself is limited in this way. He says the word is "nothing more than the feeling of absolute dependence . . . and any further content of the idea must be evolved out of this fundamental import assigned to it."[21] This is why Schleiermacher omits the doctrines of the origin of the world, angels, the devil, any link between our first parents and our own sin, eschatology and the Trinity—they seemed to him to be incapable of being derived from the experience of dependence.

The Bible. Schleiermacher's view of the Bible was subtle, but consistent with his basic presuppositions. He affirmed that Scripture is "the norm for all succeeding presentations." He agreed with most of the great theologians we have seen when he taught that each part of the Bible should be interpreted in light of the Bible's great theme, which for him was redemption in Christ. "Casual expressions" and mere "side-thoughts" should be given less emphasis than Scripture's "main subjects."[22]

But Scripture itself, he warned, should not be identified with "revelation." The latter is the event and person of Jesus Christ. Revelation from God was "in Christ" and is found in the New Testament only as the biblical authors receive radiation, as it were, from that shining light of Christ. Their acts of writing the New Testament books were no more inspired than their preaching or saying things that did not wind up in Scripture. So "inspiration" was not confined to Scripture, and "revelation" refers to Jesus Christ, not the Bible per se. In fact, not all the New Testament books "are equally fitted, by content and form, to vindicate their place in the Canon."[23]

The German theologian's attitude to the Old Testament was almost contemptuous. He wrote that if a doctrine appears only in the Old Testament and not also the New, it is not Christian. The Old Testament has neither the dignity nor the inspiration of the New, and contains instead the "spirit of the [Jewish] people . . . not the Christian Spirit." Therefore

---

[21]Ibid., p. 17.
[22]Ibid., pp. 594, 595-96.
[23]Ibid., pp. 597, 598-99.

we are not to use the Old Testament to support Christian doctrines.[24]

Even liberal Christians today, who often appeal to the psalms and prophets for moral teaching and consider Schleiermacher their mentor, might be surprised to hear their theological father saying, "It is only after *deluding* ourselves by unconscious additions and subtractions that we can suppose we are able to gather a Christian doctrine of God out of the Prophets and the Psalms." The following statement is still more alarming and makes us wonder if there is a line from Schleiermacher to the German Christians of the 1930s who ripped the Old Testament out of their Bibles: The only reason why earlier eras read the Old Testament was because of its "historical connexions *[sic]*" to the Christian faith, so that its "gradual retirement into the background" of Christian reading and worship is not to be regretted.[25]

WHAT WE CAN LEARN

1. Schleiermacher tried admirably to secure an independent footing for theology against the Enlightenment's attempts to reduce it to morality or metaphysics. But he overreacted and produced a theology that is just as problematic as Enlightenment reductionism. The result is that Schleiermacher has come to be an example of how not to do theology—or for that matter, how not to think about God. He starts from human experience rather than God's biblical revelation. The result is inevitable rejection of orthodox theology (and teaching of the apostles!) on almost every major point—from God and Christ and Trinity to redemption and Scripture and the final ends of humanity. When we think we can find God by looking inside our own hearts and minds, we start down the trail that leads to a different religion. This novel approach changes our view of God into a bigger version of ourselves. We wind up doing anthropology and not theology. We have made God into a big human with a big voice. But this god is really an idol, a larger version of ourselves. In short, we end up worshiping ourselves.

2. We learn from Schleiermacher the danger of Marcionism. Marcion was a second-century A.D. heretic who said the God of the Old Testament was evil, and the true Bible contains only the Gospel of Luke and some Pauline letters. It's no wonder that Marcion was a favorite of the Nazis,

---

[24]Ibid., pp. 116, 609, 610.
[25]Ibid., pp. 609, 610, italics added.

and that the German church of that period got rid of the Old Testament. Our modern churches don't throw the Old Testament out literally, but their failure to read or preach from Torah suggests they have adopted Schleiermacher's attitude toward it. We need to remember that the Old Testament was Jesus' Bible, and it was of *this* Bible that he said, "Until heaven and earth pass away, not an iota, not a dot, will pass from the Law [the Old Testament!] until all is accomplished" (Mt 5:18).

3. Schleiermacher teaches us the danger of relying on personal experience for authority. Personal experience of the risen Christ is a must, but we must not rely on that experience to teach us who Christ is. We must look instead to what the apostles gave us in the New Testament and their reading of the Old Testament. This is an objective revelation from God that helps correct and guide all our subjective experience. Evangelicals and Pentecostals, who rightly teach the need to experience the gospel, must nonetheless be careful not to let experience become what teaches the gospel. Otherwise they risk falling into Schleiermacher's trap of constructing a religion of humanity.

4. This should also help us remember the biblical view of human nature. We are made in the image of God and can see through nature and conscience (Rom 1–2) that there is an eternal and omnipotent God. But sin has darkened our minds and, as Calvin put it, turned them into factories of idols. We easily mistake our ideas for God's, forgetting that his ideas are as different from ours "as the heavens are higher than the earth" (Is 55:9). So we must realize that because of our sin and finitude, "no one comprehends what is truly God's except the Spirit of God" (1 Cor 2:11). Therefore we must saturate our minds with the Spirit's revelation of God in Scripture, and the church's explication of this revelation in its creeds and confessions.

5. Finally, Schleiermacher helps explain the puzzling conflicts between liberal and orthodox Christians today. Very often they use the same language but mean different things by the same words. Thus the puzzle. Schleiermacher used most of the same words the orthodox tradition had used but filled them with new meanings. Redemption is not from sin, death and the devil, and won by what happened on the cross, but instead a new consciousness in which the cross seems unnecessary. Revelation is important, but it is no longer found in both Christ and Scripture; now it is

restricted to Christ's God-consciousness. This new use of language points to our need to make sure our churches not only use the language of the orthodox tradition but also assign meanings to the words in the way the great orthodox theologians did.

A SELECTION FROM FRIEDRICH SCHLEIERMACHER'S WORKS

If . . . word and idea are always originally one, and the term "God" therefore presupposes an idea, then we shall simply say that this idea, which is nothing more than the expression of the feeling of absolute dependence, is the most direct reflection upon it and the most original idea with which we are most concerned, and is quite independent of that original knowledge (properly so called), and conditioned only by our feeling of absolute dependence. So that in the first instance God signifies for us simply that which is the co-determinant in this feeling and to which we trace our being in such a state; and any further content of the idea must be evolved out of this fundamental import assigned to it. Now this is just what is principally meant by the formula which says that to feel oneself absolutely dependent and to be conscious of being in relation with God are one and the same thing; and the reason is that absolute dependence is the fundamental relation which must include all others in itself. This last expression includes the God-consciousness in the self-consciousness in such a way that, quite in accordance with the above analysis, the two cannot be separated from each other. The feeling of absolute dependence becomes a clear self-consciousness only as this idea comes simultaneously into being. In this sense it can indeed be said that God is given to us in feeling in an original way; and if we speak of an original revelation of God to man or in man, the meaning will always be just this, that, along with the absolute dependence which characterizes not only man but all temporal existence, there is given to man also the immediate self-consciousness of it, which becomes a consciousness of God.[26]

FOR REFLECTION AND DISCUSSION

1. Was Schleiermacher right to say that true religion is not at its core dogma or morality? Explain.

2. What was the problem with Schleiermacher's belief that Christian faith is essentially a feeling?

---

[26]Schleiermacher, *Christian Faith*, pp. 17-18.

3. Are there many churches today that share this belief?

4. Is there a relationship between Schleiermacher's placing feelings at the center of religion and his rejection of many orthodox Christian doctrines?

5. What do we learn about theological method from Schleiermacher?

6. Is Schhleiermacher's attitude toward the Old Testament common today? Is this worrisome?

7. If you are in a group, let each member share what he or she found most important in this chapter.

FOR FURTHER READING

Schleiermacher, Friedrich. *On Religion: Speeches to Its Cultured Despisers.* Translated by John Oman. New York: Harper & Row, 1958.

Livingston, James C. "Friedrich Schleiermacher." In *Modern Christian Thought.* Vol. 1. 2nd ed. Upper Saddle River, N.J.: Prentice Hall, 1997.

Redeker, Martin. *Schleiermacher: Life and Thought.* Philadelphia: Fortress, 1973.

10

John Henry Newman

Anglican Theologian Who Swam the Tiber

In the last chapter we saw that Schleiermacher believed the essence of religion is piety, which he said had always been his "womb."[1] For John Henry Newman (1801-1890), on the other hand, religion is all about "dogma," those doctrines that must be believed: "From the age of fifteen, dogma has been the fundamental principle of my religion."[2] Any religion, he thought, that did not put belief at its core does not deserve the name of religion. Religion is about what is outside the human self, not some sentiment inside the person.

> I know no other religion [than what is founded on dogma]; I cannot enter into the idea of any other sort of religion; religion, as a mere sentiment, is to me a dream and a mockery. As well can there be filial love without the fact of a father, as devotion without the fact of a Supreme Being.[3]

Newman has been called "England's outstanding theologian, and Catholicism's—at least besides Leo XIII—most significant personality in the [nineteenth] century."[4] His leadership of the Oxford movement in the Church of England from 1833 to 1841 "swayed England as she had not been swayed religiously for many years."[5] When this high-church Angli-

---

[1]Friedrich Schleiermacher, *On Religion: Speeches to Its Cultured Despisers*, trans. John Oman (New York: Harper & Row, 1958), pp. 11-12.
[2]John Henry Newman, *Apologia Pro Vita Sua* (Boston: Houghton Mifflin, 1956), p. 66.
[3]Ibid.
[4]Sophocles D. Lōlē, *On the First Creed*, cited by Jaroslav Pelikan, *Christian Doctrine and Modern Culture (since 1700)* (Chicago: University of Chicago Press, 1989), p. 274.
[5]A. Dwight Culler, introduction to Newman's *Apologia*, p. vii. The Oxford movement was a

can Oxford professor—who had been at one time an evangelical and then a liberal for a short time—at last converted to Roman Catholicism in 1845, all England was shocked. Outrageous charges followed him: he had been a Jesuit in disguise all along; shortly after his conversion he bitterly repented and would give anything to return to Protestantism; he had lost his Christian faith entirely and was now an infidel hiding in Paris; he was really in Birmingham supervising torture cells for Protestant maidens.[6]

None of these were true. In fact he went on to produce some of the most influential and important theological works of the nineteenth century. When Newman was seventy-eight years old, Pope Leo XIII recognized his achievement by appointing him a cardinal of the Catholic Church.

A YOUNG EVANGELICAL AND THEN LIBERAL

Newman grew up in the Church of England when its children learned at their mothers' breasts about the Catholic Queen, Bloody Mary, who had burned three hundred Protestant martyrs at the stake during the English Reformation. "From my boyhood," Newman recalled, "I considered . . . that St. Gregory I about A.D. 600 was the first Pope that was Antichrist." Then, at age fifteen, when he fell seriously ill at boarding school, Newman experienced an evangelical conversion. He became conscious of "two and two only absolute and luminously self-evident beings, myself and my Creator." Even in his old age he remembered this as a definite experience that changed him forever: "It is difficult [for me] to realise or imagine the identity of the boy before or after August 1816. . . . I can look back at the end of seventy years as if on another person."[7]

In his early twenties Newman started to "[drift] in the direction of the Liberalism of the day." He wrote in the *Apologia Pro Vita Sua*, his religious autobiography, that "I was beginning to prefer intellectual excellence to moral." Later in his life he defined liberalism as being in principle against any dogma: it is the idea there are no religious truths that we can know for sure, so one religious belief is as good as another, and all must therefore be tolerated.

---

revival of Catholic piety in the Church of England that stressed the mystery of medievalism, the authority of the church and its ancient tradition, the objectivity of the sacraments, and the importance of moral obedience.
[6]Ibid.
[7]Newman, *Apologia*, p. 69; Culler, introduction to *Apologia*, p. xviii; Newman, *Apologia*, pp. 24, 24 n.

Liberalism in religion is the doctrine that there is no positive truth in religion, but that one creed is as good as another. And this is the teaching which is gaining substance and force daily. It is inconsistent with any recognition of any religion, as *true*. It teaches that all are to be tolerated, for all are matters of opinion. Revealed religion is not a truth, but a sentiment and a taste; not an objective fact, not miraculous; and it is the right of each individual to make it say just what strikes his fancy.[8]

Newman was a liberal for a time, but not in his personal habits. He refused to go the way of the "two-bottle orthodox," who prided themselves on drinking two bottles of port a day as a protest against "puritans" who were orthodox in belief and ascetic in their personal lives.[9]

THE CONVERSION THAT SHOOK ENGLAND

Martin Luther and John Henry Newman both took trips to Rome and were scandalized by the laxity of the Roman church. Newman was especially revolted by the Italian penchant for spitting everywhere by both men and women, even by a priest at the altar "in the most sacred part of the service." Yet Newman was also impressed by the sincerity and intelligence of young men studying for the priesthood, thinking he saw in them "a deep substratum of true Christianity."[10]

During this period Newman's brother Francis had become a Unitarian after serving as an unofficial evangelical missionary to Baghdad. Perhaps in reaction to this devastating personal blow,[11] Newman began to see in Protestantism an emphasis on feeling that seemed similar to liberalism's romantic tendencies: "[Protestants] substitute faith for Christ." Their doctrine of justification by faith points to inner experience rather than to Christ outside themselves: "To look at Christ is to be justified by faith; to think of being justified by faith is to look from Christ and to fall from grace."

---

[8]Newman, *Apologia*, p. 34; John Henry Newman, *My Campaign in Ireland*, cited in Ian Ker, *John Henry Newman: A Biography* (Oxford: Oxford University Press, 1988), p. 721.

[9]Newman, *Apologia*, p. 35.

[10]Ker, *John Henry Newman*, pp. 69, 73.

[11]Michael McClymond thinks Newman was "projecting onto the Evangelical party as a whole the unusual spiritual trajectory followed by his brother Francis" (Michael McClymond, "'Continual Self-contemplation': John Henry Newman's Critique of Evangelicalism," *Downside Review* 127 [2009]).

[Luther] found Christians in bondage to their works and observances; he released them by his doctrine of faith; and he left them in bondage to their feelings. . . . For outward signs of grace he substituted inward; for reverence towards the Church contemplation of self. And . . . whereas he preached against reliance on self, he introduced it in a more subtle shape; whereas he professed to make the written word all in all, he sacrificed it in its length and breadth to the doctrine which he had wrested from a few texts.[12]

Newman thought evangelicals were the worst, for instead of preaching Christ, they preached conversion. They directed attention "to the heart itself, not to anything external to us, whether creeds, actions, or ritual." This was "really a specious form of trusting man rather than God," and so "in its nature Rationalistic."[13]

Newman also thought evangelicals were wrong to think of conversion as being instantaneous. He denied that "there is some clearly marked date at which he began to seek God" and insisted that a person's change of heart is always "a slow work." But, as Michael McClymond notes, Newman had a difficult time interpreting what seemed to be St. Paul's sudden conversion.[14]

The long march toward Rome began when Newman decided, at the age of twenty-seven, to read in systematic fashion all two hundred volumes of the writings of the fathers of the early church.[15] His favorites became Athanasius and Chrysostom, and in Ignatius of Antioch (second century A.D.) the Oxford theologian was surprised to see "the whole system of Catholic doctrine . . . at least in outline."[16] As an Anglican he had always assumed that Canterbury had the faith of the apostles, and Rome the faith of catholicity (most Christians around the world by the time of the Reformation). But as he proceeded through the fathers, he began to

---

[12]John Henry Newman, *Lectures on the Doctrine of Justification*, cited by Ker, *John Henry Newman*, pp. 155, 339-41, in Ker, *John Henry Newman*, p. 156.

[13]John Henry Newman, *Essays Critical and Historical*, cited by Ker, *John Henry Newman*, p. 122.

[14]Not to mention his own rather sudden conversion. Ker, *John Henry Newman*, p. 79; Newman, "Christian Repentance," *Parochial and Plain Sermons*, cited in McClymond, "Continual Self-contemplation," p. 19; Newman, "Sudden Conversions," *Parochial and Plain Sermons*, cited in McClymond, "Continual Self-contemplation," p. 20

[15]John Henry Newman, *The Letters and Diaries of John Henry Newman*, ed. Charles Stephen Dessain (Oxford: Oxford University Press, 1961-1984), 1:285, cited in Ker, *John Henry Newman*, p. 28.

[16]Newman, *Apologia*, p. 67 n.

conclude that Rome had *both* apostolicity and catholicity.

The turning point came in the summer of 1839 (he was thirty-eight), when it suddenly dawned on him that the early heretics shared characteristics of Anglicans like himself, and the orthodox fathers thought like Rome. "I saw my face in that mirror, and I was a Monophysite [heretics who said Jesus had only a divine and not a human nature]."[17]

Yet he still had problems with Rome. For one thing, the history of the popes, with its immoralities and political maneuverings, was a stumbling block. But, he told himself, these things didn't stop Caiaphas or Balaam from speaking the truth. Then there was the emerging claim to papal infallibility, which was not yet declared dogma but was on its way to being so. Newman was disturbed. After all, St. Peter was not infallible at Antioch when St. Paul disagreed with him; nor was Liberius, the bishop of Rome, when he excommunicated Athanasius. Newman reassured himself, however, that "remedies spring up naturally in the Church, as in nature, if we wait for them."[18]

Newman finally decided the issue by an appeal to authority and his own fear of God. He resolved that his era's crisis of belief required a strong force to bind the church together—Protestantism's appeal to the private conscience produced only a cacophony of differing opinions. He also feared for his own salvation: "The simple question is, Can I (it is personal, not whether another, but can *I*) be saved in the English Church? Am *I* in safety, were I to die tonight?"[19]

The theology professor told himself that, after all, Rome had better answers to questions about life after death. Purgatory, with its implication of innumerable degrees of grace and sanctity among the saved, made more sense of the near-infinite variations among human beings. Besides, Protestant comparisons of Roman practice with Protestant theology were like comparing apples and oranges. Protestants ought to compare Catholic theology with their own theology, and Catholic practice with Protestant practices. If apples were compared with apples, Newman surmised, Rome would come out ahead.[20]

---

[17]Ibid., p. 121.
[18]Ker, *John Henry Newman*, pp. 631, 661, 660, 689.
[19]Ibid., p. 670; Newman, *Apologia*, pp. 219-20.
[20]Ker, *John Henry Newman*, p. 664; Newman, *Apologia*, p. 113.

In the end, Newman had begun "with feeling, . . . flirted with intellect, . . . [and] ultimately submitted his will to the will of God as interpreted first by his bishop and then by the Pope."[21] On the rainy morning of October 9, 1845, he confessed to Father Dominic, a Passionist priest, and was received into the Catholic Church.

REASON AND FAITH, PREACHING, AND PROBLEMS IN THE CHURCH

Before we get into Newman's most significant legacy, let's look quickly at some of his distinctive teachings. The first is his singular approach to the perennial question of how reason relates to faith. We must start, he said, by seeing that the "popular" or "secular" view of reason is faulty. It presumes true knowledge comes only from sense experience and logic, and that therefore reason is opposed to faith. But Newman argued this is a superficial approach, for it fails to realize that all reasoning must take for granted some things that cannot be proved—such as the uniformity of nature. We often assume that the laws of nature have always worked the way they do now, and that they always work the same way even when we are not looking. But we can't prove either.

In fact, he said, all reasoning really works by "antecedent probability." Because we trust the person who is giving us new knowledge ("I trust you because I have seen you in action, and you have never deceived me"), we give him or her the benefit of the doubt up front (antecedent), and presume that what he or she tells us is *probably* true. Any one piece of evidence given for a conclusion is weak, but when all the weak evidences are put together, the collection becomes strong. "The best illustration . . . is that of a cable which is made up of a number of separate threads, each feeble, yet together as sufficient as an iron rod."[22] So all reasoning is based on "first principles" that cannot be proved. Another way of saying this is that all reasoning is based on faith. Even that of the atheist—he cannot prove his first principle, that there is no God. So his thinking is based on faith.

Reason as it actually works in human experience—as opposed to so-called scientific reasoning we learn in science textbooks—is ad hoc and unsystematic. Newman compares it to the movements of a rock climber.

---

[21]Newman, *Apologia*, pp. xviii-xix.
[22]Ker, *John Henry Newman*, p. 620.

The mind ranges to and fro, and spreads out, and advances forward with a quickness which has become a proverb, and a subtlety and versatility which baffle investigation. It passes on from point to point, gaining one by some indication; another on a probability; then availing itself of an association; then falling back on some received law; next seizing on testimony; then committing itself to some popular impression, or some inward instinct, or some obscure memory; and thus it makes progress not unlike a clamberer on a steep cliff, who, by quick eye, prompt hand, and firm foot, *ascends how he knows not himself, by personal endowments and by practice, rather than by rule*, leaving no track behind him, and unable to teach another. . . . And such mainly is the way in which all men, gifted or not gifted, commonly reason,—not by rule, but by an inward faculty.[23]

For Newman, then, the line between reason and faith is blurred. All reasoning uses faith at some points, and religious faith is a kind of reasoning. It sees first principles in the conscience, which is the most common way God speaks to human beings, and moves from one point of knowledge to another by a variety of means, all of which use the faculty of reason.

Conscience was the basis for Newman's faith in God: "If I am asked why I believe in a God, I answer that it is because I believe in myself, for I feel it impossible to believe in my own existence . . . without believing also in the existence of Him, who lives as a . . . being in my conscience."[24]

Listening to conscience was also the surest way to gain knowledge of God: "I have always contended that obedience even to an erring conscience was the way to gain light, and that it mattered not where a man began, so [long as] he began on what came to hand, and in faith."[25]

For Newman, faith is the acceptance of testimony by those who had firsthand experience—the apostles and fathers of the church. Faith is not just intellectual but also moral. This means a proper moral state of the heart is the means to gaining truth. We protect faith not primarily with the mind but with a rightly disposed heart. We keep faith from abuse not by theological investigation first of all but by the right prepa-

---

[23]John Henry Newman, "Implicit and Explicit Reason," in *Fifteen Sermons Preached Before The University of Oxford Between A.D. 1826 and 1843*, ed. Mary Katherine Tillman (Notre Dame, Ind.: University of Notre Dame Press, 1997), p. 257, italics added.

[24]Newman, *Apologia*, p. 193.

[25]Ibid., p. 199.

ration of heart. This is why Newman said philosophers should seek truth "on their knees."[26]

Newman took these insights on faith and reason and labored over them for three decades. Eventually they resulted in *An Essay in Aid of a Grammar of Assent* (1870). The purpose of this book, which sold out on its first day and saw its second printing just a week later, was to defend Catholicism and Christianity generally against the accusation of fideism—blind faith without reasoning to support it. He reminded his readers that we give absolute assent to propositions on countless occasions in daily life and even in intellectual and moral life, when absolute proof is unavailable. We trust what our grandparents tell us about their childhoods, but don't know for sure the accuracy of their stories. We believe in atoms even though we haven't seen them. Many of us accept macroevolution as a theory with evidence supporting it, but concede there is no absolute proof for it. Probability is a practical guide we use in life and reasoning. A combination of probabilities pointing to the same truth often gives us a sense of certainty. Even on those rare occasions when our certainties are proved to have been misplaced, we still know there are some truths that are certain. Hence Christian faith that is without absolute proof can nevertheless provide a kind of certainty that warrants absolute assent.[27]

Newman is rightly famous for his preaching. Some have observed that his sermons were the best of his day. He also had advice for preachers. They should preach for holiness and not comfort. "Those who make comfort the great subject of their preaching seem to mistake the end of their ministry. *Holiness* is the great end. There must be a struggle and a trial here. Comfort is a cordial, but no one drinks cordials from morning to night."[28] Newman followed his own advice. He admitted his sermons induced "fear" and "depression," but they were meant to do so, for "we need a continual Ash-Wednesday." Not only do Christians need more repentance, but they tend not to listen very well. So preachers should focus on only one point in each sermon, and need not fear repetition: "People need

[26]Tillman, introduction to *Fifteen Sermons Preached*, esp. p. xxvii.

[27]John Henry Newman, *An Essay in Aid of a Grammar of Assent* (Garden City, N.Y.: Image Books, 1955).

[28]Cited by Ker, *John Henry Newman*, p. 21.

the same thing being said a hundred times over in order to hear it."[29]

Newman is also known for his comforting advice about the problems in Christian churches. Every age of Christians seems to bemoan the low state of the churches, and Newman's was no exception. But he had some valuable insights. To those who lamented the bad morals and religious ignorance of people in the pews, Newman said they should not be surprised, for Christ usually calls the poor, sinful and ignorant. To those who despaired their leaders' failures, Newman pointed out this wasn't the first time. During the Arian crisis, it was the laity not the bishops who held to the truth that Jesus was fully God. The bishops failed. To those who are scandalized by corruption in the church, Newman retorted that corruption is inseparable from a living church. "Things that do not admit of abuse have very little life in them." Corruption in the church goes all the way back to the Twelve—think of Judas Iscariot. It is bound up with the very idea of Christianity, and is "almost a dogma." In other words, its dogma of original sin predicts there will always be corruption.[30]

THE DEVELOPMENT OF DOCTRINE

Newman's "most influential and seminal, and indeed controversial, work" was his *Essay on the Development of Christian Doctrine* (1845; rev. ed. 1878), which stipulated that the Holy Spirit leads the church in its growing understanding of biblical revelation. It argued that all major postbiblical developments in Catholic doctrine were "hidden . . . in the Church's bosom from the first." The New Testament authors did not write everything they knew of the gospel, but in fact concealed many teachings in the form of parables and symbols that required further explanation later on. It took the church hundreds of years to explicate the meaning of the most important biblical truths, many of which were not spelled out explicitly in the Bible.[31]

Did the church therefore know more than Christ and the apostles? Only in the way that later scholars of Aristotle knew more than Aristotle:

---

[29]Ibid., pp. 113, 170, 92. Ironically, however, this brilliant preacher tended to disparage the value of preaching, presuming the Eucharist was a better teacher (McClymond, "Continual Self-Contemplation," p. 25).

[30]Ker, *John Henry Newman*, pp. 485, 482, 586.

[31]Ian Ker, foreword to *An Essay on the Development of Christian Doctrine*, ed. Ian Ker (Notre Dame, Ind.: University of Notre Dame Press, 1989), p. xxii; Newman, *The Via Media*, cited by Ker, *John Henry Newman*, p. 105.

A learned Aristotelian is one who can answer any whatever philosophical questions in the way that Aristotle would have answered them. . . . In one respect he knows more than Aristotle; because, in new emergencies after the time of Aristotle, he *can* and *does* answer what Aristotle would have answered, but for the want of opportunity did not.[32]

All new doctrines the church proclaimed in the centuries after the apostles were in the Bible in germ form. It took controversy and the guidance of the Spirit to discern the meaning of revelation for these new problems.

But the apostles would not be surprised by any of these new developments: "I wish to hold that there is nothing which the Church has defined or shall define but what an Apostle, if asked, would have been fully able to answer or would have answered, as the Church has answered, the one answering by inspiration, the other from its gift of infallibility."[33]

The gist of this proposal is that the principle of "antecedent probability" suggests that God would watch over his own work and direct and ratify those developments which faithfully explicated what he had revealed. Thus the church, like its Lord, "increased in wisdom" (Lk 2:52). Like the human mind, which "cannot reflect upon [a great idea] except piecemeal," the church must develop a great idea given in biblical revelation by a series of tests and conflicts.

Whatever the risk of corruption from intercourse with the world around, such a risk must be encountered if a great idea is duly to be understood, and much more if it is to be fully exhibited. It is elicited and expanded by trial, and battles into perfection and supremacy. . . . In time it enters upon strange territory; points of controversy alter their bearing; parties rise and fall around it; dangers and hopes appear in new relations; and old principles reappear under new forms. *It changes with them in order to remain the same. In a higher world it is otherwise, but here below to live is to change, and to be perfect is to have changed often.*[34]

Newman found evidence for development in the Bible itself. At the most obvious level, the Old Testament hides under veils and mysteries what is

---

[32]John Henry Newman, *The Theological Papers of John Henry Newman on Biblical Inspiration and on Infallibility*, ed. J. Derek Holmes (Oxford: Clarendon Press, 1972), pp. 156-59, cited by Ker, *Essay*, p. xxiv.

[33]Newman, *Theological Papers*, cited in Ker, *John Henry Newman*, p. 314.

[34]Newman, *Essay*, p. 100; Newman, "The Theory of Developments in Religious Doctrine," in *Fifteen Sermons*, p. 331; Newman, *Essay*, pp. 39-40, italics added.

later developed in much more clarity in the New Testament. Even in the Old Testament itself we can see development. For example, in Genesis God tells Abraham enigmatically that in him all nations would be blessed, but only in the prophets do we read at length about the expansion of the covenant prophesied for the Gentiles. Moses first tells Pharaoh he wants to take his people into the desert for three days to sacrifice to his God, and does not intimate his plans to leave Egypt for good. This illustrates God's pattern—he "works out *gradually* what He has determined absolutely."[35]

There are plenty of other examples. The apostle John declares he writes "no new commandment," but an old one they had "from the beginning." Then he adds, "A new commandment I am writing to you" (1 Jn 2:7-8). The old is old and yet also new because it has received new development in Jesus Christ. Jesus says, "Don't think I have come to abolish the Law and the Prophets; I have come not to abolish them but to fulfill them" (Mt 5:17-19). Newman comments, "He does not reverse, but perfects, what has gone before." Jesus' perfection of the law is a further development of the law.[36]

Then there is the idea of sacrifice. Newman says it was commanded first by Moses. Next Samuel says that "to obey is better than sacrifice." Then Hosea adds, "I want mercy and not sacrifice." Isaiah says the sacrifice of incense is an abomination to God. Malachi predicts the messianic age will see the "pure sacrifice" of wheat flour. Finally, Jesus speaks of worshiping "in spirit and in truth." When the church began to offer corporate worship, says Newman, "sacrifice was not removed, but truth and spirit [were] added." The concept and practice of sacrifice underwent profound development.[37]

Newman saw the same development in the apostolic church. At its beginning on Pentecost, Peter had still to learn that he could baptize Cornelius. Even then, more light would come from Paul's Epistles. Many other doctrines would be developed as new light was shed through the later books of the New Testament. Even after the closure of the New Testament, doctrines continued to develop.

No one doctrine can be named which starts complete at first, and gains nothing afterwards from the investigations of faith and the attacks of her-

---

[35]Newman, *Essay*, p. 70.
[36]Ibid., p. 65.
[37]Ibid., pp. 65-66.

esy. The Church went forth from the old world in haste, as the Israelites from Egypt "with their dough before it was leavened, their kneading troughs being bound up in their clothes upon their shoulders."[38]

Newman says this follows from the principle of the incarnation, which is the very heart of the good news. Just as the Word became flesh, the words of God become flesh in developed ideas as church history progresses. For example, original sin is not stated in those words in the New Testament, and is not mentioned in either the Apostle's or Nicene creeds, but it has been adopted by all the Western churches. The practice of penance, Newman taught, is not shown explicitly in the Bible. But it is a necessary consequence of baptism, since there must be a way to receive public forgiveness and readmission to the visible church after public sin (against baptismal promises).

So too for later ages in church history. In the third and fourth centuries the church came to stand for the statement that the Son of God was *homoousios* (of the same being) with the Father. This was not stated in the New Testament, but was a clear development of what was revealed there. In the first three centuries the church finally agreed on the Trinity, another unbiblical word that nevertheless fittingly summed up the apostolic witness about God. In the age of Augustine the church came eventually to agree on the classic doctrines of sin and grace, which again were logical developments of all that Scripture revealed on those subjects. The Reformation gave us new understandings of how we are saved (the doctrine of salvation), the period of Protestant orthodoxy showed us in a new way what it means for the Bible to be inspired, and the last two centuries have shown Christians in fresh ways what it means to be church. In each period, by discussion and argument against heresy, the worldwide church came to new agreement and insight. Doctrine developed as the Holy Spirit opened up deeper understanding of the blinding revelation of Jesus Christ. Newman says more is to come in every age.[39]

Newman argued that God has used this process of development to incorporate even pagan elements into Christian practice, but only after

---

[38]Ibid., p. 68.
[39]Ker, *John Henry Newman*, p. 268; Philip Schaff, *The Principle of Protestantism*, cited in Jaroslav Pelikan, *Christian Doctrine and Modern Culture (since 1700)* (Chicago: University of Chicago Press, 1989) p. 281.

Christianizing them—just as Aaron's rod swallowed the rods of Egypt's sorcerers, but kept its own identity, incorporating them into itself. So, for example, most Christians in Newman's day enjoyed holy days and seasons, used a ring in marriage, venerated images in church, and sang the "Kyrie Eleison." Yet all these things, said Newman, were originally pagan. God used the process of development to take up what was useful in them and fill them with new Christian meaning.

There were other practices accepted by most Christians, especially evangelicals, that nevertheless were not taught explicitly in the Bible: the lawfulness of bearing arms, the duty of public worship, the substitution of the first for the seventh day as the Christian sabbath, infant baptism, and the Protestant idea of *sola scriptura* (the Bible alone as a rule for faith and practice). Newman's point was that conservative Christians, who claim to base their faith on the "Bible alone," actually believe and practice things that are not taught by the Bible but which are consequences by *development* of what is revealed there.[40]

Newman anticipated objections to his theory. First, it sounded like he was saying the church got new revelation. No, he replied, "the Church does not know more than the Apostles knew." It simply draws out, bit by bit, what the apostles meant in their inspired descriptions of that blinding revelation.

And it is no wonder it takes thousands of years to draw out its meaning. For it is the revelation of the infinite God, and so

> it cannot, as it were, be mapped, or its contents catalogued; but after all our diligence, to the end of our lives and to the end of the Church, it must be an unexplored and unsubdued land, with heights and valleys, forests and streams, on the right and left of our path and close about us, full of concealed wonders and choice treasures.[41]

Another objection was that he was uncritical. Was he implying that all development is good and true, and ignoring the hosts of so-called developments that in reality are heresies? Not at all, Newman said. First of all, that is why there is a supreme authority in Rome, to distinguish true from false developments. Protestants don't have this and so go on forever fighting one another over doctrine without final resolution. Second, Newman

---

[40]Newman, *Essay*, pp. 355, 373, 58-59.
[41]Ibid., p. 71.

worked out a sophisticated set of seven "notes" of faithful development—it must correspond to its rudiments; it shows a continuity of principle; it assimilates and absorbs; it is a logical result of original teaching; it can be seen in earlier anticipations; it conserves orthodox teaching from the past; and it shows energy and permanence. In short, a faithful development is one that truly develops from what is in the biblical vision and does not conflict with "the whole counsel of God."[42]

I should add that it was his theory of development that enabled Newman first to become a Catholic, and then later to accept papal infallibility, first promulgated in 1870 at the First Vatican Council. In the *Via Media*, a book on church history he wrote while still an Anglican, Newman said that early Christianity did not contain precedents for certain ideas and practices of modern Catholicism, such as Marian devotion. But as Newman became disillusioned with the Church of England, he used his theory of development to see that Marian devotion, while not practiced explicitly in the early church in nineteenth-century manner, was there in seed form.

Early on in his Catholic life, Newman was opposed to the teaching of papal infallibility. But on this doctrine too Newman eventually came to believe that the principle of authority in the apostolic deposit pointed to an ultimate earthly authority that God could use to lead his church.

THE *DISCIPLINA ARCANI*

I have mentioned in passing that in Newman's view of the history of God's revealing himself to human beings, God often speaks at first in mysterious and cryptic ways. Old Testament prophecies, for example, were sometimes difficult or impossible to understand when they were first given, and became clear only when Jesus came to fulfill them. Jesus himself often spoke in parables, purposely hiding their meanings from the multitudes and revealing those meanings only to his disciples. He told his disciples not to throw the pearls of his teachings before swine, for the pigs would trample them.

Newman said the early church took this very seriously. Beginning in the fourth century A.D., they elaborated what they had been practicing

---

[42]Ibid., pp. 170-206.

since the beginning—the *disciplina arcani,* or "method of keeping sacred things secret." Early church fathers said they refused to share the higher truths of the faith, such as justification and Eucharist and Trinity and atonement, to pagans and even seekers. Instead, inquirers were directed to the moral teachings of the law and told they must prepare themselves morally to be able to hear and understand higher truths. Moral obedience was a means to faith. Only after seekers proved themselves by these means did the church give them more instruction. In fact, it was typically only after a year or more of church classes that would-be converts were permitted to observe the communion rite, and only after further instruction and baptism (sometimes after three years) could they take holy communion.

Newman explains that ever since "the Creator clothed Adam, concealment is in some sense the necessity of our fall." He noted that Paul said nothing of justification to the Athenians on Mars Hill and only the law and the Messiah's resurrection to Agrippa—nothing of grace. In other words, Paul and the apostles concealed the higher truths from unbelievers and shared them only when disciples had progressed to a place where they were ready to listen. This was a way in which the apostles followed God's pattern in history—not sharing all truth at once but only a bit at a time, as people were ready to hear.[43]

UNIVERSAL REVELATION

Even those who are familiar with Newman's theology often do not know that the theologian was fascinated by other religions and wrote prolifically about them. His interest in them was connected with his theory of development of doctrine, for he noted how God used non-Christian thinkers to help Christians think through the meaning of Jesus Christ. For example, Christians in the first four centuries A.D. used Greek philosophy to help develop the doctrine of the Trinity that all Christians now accept.

Newman also pointed to Moses, who was "instructed in all the wisdom of the Egyptians" (Acts 7:22), and was perhaps influenced by some of that wisdom.

> Unbelievers have accused Moses of borrowing his law from the Egyptians or other Pagans; and elaborate comparisons have been instituted, on the

---

[43]Newman, *The Via Media,* cited by Ker, *John Henry Newman,* p. 705.

part of believers also, by way of proving it; though even if proved, and so far as proved, it would show nothing more than this,—that God, who gave His law to Israel absolutely and openly, had already given some portions of it to the heathen.[44]

In this brief quote Newman refers to "universal revelation." By this he meant a global diffusion of divine truth, scattered unequally around the world in all time and all places. He said the church is the ordinary channel of this revelation and has the fullest access to it through the Bible (which he called the "unadulterated and complete revelation") and sacraments. But through what Newman called "traditional religion," God has spoken to human beings outside of Christianity and Judaism, never leaving himself without a witness but in every nation accepting those who feared and obeyed him.[45]

The witness can be found in four places: philosophy, natural religion and conscience, the arts, and other religions. Newman was especially influenced by Clement of Alexandria, who proposed that God taught the Greeks through Greek philosophy. Therefore for Newman, "The Greek poets and sages were in a certain sense prophets, for 'thoughts beyond their thoughts to those high bards were given.' " If Palestine had been the seat and foundation of supernatural truth, "Attica [ancient Greece] was chosen by Providence as the home and center of intellectual excellence." Newman thought God had inspired Plato, Aristotle, Sophocles, Homer and Euripides.[46]

Natural religion was the second channel through which God disseminates truth. By natural religion he meant what we can know about God through nature and conscience. Conscience, Newman said, teaches us not only that God exists but also that our supreme judge is holy, just and powerful.[47]

The third and fourth channels for universal revelation are poetry and art and music, on the one hand, and world religions, on the other. "There is nothing unreasonable in the notion that there may have been heathen

---

[44]John Henry Newman, *Discussions and Arguments on Various Subjects*, cited by Francis McGrath, *John Henry Newman: Universal Revelation* (Macon, Ga.: Mercer University Press, 1997), pp. 75-76.

[45]John Henry Newman, *The Arians of the Fourth Century* (Westminster, Md.: Christian Classics, 1968), pp. 83-84.

[46]Newman, *Apologia*, p. 46.

[47]McGrath, *John Henry Newman*, p. 19.

poets and sages . . . in a certain extent divinely illuminated, and organs through whom religious and moral truth was conveyed to their countrymen." In fact, he added, there is something "true and divinely revealed" in every religion around the globe, though those truths and revelations are mixed and sometimes overwhelmed by "impieties" inspired by the "corrupt will and understanding of men." Most teach "the power and presence of an invisible God, of His moral law and governance, of the obligation of duty, and the certainty of a just judgment, and of reward and punishment, as eventually dispensed to individuals." Some of them also teach Christian doctrines such as the Trinity, washing, divine Word, incarnation, angels, demons, new birth and sacramental virtue.[48]

According to Newman, at certain times God gave truth to his church through paganism, and the Holy Spirit guided the church to collect these truths but then purify them by sifting them through the sieve of biblical revelation.

> As Adam gave names to the animals around him, so the Church from the first looked around the earth noting and visiting the doctrines she found. She began in Chaldea, and then sojourned among the Canaanites, and went down into Egypt, and then passed into Arabia, till she rested in her own land. Then to the merchants of Tyre, the wisdom of the East, luxury of Sheba, Babylon, the schools of Greece, sitting in the midst of the doctors [Latin for "teachers"], both listening and asking questions, claiming to herself what they said rightly, supplying their defects, completing their beginnings, expanding their surmises, and gradually, by means of them enlarging the range and refining the sense of her own teaching. In this way she has sucked the milk of the Gentiles and sucked the breasts of kings.[49]

Newman said God has always acted by the principle of "addition." He does not destroy pagan wisdom but adds what is necessary to purify and complete it. He "does not begin anew but uses the existing system." God does not undo the past but fulfills and perfects it. Therefore a pagan religious mind, "sincerely attached to some form of heathenism . . . would be drawn off from error into truth, not by losing what it had, but by gaining what it had not, not by being unclothed, but by being 'clothed upon.' . . . True conversion is ever of a positive, not a negative character."

---

[48]Newman, *Arians*, pp. 82, 80; Newman, *Essay*, p. 380.
[49]Newman, *Essay*, p. 380.

Newman, then, would advise the Christian missionary not to assume all pagan beliefs and practices are corrupt, or that all pagans will be damned, but to aim to recover and then reverse "the essential principles of [pagan] belief."[50] The Christian missionary will use his or her own biblical faith to recognize truth in a religion and also try to correct falsehood.

Now that we have gotten this far, please don't mistake what Newman is saying here. He is not saying that a pagan will be saved as a pagan. As I understand him, he is saying that God has mysteriously been leading some pagans on a long pilgrimage to his triune self, even while they are pagans. If they are headed toward him, they will at some point recognize that Jesus is Lord of the cosmos and has saved them by his death and resurrection. At that point they will have to repent of the false beliefs and practices in their former religion and convert to full faith in Christ. But Newman's point is that God uses nature and conscience and limited truths within their religions to lead some (not all!) pagans to the gospel, at some time and in some way God alone knows. This is all part of his massive and mysterious plan to gradually unfold, by progressive development, his people's understanding of himself.

WHAT WE CAN LEARN

1. Protestant readers of this book won't be able to accept Newman's conclusion that biblical truth developed into Roman Catholic doctrine. But they may, and should, see that there has been an indisputable development of doctrine over time. The worldwide body of Christians does indeed agree on doctrines such as Trinity and original sin, which are not named as such in the Bible. Protestants should therefore consider the possibility that God's Spirit has indeed been guiding the church in its understanding of what Scripture and Jesus Christ mean. This means, further, that we should listen to Athanasius, Augustine and many of the other great theologians as we read the Bible, and not think we can make complete sense of the Bible without their help.

2. Evangelicals and Lutherans especially can learn from the *disciplina arcani*. Too often we have thrown pearls before swine in our evangelism

---

[50]Newman, *Essays Critical and Historical*, cited in McGrath, *John Henry Newman*, p. 77; Newman, *Essay*, pp. 356-57, 200-201; Newman, *Arians*, p. 84.

and Christian education. Lutherans have forgotten that law must come before gospel if the gospel is to be understood, and evangelicals have sometimes pronounced people saved before time has proven the solidity of conversion. We Christians generally have been too willing to blabber the mysteries of the faith to anyone we can get to listen, forgetting that "the natural person does not accept the things of the Spirit of God, . . . and he is not able to understand them" (1 Cor 2:14). We have both said too much (when we explain the intricacies of atonement and justification to unbelievers) and too little (reducing the gospel and all the Bible to justification by faith).

3. Newman helps free us from the false presumptions of the scientific Enlightenment, such as the idea that the only kind of reason is that which uses sensory experience and testing in a science lab. Newman takes us back to the conclusions of most of the world's great thinkers before the Enlightenment, who agreed that reason can tell us there is a God who is all-powerful and holy, and will judge us. He also shows us that even the reason of modern science is based on faith, thus refuting the modern proverb that reason is opposed to faith.

4. The Oxford don would force many conservative Christians today to check the object of their trust. Are they trusting in Christ or their conversion? The Savior or their own experience? Too often we are more focused on a theology of salvation than on the One who saves us.

5. Newman has some helpful advice for preachers. He warns them not to preach a majority of sermons on comfort. Most of us need to be called to holiness—a call which tends to afflict us when we are comfortable. Because we tend to be complacent and lazy, preachers who only preach comfort for the afflicted will leave us unholy.

A SELECTION FROM JOHN HENRY NEWMAN'S WORKS

Great questions exist in the subject-matter of which Scripture treats, which Scripture does not solve; questions too so real, so practical, that they must be answered, and, unless we suppose a new revelation, answered by means of the revelation which we have, that is, by development. Such is the question of the Canon of Scripture and its inspiration: that is, whether Christianity depends upon a written document such as Judaism;—if so, on what writings and how many;—whether that document is self-interpreting, or requires a comment, and

whether any authoritative comment or commentator is provided;—whether the
revelation and the document are commensurate, or the one outruns the other;—
all these questions surely find no solution on the surface of Scripture, nor indeed
under the surface in the case of most men, however long and diligent might be
their study of it. Nor were these difficulties settled by authority, as far as we
know, at the commencement of the religion; yet surely it is quite conceivable that
an Apostle might have dissipated them all in a few words, had Divine Wisdom
thought fit. But in matter of fact the decision has been left to time, to the slow
process of thought, to the influence of mind upon mind, the issues of controversy,
and the growth of opinion.[51]

For Reflection and Discussion

1. Is there a danger of trusting more in our conversion than in Christ?

2. What do you make of Newman's conversion to Catholicism? Were his reasons reasonable?

3. What of antecedent probability and the role of conscience? If you are in a group, have someone explain each and then have the group discuss whether he or she is right.

4. Newman thought too much preaching was priestly rather than prophetic—that more sermons ought to aim at holiness rather than comfort. Do you agree? Why?

5. Are you surprised by Newman's doctrine of development of doctrine? Does this mean there is new revelation or simply new illumination of the same revelation?

6. Does the *disciplina arcani* suggest that we say too much to seekers? Do you agree?

7. Does Newman's theory of universal revelation seem biblical? Does it help us to understand other religions?

For Further Reading

Newman, John Henry. *Fifteen Sermons Preached Before the University of Oxford Between A.D. 1826 and 1843.* Edited by Mary Katherine Tillman. Notre Dame, Ind.: University of Notre Dame Press, 1997.

---

[51]Newman, *Essay*, p. 60.

————. *Parochial and Plain Sermons*. Fort Collins, Colo.: Ignatius, 1997.

Jaki, Stanley L. *Newman's Challenge*. Grand Rapids: Eerdmans, 2000.

Ker, Ian. *John Henry Newman: A Biography*. Oxford: Oxford University Press, 1988.

11

Karl Barth

Most Influential Twentieth-Century Theologian

Karl Barth (1886-1968) was raised in the German Reformed Church in Switzerland. Both of his grandfathers had been pastors, and his father was a theological lecturer at Basel.

Barth was trained in the theological liberalism started by Schleiermacher. As a young pastor in Calvin's church in Geneva, he believed that the kingdom of God is a way of life that helps the disadvantaged, tries to abolish private property through "Christian socialism," and enlists fellow Christians in a nonviolent social revolution. He was "extremely hesitant to affirm a bodily resurrection of Jesus," attacked the theology of Chalcedon (Jesus as fully man and fully God), and said the Ten Commandments were "too much for our needs and sometimes too little."[1]

But World War I changed all that. It began on the first day of the war (August 1, 1914) when he discovered that all his professors had signed a manifesto supporting the war policy of the Kaiser. "It was like the twilight of the gods when I . . . discovered how religion and scholarship could be changed completely, into intellectual 42 cm cannons." Barth concluded that his professors' moral myopia had cast a shadow on the liberal theology they had taught him: their "ethical failure" suggested that "their exegetical

---

[1]Bruce L. McCormack, *Karl Barth's Critically Realistic Dialectical Theology: Its Genesis and Development 1909-1936* (Oxford: Clarendon, 1995), p. 103; Eberhard Busch, *Karl Barth: His Life from Letters and Autobiographical Texts* (Grand Rapids: Eerdmans, 1994), p. 54. Because Busch's citations of Barth's statements from his published works are so fragmentary and tedious, I have decided to simply provide the page numbers in Busch; the reader who wants to find the precise location of these disparate quotations can find their original locations there.

and dogmatic presuppositions could not be in order."[2]

Barth moved to a Reformed church in a village near the German border, and from there watched the carnage of World War I. He could almost hear the boom of the big guns from his study. The near-endless bloodbath of the war convinced him and his whole generation that liberalism's faith in human progress and goodness was naive. He also discovered that his liberal theology brought no relief to his grief-stricken parishioners. Of his sermons in this period, he said, "I always seemed to be beating my head against a brick wall. . . . I and the people of Safenwil [his village] were always . . . looking at each other through a pane of glass." He said he usually felt "awkward" in the pulpit, and his people looked at him with "bored faces." After a while, his parishioners voted with their feet, and the pews became "largely empty."[3]

This drove Barth to question what he had been taught. He went back to the Bible, and tried to read it "as though I had never read it before." He went first to Paul's epistle to the Romans.

> During the work it was often as though I caught a breath from afar, from Asia Minor or Corinth, something primaeval, from the ancient East, indefinably sunny, wild, original, that somehow is hidden behind these sentences. Paul—what a man he must have been and what men also those for whom he could so sketch and hint at these pithy things in a few muddled fragments! . . . And then *behind* Paul: what realities those must have been that could excite the man in such a way! What a lot of far-fetched stuff we compile about his remarks, when perhaps ninety-nine per cent of their real content escapes us![4]

Barth also went back to Augustine, Luther and Calvin. In 1919 he published his first book, *Der Römerbrief (The Epistle to the Romans)*, and expanded it in 1922. It was a radical criticism of liberal theology as focused on humanity rather than God, simply speaking about humans "in an exalted tone." Using the work of Søren Kierkegaard, he argued for the "infinite qualitative difference" between God and humanity—God is Wholly Other. The first thing we need to realize as human beings is that God is God and we are not: "God is in heaven and man is on the earth!" In fact,

[2]Busch, *Karl Barth*, p. 81.
[3]Ibid., pp. 63, 64, 66, 64.
[4]Ibid., pp. 98-99.

we are under God's judgment, and have no hope for release apart from the grace of God coming to us from outside of ourselves.[5]

The book "fell like a bombshell upon the playground of the theologians." Rudolf Bultmann, the German New Testament scholar, called it "enthusiastic revivalism." Liberal church historian Adolf von Harnack compared Barth to Thomas Müntzer, the radical reformer of the sixteenth century who said the end of the world was at hand. But the book was received enthusiastically by Christians all over Europe, especially those who felt the Great War represented the failure of the best civilization in history. Barth seemed to make sense of the failure.[6]

Barth went on to write his massive twelve-volume *Church Dogmatics*, which has become recognized widely as "the most monumental Protestant systematic theology since Calvin's *Institutes*." Over the years of writing these volumes (which grew to twelve million words on nine thousand pages), from 1927 until his death, Barth rejected his earlier existentialism (the idea that we find our meaning in our own free choices) and dialectic approach (going back and forth between contrasting theological ideas to seek understanding of God), both of which seemed to be human-centered. They appeared to rely on our own powers to see God. As he wrote the *Church Dogmatics* he came to see more and more the reality of God's *self*-revelation in Jesus Christ. We do not need to work to see God; our job instead is to receive in faith God's own Word about himself.[7]

Like Schleiermacher, Barth was politically involved. He became an early critic of Nazism while teaching in Germany, preaching that Jesus was a Jew in 1933 (some got up and left in protest), and refusing to give the Hitler salute at the beginning of his lectures. In 1934 he was the lead author of the Barmen Declaration, a public statement from the "Confessing Church" that Jesus Christ alone can be a source for church proclamation. While its intent was clearly to denounce Nazism, Barth later regretted that the statement said nothing specifically about Jewish persecution. In 1935, after being banned from speaking in public and fined for not giving the

---

[5]Ibid., pp. 90-91, 99.
[6]Busch, *Karl Barth*, p. 102.
[7]Jaroslav Pelikan, *Christian Doctrine and Modern Culture (since 1700)* (Chicago: University of Chicago Press, 1989), pp. 299-300; for this paragraph and parts of the preceding, I am indebted to an unpublished paper by my colleague Paul Hinlicky, "Barth on the Baptism in the Holy Spirit," written in the late 1990s.

Hitler salute, Barth was dismissed from his teaching job. Almost immediately he was offered a chair of theology in neutral Basel (Switzerland).

UNDERMINING LIBERALISM

One of Barth's great achievements was to identify the inner workings of theological liberalism and to expose its inner logic. Its basic method, he showed, is to assume that we human beings can find truth and reality through our own consciousness and explorations of the world. So we first find in ourselves and the world what we take to be the true, the good and the beautiful. Then we go to the Bible and Christian tradition and see what lines up with what we have found. If something in the Bible or the creeds agrees with what we already know to be good and true, we accept it. If not, we throw it out and conclude that the Bible and Christian orthodoxy are wrong on those points.

Let's take, for example, the idea of love. Is it real? What does it mean? We go to the best of human thinking and experience on this—at least according to what people think today—and declare this to be the true meaning of love. If we have concluded that love is a feeling, then we cannot accept the Bible's determination that love is more a commitment and action than a feeling. We also decide what God's love is by extrapolating from our human experience. If we find our own love to be a warm feeling, then God's love must be the same, but much bigger and stronger. If our own feeling of love would never permit us to declare that something is a sin that deserves punishment, then God too would never condemn sin or judge sinners.

According to this liberal method, said Barth, God is an "idealized version of man."[8] He becomes the object of our human knowledge, which means he corresponds to our own ideas and experience. In that sense, we can know his inner essence and what he will do because we know ourselves, for he is but a larger version of ourselves.

Barth said the liberal method of thinking about God wipes out the infinite qualitative difference between humans and God. It presumes that the Bible is a book of human thoughts about God instead of God's thoughts about human beings.

---

[8]Hinlicky, "Barth on the Baptism in the Holy Spirit."

This rejection of liberal theology, with its assumption that God can be found within human consciousness, called into question a string of movements that had spun off from the Enlightenment: Romanticism (which assumed truth within human feeling), idealism (which saw reality as created by human thoughts), pietism (which found salvation within human religious experience) and humanism (which made human experience and thinking the measure of what is good and true). Barth thought even "revivalism" and "Biblicism" were based on the Enlightenment, since the first put too much emphasis on experience and the second rejected tradition.[9]

Barth even decided the first edition of his *Epistle to the Romans* was pantheistic, placing God within human experience too much, and replaced it in his second edition with a sharp emphasis on the sovereignty of God in his gracious initiatives to humanity. He complained that Paul Tillich, another German theologian who resisted the Nazis, had an "antipathy to orthodoxy" because he assumed revelation from God was everywhere and accessible to anyone. Barth denied this, saying revelation from God is a miraculous event that occurs only if God so chooses.[10]

ANALOGY OF BEING AND SYSTEMS

Barth believed the liberal theological method was being used in a new and destructive way by current applications of the Roman Catholic doctrine of the "analogy of being." This was the idea, best elaborated by Thomas Aquinas, that the being of things in the world have some similarity to the being of God because God created the world. It doesn't mean that God is simply a much larger version of beings "down here," but that beings in the world are signposts to God. Human fatherhood, for example, tells us something about God's fatherhood, without being identical to God's fatherhood. The idea is that we can start with some aspect of creation to tell us something about God, in addition to starting with revelation.

For Barth, this idea of continuity between God and humanity threatens to make humans both their own creator and reconciler. Instead, he says, only the event of revelation (when God reveals to us something of Jesus Christ) shows us anything of God. Because the analogy of being presumes

---

[9]Biblicism is attachment to Bible texts without considering their relation to the whole message of the Bible and Christian doctrinal tradition (Busch, *Karl Barth*, pp. 100, 119, 178).
[10]Ibid., p. 137.

there is something inherent in us that shows us God, it is "*the* invention of Anti-Christ."[11] The other problem with this analogy is that it uses the creation as a norm or standard for doing theology. Barth said that revelation is needed for us to know what in creation is a signpost, and then also to know how to interpret it. Otherwise, for example, how would the Afrikaner church in South Africa have known if apartheid, based on created racial differences, was true to God's purposes for creation?

Barth wanted to replace the analogy of being, which he said came from Augustine and is taught by Roman Catholicism, with the analogy of faith, which is given by God in the event of revelation. Catholics and liberals spoke of a "point of contact" in human nature and experience that can point human beings to God, but Barth said the only point of contact is the Word of God, Jesus Christ, who comes to us from God.

Barth talked about the "event" of revelation in order to stress God's freedom. This is a major theme that reappears time and again in his *Church Dogmatics*. God does not need us in order for him to be the living God; he is perfectly complete without us. As Jonathan Edwards asserted in his *End for Which God Created the World,* Barth says the same—God was happy and fulfilled, as it were, in his inter-trinitarian relations through all of eternity before the creation. The Father loved the Son and the Son loved the Father, in the unity of the Holy Spirit. That trinitarian God was free to create or not create. He created in an act of freedom; nothing outside or inside of God was required or needed. God's choice to redeem was also a free act. We have no innate capacity to know God (contra Schleiermacher) and have no ability to overcome our alienation from God because of sin (contra all Pelagian systems). Barth stressed God's sovereignty of grace and the ongoing activity of grace: our relationship with God is never a possession of ours but instead is continually reestablished by God anew based on his freedom and good pleasure.

Barth was also opposed to all talk of theological or philosophical "systems" or even "systematic theology." The problem with systems, for Barth, is that they presume there is some pattern of thinking or action that autonomous reason can see, with or without revelation. But the true identity of Jesus is known only to those who by the Spirit recognize him as the

---

[11]Ibid., pp. 214-15.

self-revelation of God. Alister McGrath suggests the thought experiment of imagining two men at Golgotha in A.D. 30. One says, "Look at that common criminal dying between those two thieves." The other observes, "It is the Son of God dying for me." Only reason informed by revelation can see the true object of theology, God in Jesus Christ. But "systems" seem to suppose there is an intellectual structure pointing definitively to God that anyone can see. Besides, systems presume they can systematize what eludes all human systematizing—the infinite and mysterious God. They suggest they can capture Jesus Christ in a mental package. They leave no room for anomalies, such as the discrepancy between the doctrine that God has reconciled the world and the appearance of a world that seems to be unreconciled. Good theology leaves such anomalies standing without trying to systematize them. Therefore true theology is more musical than architectural. That is, it must not suppose that it can contain God as an architectural drawing comprehensively renders a building, but should point to mysteries as great music suggests heights and depths that cannot be captured.[12]

GOSPEL AND LAW

Barth appreciated the Lutheran teaching that law (which is a term for what God demands of us and thereby shows us our sin and condemnation) must precede gospel (which is the good news of salvation from sin and condemnation through the work of Christ). But Barth felt the danger of always reading the law first is that we interpret it apart from the revelation of Jesus Christ and therefore misinterpret it. God's commands to Israel cannot be understood without the realization of how all those commands were fulfilled by Christ. For example, the command to stone the adulterer (Deut 22:23-24) can best be seen by reading how Jesus protected the adulteress from stoning (Jn 8:1-11) and went on to die the death she deserved.

In addition, Barth taught, the law was given *after* God had redeemed Israel, and as a blessing of instruction on how to live the best life. So the law *is* grace and gospel. Therefore where Lutherans might see only law, the Reformed theologian Barth saw gospel as well. The command to "keep

---

[12]Alister McGrath, *Christian Theology: An Introduction* (Oxford, Blackwell, 1994), p. 262; George Hunsinger, *How to Read Karl Barth: The Shape of His Theology* (New York: Oxford University Press, 1991), pp. 34, 29.

the sabbath holy," for example, was not only given to show us our sin (when we don't keep the sabbath holy) but also to show us the best way to encounter God on a regular basis, by listening to God's Word in holy assembly. Therefore it is grace.

PREACHING

Barth believed the pulpit is "the real arena of the Kingdom of God." But the problem is that too many preachers think it is the time for them to proclaim their own ideas about the meaning of the world or current events. True Christian preaching, he said, is simply the "interpretation of Scripture." Preachers may occasionally take up the "questions of the day," but they should never devote a whole sermon or series of sermons to them. Barth said his preaching was most effective when he chose not to rely on human analogies or his own rhetorical skill but simply explained the biblical text.

> Preaching on themes (the arrogant view that the preacher has something of his own to say to the congregation as well as, or in with, his interpretation of Scripture—*analogia entis!* [analogy of being]) was and is quite simply the result of the neo-Protestant combination of biblical and natural theology in practical terms. Once the preacher wants his sermon to fulfill a second function over and above the service of the divine Word, and plans it that way, this second function wins the day and the preaching ceases to serve the Word.[13]

In 1934 Barth published his famous *Nein! (No!)* against fellow Swiss theologian Emil Brunner, who wanted to retain natural theology—the idea that nature can show us something definitive about God. Brunner said the preacher should seek a point of contact in human experience to help explain the Word. Barth replied that the Word can take care of itself and introduce itself. It does not depend on anything creaturely to communicate itself to human beings.

THE NATURE AND TASK OF THEOLOGY

Barth has influenced both Protestant and Catholic theology in a number of ways. But his most lasting legacy may be his reformulation of theology's nature and task. After nearly two centuries of Protestants

---

[13]Busch, *Karl Barth*, pp. 162, 270, 220, 248.

and some Catholics focusing theology on the human subject, Barth launched his own "reverse Copernican revolution" by turning to the *divine* subject—God. Even the task of interpreting God's self-revelation in Scripture—which is theology's central task—is itself a part of the divine self-communication. In other words, if God is truly recognized when the Christian tries to read and understand the message of Scripture, and when the theologian does the same for a larger audience, it is because God is actively revealing himself to those believers and the world. This is the way in which, as John Webster has put it, exegesis (understanding the biblical text) becomes part of sanctification (becoming holy). God is not an object of our study, where we can grasp his essence or totality, but in our study of the Word of God we find God revealing himself to us and sharing with us his holiness.[14]

The ruling assumption Barth makes is that God alone can make God known. Liberal theology had assumed that God was an object we could know by looking at ourselves and studying his traces in nature. But Barth said the true task of theology was to wait to receive in humility and trust God's self-revelation in the Bible. Once he described theology as simply "the description of the reality of the Word of God which addresses man." Another time he said, following Anselm of Canterbury, that theology is "faith seeking understanding . . . on the way to the final 'vision of God.' " It is not the rejection of reason in favor of faith but the use of reason within the limits of revelation. In sum, it is *Nach-Denken*, "thinking afterwards." We are to wait for God to open up the Word of God to us, receive that Word in faith, and then (afterward) think through its meaning for us and our lives. That is the nature and task of theology.[15]

Theology then is a response to God's self-revelation. Its agenda is set not by human questions but by the demands and vision in the revelation of God's Word. Its most important task is to study and exegete the Bible. In 1935, just before leaving Germany, he bade farewell to his Bonn pupils

---

[14]Kevin Vanhoozer, "A Person of the Book? Barth on Biblical Authority and Interpretation," in *Karl Barth and Evangelical Theology*, ed. Sung Wook Chung (Grand Rapids: Baker Academic, 2006), p. 53; John Webster, "Reading the Bible: the Example of Barth and Bonhoeffer," in *Word and Church: Essays in Christian Dogmatics* (Edinburgh: T & T Clark, 2001), p. 93, cited in Vanhoozer, "A Person of the Book?" p. 53.

[15]Busch, *Karl Barth*, pp. 182, 206; Hunsinger, *How to Read Karl Barth*, p. 49; McGrath, *Christian Theology*, p. 261.

with these words: "And now the end has come. So listen to my last piece of advice: exegesis, exegesis, and yet more exegesis! Keep to the Word, to the scripture that has been given us."[16]

But if saturation in the Bible is critical for theology, Barth did not believe the Bible itself is revelation. We will discuss this more shortly, but revelation for Barth was an "encounter with a crucified man," not a collection of words on a printed page. The foundation for revelation was the resurrected Jesus himself, who as the living Word of God continues to speak for and vindicate himself. Jesus Christ today *uses* the written Word and preaching of that written Word to reveal himself to human beings.[17]

Therefore the subject of theology is not religious experience or ideas about life and salvation, or an abstract God, or even the Creator, but "Jesus Christ the Word of God as he is attested in the Bible." The subject is not Christology but Christ himself:

> Sometimes I don't like the word Christology very much. It's not a matter of christology, nor even of christocentricity and a christological orientation, but of *Christ himself.* Any preoccupation with Christology—and I have been preoccupied a little with that—can only be a critical help towards coming to the point where we may have the experience of the disciples on the Mount of Transfiguration: "They saw no one but Jesus alone."[18]

This of course required a method entirely different from what Barth had been taught. No longer was theology considered a detached intellectual discipline for which faith was unnecessary and whose goal was a neutral assessment of the implications of religious experience. Now theology was to be done as a member of the historic church, in submission to its creeds and confessions. This is why he titled his life project *Church Dogmatics.*

Theology must also be bathed in prayer. It was an intellectual discipline that was spiritual as well, and required the illumination of the Holy Spirit to proceed successfully.

And it was a discipline. Theology is not "free," but must be disciplined by its boundaries and guides—the Scriptures and church fathers. Every

---

[16]Busch, *Karl Barth*, p. 259.
[17]Ibid., pp. 114, 207.
[18]Ibid., pp. 279, 411.

Christian doctrine must cohere both with the narrative of Scripture and the network of other Christian doctrines derived from Scripture. The fathers, along with the Reformers, are indispensable helps to theology as it seeks to find this coherence.[19]

Theology is free to use concepts outside of its field, but it must approach them critically in the light of the revelation of the triune God. While Schleiermacher relegated the Trinity to an appendix, Barth introduced it early on in the *Church Dogmatics* and made it the center of God's identity and therefore of theology itself. All concepts from outside theology therefore must be baptized and born again by passing through the light of trinitarian reality. For example, theology can take from philosophy the concept of "nothingness" (as the object of human anxiety and the essence of ultimate reality), declaring that it has no existence of its own but is a philosophical counterpart to what the Bible calls "chaos." Since Scripture tells us the triune God conquered chaos and is fully in charge of the cosmos, nothingness must be treated as one description of the forces of evil whose power Christ destroyed at the cross but which will be finally destroyed only at the end of the world.[20]

Two other marks of Christian theology remain for Barth. First, it treats the Bible as a literary and theological whole, not a set of discrete books. It must assume, with the church fathers and Reformers, that the Bible has ultimately one author and one story. It is not, as some historical critics have assumed, a set of separate books with contradictory messages. Therefore Barth accepts in principle the Christian tradition of typology, in which the Old Testament is fulfilled in the story of Christ and his kingdom, as we saw in fathers such as Origen.

Second, theology is Christian only if it is trinitarian. Barth focused on Christ, but only as the second member of the Trinity. After several centuries of Protestant theology that had downplayed or ignored the Trinity (remember, Schleiermacher put the Trinity in an appendix at the back of his theology), Barth started a revival of theological recognition that, as he put it, "the Trinity . . . marks out the Christian doctrine of God as Christian."[21]

---

[19]Busch, *Karl Barth*, pp. 211, 345.
[20]Hunsinger, *How to Read Karl Barth*, p. 62.
[21]Barth, quoted in ibid., p. 213.

BARTH'S VIEW OF BIBLICAL INSPIRATION

For all the good that Barth brought to Christian theology, he also introduced some skewed perspectives. The first is his view of Scripture. You will recall that he said the Bible by itself is not the Word of God, but can *become* the Word of God when the Holy Spirit makes it come alive for its reader. The Bible is not revelation itself but a *witness* to revelation. The biblical authors were inspired in their reception of revelation even though they recorded them in the words of ordinary human language with all its limitations. So the texts alone could not serve God's purposes without a fresh work of the Holy Spirit to connect them with the living Word. Of course, all our great theologians said the same. But unlike them (with the exception of Schleiermacher), Barth was not willing to identify the biblical text itself as the Word of God.

Barth was rightly reacting against dry and sterile versions of orthodoxy that seemed to presume that mental assent to Christian doctrine is enough. And he was right to stress that the object of theology was the reality of Christ and the triune God, not the biblical words per se. But Barth marginalized the inspiration of the Bible and failed to give proper attention to the Spirit's work in superintending the writing process.

Barth's view of the Bible was based on his motif of actualism, which thinks in terms of events and relationships rather than things or substances. Barth said this motif comes from revelation itself. God's being, Barth taught, is always a being in act. Just as our relationship to God is never possessed once and for all, but is continually established anew by the ongoing activity of grace, so revelation is always an event or happening and never a thing.[22] Therefore Barth could never say the Bible, which is a thing, *is* the Word of God, which is continually established anew according to the divine good pleasure. The Spirit often uses the Bible to communicate a dynamic and living Word to a person who reads it or hears it, but apart from that dynamic illumination of the Spirit, the Bible is not the Word of God that conveys the self-revelation of God. So the Bible in and of itself is not the Word or revelation of God.

Barth's understanding of the relation of revelation to Scripture does not do justice to the Bible's own witness to itself. New Testament authors re-

---

[22]Hunsinger, *How to Read Karl Barth*, pp. 30-32, 76-102; Barth, *Church Dogmatics* 2/1 (Edinburgh: T & T Clark, 1961), pp. 257-321.

gard Old Testament passages as authoritative utterances of God (Mt 19:4-5; Acts 4:25-26; Heb 1:5-13; 3:7-11). The question, Have you not read . . . ? is virtually the equivalent of "Do you not know that God has said . . ." (Mt 12:3; 21:16; 22:31; Mk 2:25; 12:10, 26; Lk 6:3). The phrase "it is written" carries the full weight of divine authority (Mt 11:10; 21:13; 26:24, 31; Mk 9:12-13; 11:17; 14:21, 27; Lk 7:27; 19:46). The New Testament authors clearly believed that if something was written in the Old Testament, it was God's Word—not just a witness to God's Word. Sometimes "God" and "Scripture" are used interchangeably (Rom 9:17 [Ex 9:16]; Gal 3:8 [Gen 12:3]; Mt 19:4-5; [Gen. 2:24]). In other words, Scripture itself claims that when it speaks, God speaks.

So while Scripture claims that its *written* deposit was inspired by the Spirit (2 Tim 3:16; 2 Pet 1:20-21; 3:2, 15-16; 1 Tim 5:18), Barth refuses to separate the inspiration of the writers of Scripture from the subsequent illumination of the readers of Scripture. Thus for Barth the work of the Spirit in illuminating readers of the Bible is essential to the very conception of what the Word of God is. Geoffrey W. Bromiley, chief translator of Barth's *Church Dogmatics*, concludes that Barth stressed the present ministry of the Holy Spirit at the expense of the once-for-all work of the Spirit in the *writing* of Scripture.[23] While Barth therefore agreed with Calvin and church tradition that God's Spirit "confirmed" the Bible as God's Word, he failed to affirm clearly their conviction that the Spirit also "dispensed" the Word in the formation of the Bible.[24]

BARTH ON ELECTION

Barth also departed from Augustinian and Calvinist tradition on election, the idea that God has elected some (not all) for salvation. He strayed even further on the question of whether any are lost. Barth held to double predestination (that God not only elected for salvation but also permitted by divine decree damnation for unrepentance) but said the damnation took place on the cross of Christ. He opposed any views that specific individuals or groups of people were either chosen for salvation or rejected—inde-

---

[23]Geoffrey W. Bromiley, *Historical Theology: An Introduction* (Grand Rapids: Eerdmans, 1978), pp. 420-21.
[24]John Calvin, *Institutes of the Christian Religion*, ed. John T. McNeill, trans. Ford Lewis Battles (Philadelphia: Westminster Press, 1960), p. 95.

pendent of or prior to God's choice of Jesus Christ.

Barth held instead that Jesus is the one who was elected, both for salvation and for damnation. Many critics have charged that this part of his theology amounts to universalism—the idea that everyone is eventually saved and no one will be damned forever. Barth retorted, "I don't believe in universalism," but he also said "I do believe in Jesus Christ, the reconciler of all." Emil Brunner, whom Barth lambasted for his natural theology, said this amounted to universalism and obliterated the need for conversion.

> What does this statement, "that Jesus is the only really rejected person," mean for the situation of humanity? Evidently this: That there is no possibility of condemnation. . . . The decision has already been made in Jesus Christ—for all of humanity. Whether they know it or not, believe it or not, is not so important. They are like people who seem to be perishing in a stormy sea. But in reality they are not in a sea in which one can drown, but in shallow waters, in which it is impossible to drown. Only they do not know it.[25]

Given Barth's view of election, it might indeed follow that conversion seems unnecessary for salvation. Yet this conflicts with Barth's insistence that salvation includes a response elicited by the Spirit. Therefore many have found Barth's view of election at least logically inconsistent. Others have traced the World Council of Churches' 1973 call for a "moratorium" on missions to, at least in part, Barth's theology of election.

NO REVELATION IN NATURE?

We have seen already that Barth fought hard to defend Christian revelation against the German Christian religion, which found revelation in German blood and soil. In what seems to have been an overreaction, Barth denied any revelation in nature that could serve as a basis for Christian theology. Toward the end of his career, he acknowledged "lights" in creation that exude a certain "luminosity" and testify to creation as a *theatrum gloriae Dei* (a theater displaying the glory of God).[26] But earlier, he seemed to deny revelation in nature at all (and this denial has been remembered more than his later qualifications). For example, he protested that the bib-

---

[25]Busch, *Karl Barth*, p. 394; Emil Brunner, quoted in McGrath, *Christian Theology*, p. 402.
[26]Barth, *Church Dogmatics* 2/3.1, pp. 139-40.

lical passages typically used to support knowledge of God in nature have been misinterpreted by generations of readers, particularly since the Enlightenment. The Old Testament, he claimed, shows that no one outside of Israel knew the true God, and Paul explained that knowledge of God gained through nature leads only to condemnation.[27] In his battle with Brunner over natural theology and revelation, Barth insisted that testimonies of God in nature are not revelation because they are invariably misunderstood; they falsify rather than illumine. The only true knowledge we have of God is in the face of Christ (2 Cor 4:6).[28]

The voices of the cosmos in Psalm 19:3 are dumb, he wrote, because the text says "their voice is not heard." But the psalmist probably meant that there is no *audible* voice, for he goes on to say that that voice "goes out through *all* the earth, / and their words to the *end* of the world" (v. 4, italics added). This seems to speak of God's revelation going to those who have *not* heard of the Lord of Israel—not just to Israelites, as Barth had suggested. Furthermore, Paul made it clear that the revelation of God's law is made to *every* human heart (Rom 2:14). And in Romans 1:19-21 he used five words to emphasize that God's revelation is seen and heard even by those who rebel against him:

> For what can be *known* about God is plain to them, because God has *shown* it to them. Ever since the creation of the world his eternal power and divine nature, invisible though they are, have been *understood* and *seen* through the thing he has made. So they are without excuse; for though they *knew* God, they did not honor him as God or give thanks to him. (NRSV)

Barth accurately noted that many biblical writers suggest that these voices are not heard properly. But the passages from Psalm 19 and Romans 1–2, and others besides, nevertheless indicate that there is genuine disclosure of God given through the cosmos and humans—even if that disclosure is not properly understood by many. Condemnation is indeed the result of some of this revelation (Rom 1:20), but Scripture also hints that the Spirit uses this revelation, no doubt in conjunction with others, to lead some closer to God (Rom 2:15; Acts 17:27). As G. C. Berkouwer put it,

[27]Ibid., 2/1, pp. 130-33.
[28]Karl Barth, *Nein! Antwort an Emil Brunner,* Theologische Existenz heute 14 (Munich: Chr. Kaiser Verlag, 1934); Eng. trans. in Karl Barth and Emil Brunner, *Natural Theology: Comprising "Nature and Grace"* (London: G. Bles, 1946).

Barth's interpretation seems to be special pleading: "[Barth's exegesis] is more the result of an *a priori* view of revelation than an unprejudiced reading of the text itself."[29]

WHAT WE CAN LEARN FROM BARTH

1. We should now be able to recognize a liberal theological method, thanks to Barth. It starts with the world and ourselves, thinking it can find truth and goodness and beauty there. Then it goes to the Bible and decides what can be believed in the Bible based on what it already knows from outside the Bible. We should beware of this method, for it seeks to infiltrate the theology even of those who claim to be orthodox and evangelical.

2. Barth helps us remember that the Christian faith is based on revelation. God has already revealed himself in Israel—in Jesus and Scripture. Our theology should therefore move from above to below. We should seek to understand what is here below by looking through the prism of what has been revealed from above.

3. Barth boldly declared the independence of theology, freeing Christian theologians from having to apologize for what they do. Friedrich Schleiermacher made the same declaration, but on a foundation of sand. Barth insisted, and demonstrated by his own erudition and courage, that theology does not need to lean on other disciplines outside itself, for it is rooted in God's revelation in history and the Word. Theologians have been emboldened by Barth to do their work with confidence and forthrightness. They have learned from their tutor that they don't need to make Christian theology palatable to the modern mind, for the gospel contains its own authentication from the Holy Spirit. Barth's "irrelevant" theology has proven more relevant over the long haul than many apologetic theologies such as those constructed by Schleiermacher, Ernst Troeltsch and Paul Tillich. One of the many festschrifts (celebratory volumes by students and colleagues) for Barth was titled *Parrhesia*, which was a favorite word of Paul and means "boldness" and "freedom of speech." This is an important aspect of Barth's genius.

4. Even if Barth had a flawed view of inspiration, he nevertheless re-

---

[29]G. C. Berkouwer, *General Revelation* (Grand Rapids: Eerdmans, 1983), p. 154, cited in Gabriel Fackre, *The Doctrine of Revelation: A Narrative Interpretation* (Grand Rapids: Eerdmans, 1997), p. 50.

minds us that we need to bathe ourselves in Scripture and prayer every day if we are to do or understand theology properly.

5. He shows us also that Christian theology starts with the trinitarian God's self-revelation in Scripture. Theology that doesn't start with the Trinity is not Christian; neither is theology that doesn't reflect in a disciplined way on Scripture.

6. Barth is also an excellent reminder that we cannot understand Scripture without the Holy Spirit's illumination. Thus the need to pray every time we read Scripture, asking God to illuminate for us what he has already revealed. As Barth taught, God is the only one who can show us God.

A SELECTION FROM KARL BARTH'S WORKS

The voice which reigns, the voice by which we were taught by God Himself concerning God, was the voice of Jesus Christ. Along all the path now behind us we could not take a single step without stumbling again and again across that name. And "across that name" does not mean across an empty title. . . . [W]hen theology allows itself on any pretext to be jostled away from that name, God is inevitably crowded out by a hypostatised image of man. Theology must begin with Jesus Christ, and not with general principles, however better, or, at any rate, more relevant and illuminating, they may appear to be: as though He were a continuation of the knowledge and Word of God, and not its root and origin, not indeed the very Word of God itself. Theology must also end with Him, and not with supposedly self-evident general conclusions from what is particularly enclosed and disclosed in Him: as though the fruits could be shaken from this tree; as though in the things of God there were anything general which we could know and designate in addition to and even independently of this particular. The obscurities and ambiguities of our way were illuminated in the measure that we held fast to that name and in the measure that we let Him be the first and the last, according to the testimony of Holy Scripture. Against all the imaginations and errors in which we seem to be so hopelessly entangled when we try to speak of God, God will indeed maintain Himself if we will only allow the name of Jesus Christ to be maintained in our thinking as the beginning and the end of all our thoughts.[30]

---

[30]Karl Barth, *Church Dogmatics: A Selection*, ed. G. W. Bromiley (New York: Harper Torchbooks, 1962), pp. 87-88.

FOR REFLECTION AND DISCUSSION

1. Describe Barth's "conversion" from liberalism to orthodoxy. If you are in a group, find out if anyone in the group has gone through a similar transformation.

2. How does Barth define liberalism? What is an example of using that method?

3. Why did he have problems with the analogy of being? With systems?

4. What can we learn from his view of biblical law and his understanding of preaching?

5. According to Barth, what is the proper way to do theology?

6. Explain Barth's views of (1) biblical inspiration and (2) election. Evaluate them.

7. Do you think God reveals himself in nature?

FOR FURTHER READING

Barth, Karl. *Church Dogmatics: A Selection*. Edited by G. W. Bromiley. New York: Harper Torchbooks, 1962.

Busch, Eberhard. *Karl Barth: His Life from Letters and Autobiographical Texts*. Grand Rapids: Eerdmans, 1994.

Hart, Trevor. *Regarding Karl Barth: Toward a Reading of His Theology*. Downers Grove, Ill.: InterVarsity Press, 1999.

12

Hans Urs von Balthasar

Stellar Catholic Theologian
of the Twentieth Century

One of the foremost Catholic theologians of our day says Hans Urs von Balthasar (1905-1988) is "widely regarded as the greatest Catholic theologian of the [twentieth] century" and "by far the most discussed Catholic theologian at present."[1] The German Jesuit Karl Rahner has made a deep impact on professional Catholic theologians of the twentieth century, and the French Dominican Yves Congar has been called the father of Vatican II because of his influential writings on ecumenism and other subjects the Council took up. Pope John Paul II, who is beginning to be hailed as one of the greatest popes ever, was also a formidable theologian. But Balthasar's star has been rising in recent decades, as his idiosyncratic theology has attracted more and more positive attention in both academic and nonscholarly circles.[2]

Who was this great Christian mind—whom most Christians have never heard of but about whom there is growing fascination? Readers of this book will be curious to learn that his career is connected with Barth's. A fellow Swiss, Balthasar made a name for himself by writing a book about Barth's theology that Barth called "incomparably more powerful than that of most of the books" about his theology. Balthasar said he got his "vision of a comprehensive biblical theology" from Barth and was in-

---

[1] Fergus Kerr, *Twentieth-Century Catholic Theologians* (Malden, Mass.: Blackwell, 2007), pp. 121, 144.
[2] Ibid.

spired by Barth's discussion of God's beauty and glory in *Church Dogmatics* 2/1 to make that the theme of his own sixteen-volume theological series, The Glory of the Lord. In Balthasar's work you can see themes that sound remarkably similar to Barth's—that the Word of God contains its own "proof" of its divine origin, that Christian faith cannot be derived from any philosophy or reduced to a system, that our ideas of God cannot be constructed by extrapolating from the best human qualities, and that we can know God only by his own self-revelation.[3]

There were also personal connections between Barth and Balthasar. Balthasar's theological partner Adrienne von Speyr, the female Swiss Protestant who converted to Catholicism, was best friend to Karl Barth's brother. Balthasar (who "could have been a professional pianist"), Speyr and Barth spent "almost twenty-four hours" listening to records of Mozart one time in the winter of 1948-1949; this feast of music on vinyl motivated Barth to buy his own record player and Mozart records.[4]

Curiously, both Balthasar and Barth said they were intellectually indebted to a brilliant female colleague, with whom each worked in close proximity. Balthasar went so far as to say that a good part of his best thinking was a "translation" of Speyr's mystical visions.[5]

The professional and personal relationships connecting these two Swiss theologians may help explain why they shared a similar view of Scripture and both developed eschatologies (theologies of last things) that verged on universalism, the belief that all will be saved in the end. We'll look at the latter a bit later.

---

[3]Hans Urs von Balthasar, *The Theology of Karl Barth: Exposition and Interpretation*, trans. Edward T. Oakes (1951; reprint, San Francisco: Ignatius, 1992); John Webster, "Balthasar and Karl Barth," in *The Cambridge Companion to Hans Urs von Balthasar*, ed. Edward T. Oakes and David Moss (Cambridge: Cambridge University Press, 2004), p. 241; Kerr, *Twentieth-Century Catholic Theologians*, p. 129.

[4]Kerr, *Twentieth-Century Catholic Theologians*, pp. 122n., 121; Eberhard Busch, *Karl Barth: His Life from Letters and Autobiographical Texts* (Grand Rapids: Eerdmans, 1994), p. 362.

[5]Hans Ur von Balthasar, *My Work in Retrospect* (San Francisco: Communio Books, 1993), p. 105. Balthasar was criticized for his close collaboration with Speyr, but Barth's reputation has suffered more from his relationship with Charlotte von Kirschbaum, who was theological assistant and researcher for sections of the *Church Dogmatics*. Kirschbaum lived in the Barth home, went on vacations alone with Barth, and in 1962 the two shared a room at Princeton Theological Seminary. There was and remains fierce debate over whether they were lovers. See Suzanne Selinger, *Charlotte von Kirschbaum and Karl Barth: A Study in Biography and the History of Theology* (University Park: Penn State University Press, 1998); Renate Kobler, *In the Shadow of Karl Barth: Charlotte Von Kirschbaum* (Philadelphia: Westminster John Knox Press, 1989).

AN UNUSUAL LIFE

Balthasar came from noble Swiss stock—thus the "von" in his name. Extraordinarily gifted in music and literature, he joined the Jesuits in 1929 but found their theological training to be "dreary." He was angry that modern Catholic interpretations of Thomas Aquinas stripped theology of God's glory, and lamented that as a result the only place to see that glory was in the work of poets, artists and great scientists.[6]

Balthasar was saved from utter desolation in his theological training by meeting the great Patristics scholar, Henri de Lubac.[7] De Lubac pointed him to Origen, who became Balthasar's favorite theologian. Balthasar said Origen was the key that opened to view the riches of the fathers, the early Middle Ages and even Hegel and Barth.

It was during this period that Balthasar also met Speyr, who was then one of Switzerland's very few female physicians. Under Balthasar's spiritual direction, she was received into the Catholic Church in 1940. Her visions, sixty published volumes of which she dictated to him, were so integral to his "basic perspective" that he spoke of his last volume in *The Glory of the Lord* as "our theology."[8]

Balthasar's partnership with Speyr prompted him in 1945 to found a secular institute that functioned as a religious order for laypeople, but without special dress or communal living. Its purpose was to help laypeople live out the practical implications for faith as interpreted by Balthasar. In 1950, after "painful negotiations" trying to get the Society of Jesus (the Jesuits) to recognize the order, Balthasar decided to quit the Jesuits.[9]

If the Jesuits felt uncomfortable about the new institute Balthasar and Speyr ran, the larger Church felt even more discomfort when Balthasar published his book on Barth in 1951. Balthasar seemed too accepting of a Protestant theologian who attacked the heart of Catholic method, its analogy of being (see chap. 11). To make matters worse, Pope Pius XII had just declared that God's existence can be proved by reason—a notion that Barth had flatly denied. Balthasar tried to mediate by saying that unfallen reason could in theory prove God's existence, but that the existing proofs

---

[6]Kerr, *Twentieth-Century Catholic Theologians*, p. 122.
[7]Patristics have to do with the fathers of the church from roughly the second to the eighth centuries.
[8]Balthasar, quoted in Kerr, *Twentieth-Century Catholic Theologians*, pp. 129, 141.
[9]Kerr, *Twentieth-Century Catholic Theologians*, p. 123.

had used fallen reason. This distinction was lost on most Catholic interpreters, so that when the Second Vatican Council opened in 1962, Balthasar was not invited.

In 1985 he tried to return to the Jesuits, but failed. He was finally vindicated in 1988 by being nominated to become a cardinal, but died three days before he was admitted to the office.

A NEW VERSION OF THE ANALOGY OF BEING

Balthasar was a keen student of Protestant theology, having been convinced by Barth that Protestant theology is important and that Catholic theologians must be in dialogue with their Protestant counterparts. We have already seen that Barth apparently helped Balthasar sharpen his view of theology as centered in Christ and the Bible. Balthasar learned from Luther, and Barth's presentation of Luther, that the definition of a Christian is the person who *hears* God's Word and responds to it. He was also convinced, perhaps as a result of his deep study of Barth and Protestantism, that Christian proclamation should never be "de-biblicized." Preaching should focus not on platitudes or eternal principles but on the "dramatic" biblical story in which God comes to earth in Israel and Christ to defeat evil.[10]

Balthasar did not accept Barth's renunciation of the analogy of being, however. You may remember from chapter eleven that the analogy of being is an approach to nature that finds traces of God in it. (Catholics have traditionally used this more than Protestants, but some Protestant theologians have followed a similar approach without naming it as such.) Beings in this world are signposts to God, since God created the world. If things in this world were fashioned by God, then there must be earmarks of the Designer in those things. By examining those things, we can say something about the One who fashioned them—even if we cannot say very much. Barth said this makes human beings their own creator and redeemer, since they can find in themselves whatever they need to lead them to God.[11] Other Reformed theologians have said that *analogia entis* (Latin for "analogy of being") tends to place God and creation within a larger context of being, but there is no larger context for God.

---

[10]Balthasar, *My Work in Retrospect*, pp. 52, 89-90, 100.
[11]Ironically, Balthasar writes that he found the analogy of being within Barth's own thinking.

Balthasar said Barth was attacking a straw man—a "fraudulent" version of the analogy of being that could be found in "neo-Thomist" textbooks but which distorted what Thomas himself had to say. These modern Thomists presented a secularized account of the human capacity for God. But Thomas and his best interpreters, according to Balthasar, said that if there is any human capacity to find and know something of God, it is only by grace. There is no "pure nature" that can see the true God on its own. As Balthasar expressed it, the Word made flesh "came to his own." He did not merely go to a foreign "far country," as Barth put it, but came to a people who had already been prepared by that Word to recognize him.[12]

So this is an analogy of being that shows signs of responding to a Barthian critique. On the one hand, Balthasar says all worldly being is "epiphanic," which means that every being in the world "shows" or points to the being of God and his love shown in Christ. So the surrender in all human love is a token of Christ's surrender to the will of his Father. The pattern we see in all of nature that death is necessary for new life is a pointer to Christ's death being necessary for his resurrection. These are two of the innumerable ways in which God is the "fulfillment" of "the world's being."[13]

But on the other hand, this is not the analogy of being that Barth had seen and rejected, in which it was supposed that anyone, even a non-Christian using his reason, could see the true God by looking long and hard enough at this world. Balthasar insisted the true analogy was different in two ways: first, the person without grace cannot see God by looking at the beings in this world; and second, the analogy of being points to Jesus Christ, not some vague theism.[14]

YET STILL TRIUMPHANTLY CATHOLIC

But if Balthasar sounded a bit Protestant in his version of the analogy of being, his theology resounded with traditional Catholic themes: that one should return to Catholic tradition for guidance, that grace does not destroy but perfects nature, that faith and reason finally agree, that the

---

[12]Webster, "Balthasar and Karl Barth," pp. 249-50.
[13]Hans Ur von Balthasar, *Epilogue*, trans. Edward T. Oakes (San Francisco: Ignatius, 2004), pp. 59, 109; Hans Ur von Balthasar, *The Grain of Wheat: Aphorisms*, trans. Erasmo Leiva-Merikakis (San Francisco: Ignatius, 1995), p. 31; Hans Ur von Balthasar, "The Fathers, the Scholastics, and Ourselves," *Communio* 24 (1997): 391.
[14]Webster, "Balthasar and Karl Barth," p. 249.

Church helps earn salvation and redeem the world by its cooperation with Christ, and that we can offer up our suffering as part of Christ's atonement. In fact, the degree to which we belong to Christ is measured by the degree to which we participate "in the visible, sacramental and hierarchical organism" of the Catholic Church.[15]

Yet Balthasar was not a liberal Catholic. He denounced both Karl Rahner's idea that non-Christians could be "anonymous Christians" and Hans Küng's modernist tendencies. He came out against Eastern meditation, women priests, feminism and modern biblical exegesis.[16]

At times Balthasar was triumphalist in his fulminations against Protestantism. He complained that Protestants have a perverse doctrine of original sin—one which eliminates all traces of goodness in the fallen person, so that they wrongly think all human activity is "nothing but idle sin and inanity." They reject self-love and depreciate "secondary causes," the idea that we have a role in causing what we do. In this way Protestants "annihilate" a human's inner core. The religious result is that Protestants "are like beggars who are continually knocking at doors . . . hear a friendly 'Come in!', but they do not enter because they feel that 'beggars belong in the street.' " This is why Protestants are "passive," remaining on the "lowest step" of "minimum activity" and refusing to get on with "man's cooperation in the work of redemption." No wonder they lack the gusto of Catholics, for they have eliminated the aesthetic (the beautiful) in religion, which has deprived them "of the contemplative dimension of the act of faith." They have "stop[ped] up the wellspring of joy." Catholics therefore should not be reluctant to acknowledge the "superiority" of their tradition, and they should stop trying "to imitate the anguished 'existentialist' tone of their Protestant counterparts, [for] that garment does not fit them any better than his father's top hat fit Little Johnny Upstart."[17]

Balthasar was just as convinced of the superiority of the Roman tradition over Eastern Orthodoxy. The millennium-old sticking point between

---

[15]Balthasar, "Fathers, the Scholastics, and Ourselves," p. 351; Kerr, *Twentieth-Century Catholic Theologians*, p. 131; Balthasar, "Fathers, the Scholastics, and Ourselves," p. 365; Balthasar, *Grain of Wheat*, p. 47; Balthasar, "Fathers, the Scholastics, and Ourselves," p. 364.

[16]Kerr, *Twentieth-Century Catholic Theologians*, p. 124.

[17]Balthasar, *Grain of Wheat*, p. 93; Balthasar, "Fathers, the Scholastics, and Ourselves," p. 353; Balthasar, *Grain of Wheat*, pp. 116, 120-21; Kerr, *Twentieth-Century Catholic Theologians*, p. 131; Balthasar, *Grain of Wheat*, pp. 96, 120.

Rome and the East—Rome's insertion of *filioque* ("and from the Son") in the Nicene Creed portion about the procession of the Holy Spirit—reflects a difference "deeper than one thinks." For the Eastern Church is still essentially Platonist, which means it sees the world (and the Spirit) as an "egression" of the Father in such a way that matter is less real than spirit, and so the incarnation is "provisional" and resurrection of the flesh a "disturbance." This is why monophysitism (Christ had only one nature) and docetism (Christ only seemed to have a human nature) have been so prevalent in the East.[18]

THEOLOGY AT PRAYER

In an era when much academic theology lacks a sense for the holy, Balthasar is refreshing. He believed "theology is essentially an act of adoration and prayer," and lamented the replacement of "theology at prayer" with "theology at the desk." Academic theology, he observed, has "lost the accent and tone with which one should speak of what is holy," while at the same time theology in the churches often "degenerated into unctuous, platitudinous piety."[19]

The problem, Balthasar said, is that good theology requires a good heart. Higher knowledge "presupposes the moral preparation of the soul." Every good thinker must be religious because "our thinking and loving" need to "penetrate like X-rays through the flesh of things and expose the divine skeleton within them." It is no wonder that some theologians seem tone deaf and blind: all truth is "objective," but only morally and spiritually sensitive minds can hear and see it.[20]

Here are two examples of the spiritual insight possessed by this eminent theologian:

> We constantly flee from God into a distance that is theoretical, rhetorical, sentimental, aesthetic, or, most frequently, pious. Or we flee from him to external works. And yet, the best thing would be to surrender one's naked heart to the fire of this all-penetrating glance. The heart would then itself have to catch fire.
>
> Every description of mysticism must start with the insight that God's

---

[18]Balthasar, "Fathers, the Scholastics, and Ourselves," pp. 374-76.
[19]Kerr, *Twentieth-Century Catholic Theologians*, p. 137.
[20]Balthasar, *Grain of Wheat*, pp. 19, 22, 19.

ways with souls cannot be reduced to a system. The experiences of Teresa of Ávila, for instance, are wholly individual and not even particularly typical, since they are to a large extent conditioned by her character. The only set framework remains the life of Jesus, which constitutes the canon for all ways of perfection.[21]

THEOLOGY THAT STARTS WITH GOD'S GLORY

Like Jonathan Edwards, Balthasar centered his theology in God's beauty, which he said is synonymous with God's glory. Balthasar thought the theology he had been trained in was so rationalistic that it had leeched out all the beauty and glory at true theology's heart. He felt it was necessary to restore beauty to the inner structure of theology and came to believe that "starting with aesthetics" in theology "is ultimately the only appropriate stance."[22]

But for Balthasar, the beauty and glory are not there for our sake but for God's:

> God does not come primarily as a teacher for us ("true"), as a useful "redeemer" for us ("good"), but to display and to radiate himself, the splendor of his eternal triune love in that "disinterestedness" [absence of self-concern] that true love has in common with true beauty. For the glory of God the world was created; through it and for its sake the world is also redeemed.[23]

The essence of God's beauty is "eternal love descending into the uttermost darkness." This is not beauty in the modern or philosophical sense but the archetype of all true "beauty in glory"—"the splendor of the divinity of God himself as manifested in the life, death, and Resurrection of Jesus and reflected, according to Paul, in Christians who look upon their Lord."

Like Edwards, then, Balthasar made beauty the keystone of his life project and defined that beauty in terms of Jesus Christ. Also like Edwards, Balthasar said the beauty could not be seen by just anyone, but only by "the person who is touched by a ray of this glory and has an incipient sensibility for what disinterested love is." Only this person can "learn to see the presence of divine love in Jesus Christ."[24]

---

[21]Ibid., pp. 3, 119.
[22]Balthasar, *My Work in Retrospect*, p. 81.
[23]Ibid., p. 80.
[24]Ibid., pp. 85, 96, 85.

A CONTROVERSIAL TAKE ON HOLY SATURDAY

Oddly, though, it may have been this understanding of beauty that drew fire from critics before Balthasar died, and it has resurfaced recently. Balthasar said that God's beauty consists precisely in his "descending" into the uttermost darkness for humanity. This meant, in an "adventurous" innovation that seemed to critics to have departed from Christian tradition (but which Balthasar believed was latent within the tradition), that Jesus' suffering did not end on the cross, but in fact became even more severe on Holy Saturday when in his human soul he experienced the "ultimate alienation" of the damned.[25]

Balthasar got this innovation from his female collaborator, Adrienne von Speyr, who for twenty-four years relived Christ's passion every Holy Week. She told Balthasar that during these trances she descended with Jesus to hell, where there was no faith or hope or love, only sin. This was the completion of Christ's passion and was therefore crucial for the salvation of humanity.

During Balthasar's lifetime there was gossip about his heavy reliance upon Speyr's mystical experiences, and more recently he has come under strong theological criticism for rejecting what had been universally believed by Christians until the sixteenth-century Reformation. All Christians until then believed that Christ went to "hell" on Holy Saturday for two reasons: to liberate the fathers of the Old Testament period from "limbo" or Sheol, and to proclaim his victory to Satan and the damned. Protestants have always agreed with Catholics that Christ's sufferings ended on the cross, so that when Jesus said, "It is finished" (Jn 19:30), his afflictions ceased.[26]

Balthasar's teaching that Jesus continued to suffer after his body's death, that this suffering was even greater than that on the cross, and that the suffering in hell was necessary before he could be raised from the dead, were all departures from tradition. And they had little to support them but the mystical visions of his friend Speyr.[27]

---

[25]Kerr, *Twentieth-Century Catholic Theologians*, p. 134; Geoffrey Wainwright, "Eschatology," in *The Cambridge Companion to Hans Urs von Balthasar*, ed. Edward T. Oakes and David Moss (Cambridge: Cambridge University Press, 2004), p. 118.

[26]Kerr, *Twentieth-Century Catholic Theologians*, pp. 123, 134-35; for trenchant criticism of this innovation, see Alyssa Lyra Pitstick, *Light in Darkness: Hans Urs von Balthasar and the Catholic Doctrine of Christ's Descent into Hell* (Grand Rapids: Eerdmans, 2007).

[27]Strangely enough, charismatic leaders Kenneth Hagin Sr. and Kenneth Copeland teach a similar view of Holy Saturday (see William P. Atkinson, *The "Spiritual Death" of Jesus: A Pentecostal Investigation* [Leiden: Brill, 2009]).

UNIVERSAL HOPE

In his eschatology (doctrines of last things), Balthasar may not have departed from tradition, but he stretched it to near its breaking point. Many centuries ago the universal church condemned the Origenist belief in the eventual salvation of everyone as heresy.[28] Balthasar, who considered Origen to be the brightest star among the fathers, skirted close to this heresy by saying Christians have an "obligation" to *hope* for the salvation of all. He said this is "commanded" by God's Word when it says that love "hopes all things" (1 Cor 13:7). After all, Balthasar reasoned, we do not know if human beings are capable of denying Christ to the very end, when they are faced with his compelling beauty and love.[29] As you will recall, Barth's eschatology was similar. Although Balthasar did not use Barth's theory of election per se, the two Swiss theologians agreed that while universal salvation is not promised by Scripture or the tradition, we are obliged as believers to hope for it in the light of Christ's grace and God's freedom.

Balthasar admitted there was a set of texts in the New Testament that spoke of those "lost for eternity." But he said there was also a set of texts, such as the passages where Christ says he will "draw all people to myself" (Jn 12:32) and Peter says "God does not wish that any should perish" (2 Pet 3:9), that suggests the salvation of all. Because of this second set of texts, Balthasar believed the passages about hell may refer to an unpopulated hell, which is created by humans, not God. He said that "God gives man the capacity to make a (negative) choice against God that seems *for man* to be definitive, but which need not be taken *by God* as definitive." He liked Edith Stein's suggestion that God can "outwit" his human creatures.[30]

The trouble with this line of argument is that Balthasar appears to be doing what he himself said was illegitimate—subordinating one set of biblical texts to another. And even the texts he prefers do not necessarily say what he wants them to say: God does not wish any to perish, but he also does not wish any to sin. So the fact that God does not want his human creatures to do something does not mean that he prevents them from do-

---

[28]Origenist refers to followers of Origen, not necessarily Origen himself. Since many of Origen's texts come to us from those who opposed him, and we know these texts were doctored, we are not sure that Origen taught everything these texts claim he taught.

[29]Balthasar, *Epilogue*, p. 122.

[30]Wainwright, "Eschatology," pp. 122, 123, 125.

ing it. He may not want them to perish, but he won't prevent them from perishing if they so choose. Another text Balthasar prefers appears to undermine his universal hope: "God . . . is the Savior of all people, *especially* of those who believe" (1 Tim 4:10, italics added). One wonders why believers are singled out.[31]

Balthasar hopes for God's love to be so overwhelming that every creature will freely decide for him. But some critics say that this seems to ignore the psychological and biblical suggestions that there will always be some who, in their freedom, stubbornly refuse that love. It also goes against the grain of Catholic thinking, which tends to put more stock in human freedom than Protestants do.

A GRAND SYNTHESIS OF PHILOSOPHY, THEOLOGY AND THE RELIGIONS

Balthasar's greatest legacy may be his all-encompassing vision for theology as a way to think through all of human philosophy and religion by using the prism of the glory of God in Christ. Many theologians have *said* something similar, but very few have had as much knowledge of both philosophy and the religions to pull it off.

You might say he had an advantage over Protestants. Protestant theologians have usually worked with the assumption that much of philosophy and all of the religions except Judaism have represented human overreaching or demonic deception. But the Catholic tradition, beginning with the Greek fathers, has seen the Logos at work guiding whole civilizations closer to the truth. Of course the fathers and their successors also saw much error in these civilizations and believed some of it was demonic. But they also saw truth, if only here and there, and believed it was given by Christ himself working behind the scenes, as it were.

Balthasar was heir to this tradition. Because of his vast learning, he was able to develop it in unprecedented ways. He believed, with Augustine and Aquinas, that God has placed a hunger for himself in every human being, and it is because of this hunger that pagans "search for God and perhaps grope for him and find him" (Acts 17:27 NRSV).

As Balthasar put it, Christ was guiding Plato and Aristotle and the

---

[31]Ibid., p. 122.

world religions in their "groping." This is why all that is true and good and beautiful in those philosophies and religions finds its fulfillment in him— because he gave those truths to them in the first place. "Revelation decided upon by God's free initiative" to select pagans "both directs and fulfills [their] search at the same time."[32]

Christ has shed the rays of his truth not only from the inside of the world's philosophies and religions, but also from the outside. "Today the yeast of Christianity has penetrated the whole of mankind." It is historically plausible, for example, that what popular Hinduism and Buddhism know of grace was taken indirectly from Christian missionaries many centuries ago.[33]

If Christ fulfills the best of all pagan dreams, his followers have also learned from some of them. "Everything meaningful for man and the world in the religions [and philosophies] of mankind is integrated." So, for example, Christian faith learned "participation" in God from Platonism during the Patristic era; it learned about secondary causes and nature from Aristotelian philosophy during the Scholastic period; and it learned about the historically unique and concrete from modern philosophy.[34]

Christ not only fulfills pagan truth and leads pagans toward truth, but he also shows Israel, who had the highest truth till that time, that he unites

> what could not be united "in past times": the High Priest and the slain Lamb, the King and the Servant, the Temple and the worshipper inside the Temple, the sacred and the profane, and finally his origin in God and his birth as man. And he does this, when all is said and done, not by shattering the old tablets of the Law, but by "fulfil[ling] the scripture" (Jn 19:28).[35]

In other words, Christ integrates and fulfills what is true and good in all the religions and philosophies of humanity, including his own Judaism.

PHILOSOPHERS FEEDING ON CHRISTIAN BONES

Let's look a bit more closely at Balthasar's integration of Western philosophy. He says that most of the philosophers are inspired by the same desire for ultimate truth that drives theologians, and their philosophies are there

---

[32]Balthasar, *Epilogue*, p. 17.
[33]Ibid., p. 18.
[34]Ibid., p. 37; Balthasar, "Fathers, the Scholastics, and Ourselves," pp. 380-89.
[35]Balthasar, *Epilogue*, p. 94.

fore rival theologies. In the ancient world, for example, Philo's philosophy was "to a large extent a secularized theology of revelation." Gnosticism was a "classical example of secularized Christianity." Modern philosophy is no different—it is "a kind of refuse product of formerly Christian (more precisely, theological) intellectual contents." Balthasar wrote about the Christian motifs, for instance, in German idealism and French existentialism. This process of philosophy using Christian ideas takes the "form of a vampire, sucking at the living veins of what is Christian in order to transfuse the blood into other organisms." Philosophers don't realize it, but in this way they are dependent on Christ for truth: "Philosophy looks up to Christ with the same worried expectation of a dog looking at his master: Will he make up his mind to throw him the bone that will busy him for the rest of the day?"[36]

Christian theology should use philosophy as a tool, but it must be careful. Theologians should remember that their object of study is different: philosophers search the being of this world, but theologians explore God's self-revelation in the Logos. Confrontation is "unavoidable." A "wise man" does not try to "harmonize" every "philosophical system" with Christian theology. Theologians must know that when they decide what is finally true, God's self-revelation is their ultimate norm. They may pick up a "fragment or stone . . . from a pagan or heretical stream, but they [need to] know how to cleanse it and to polish it until that radiance shines forth which shows that it is a fragment of the total glorification of God." Balthasar used Paul for emphasis: "Test *everything;* hold fast to what is good" (1 Thess 5:21, italics added).[37]

But through this process of sifting and testing, philosophy can help theology develop itself. Therefore "theologians ought to delight in making everything that the natural spirit can offer into the footstool for the Word of God." If they use theological discernment, with God's self-revelation as their standard, "the gold, frankincense, and myrrh of human thought . . . [will] share in the transforming power of the fire that must catch hold of everything that is to become eternal."[38]

---

[36]Balthasar, "On the Tasks of Catholic Philosophy in Our Time," *Communio* 20 (spring 1993): 170, 165, 167; Balthasar, *Grain of Wheat,* p. 53.

[37]Balthasar, "Catholic Philosophy," p. 151; Balthasar, *Grain of Wheat,* p. 26; Balthasar, "Catholic Philosophy," p. 156.

[38]"Catholic Philosophy," p. 187.

THE SECRET WORK OF THE LOGOS IN THE RELIGIONS

Balthasar did the same with the world religions. He tested them for truth, rejoicing in the secret work of the Logos, but he also showed their sharp differences with Christian theology.

First, the truth. Balthasar wrote in considerable detail about the seeds sown by the Logos in the world religions, and said that Christian theology should both recognize these seeds and use them. If Thomas Aquinas "had known Buddha and Lao-Tse, there is no doubt that he would have drawn them too into the *summa* of what he thought, and would have given them the place appropriate to them." Balthasar argued that "if we are to be ready at all times 'to make a defense' of our faith (1 Pet 3:15)," we must be familiar with the world religions and be able to discuss both their truth and where they differ with Christian revelation. For example, we should acknowledge the Christlike ideal of self-surrender in the Buddhist *bodhisattva*, who denies himself the joy of entering nirvana so that he can go back to the world of suffering to help others.[39]

But Christian theology should also know the deficiencies of the religions in comparison with Christianity. Other religions try to free humanity from suffering and death, but it is precisely these things that "become in Christianity the highest proof for God *being* love." God partners with a whole people in Judaism, with the *ummah* (community) in Islam, but with the individual in Christianity, "who retains his ultimate dignity by being a brother or sister of Christ." The monism (all is one) in Daoism, Buddhism and Islamic Sufism "destroys the reality of man in his finitude," but in union with Christ the individual is still an individual. Daoism, Stoicism and Sufism teach "religious indifference" to this world, but Christ calls us to make an "offer of readiness" to serve in the world. Shinto does not discuss "what lies beyond death" and Confucianism is "ultimately nonreligious," while Christ promises eternal life both now and forever.[40]

WHAT WE CAN LEARN

1. Protestants and Catholics should learn from each other. A Jesuit friend once told me he was surprised to discover, long after he had finished his theological training, that Protestants also do theology. I know Protestant

---

[39]Balthasar, "Catholic Philosophy," p. 156; Balthasar, *Epilogue*, pp. 16, 72.
[40]Balthasar, *Epilogue*, pp. 36, 35, 34, 36, 21.

ministers who are blissfully ignorant of what Catholics actually believe. Many theologians would say Balthasar's theology was improved by his reading Luther and Barth. I daresay some Protestant readers of this book might say they have discovered rich veins of gold in the writings of the Catholic theologians sketched here.

2. Prayer is essential for theology. Other theologians in this book have said the same, but Balthasar's admonition has particular resonance because he wrote in an era when academic theology was the gold standard, and, as he put it, too much of that theology lacked a sense for the holy. Balthasar added that a worshiping community is also necessary for good theology, both for input from fellow believers and the reminder that worship is the purpose of theology.

3. Theology is for the sake of God's glory. So are we, and so are creation and redemption. In a word that is at first off-putting, Balthasar admonishes us that Christ came primarily not to save us but to glorify his Father. This reminds us that our theology needs to be more about God and less about us.

4. The most-repeated command in the Bible, "Be not afraid," is well put to Christians as they face rival philosophies and theologies, even those that are explicitly anti-Christian. We should follow Balthasar's example of critically evaluating them by the light of God's self-revelation in Christ, and then "plundering the Egyptians" by using for Christian purposes the treasures which the Logos has given them. We need not fear.

A SELECTION FROM HANS URS VON BALTHASAR'S WORKS

The edifying principle in Protestantism rests on a process of downward leveling: before God and from the divine perspective, all human activity, all so-called religion, is nothing but idle sin and inanity. For man, the only genuine humility that saves is for him to acknowledge this and cling exclusively to God's grace. The edifying principle in Catholicism rests on this: that the omnipotence of grace is so great that it can take into account even man's powerless striving, and that, although God does everything, still this never happens without man.

◆　◆　◆

Truth is not like a flat piece of paper. It has a body, a third dimension. It has gradations, is hierarchical. What is true at one level is not necessarily true at another. For the person who has scaled the whole of truth it is possible to describe the positions of these levels and their relation to one another. The higher a level lies, the more a knowledge of it presupposes the moral preparation of the soul. This structure of truth makes blockheads think that truth is subjective. All truth is in fact objective, but not for everyone.[41]

FOR REFLECTION AND DISCUSSION

1. How did Balthasar defend the Catholic analogy of being? Did he persuade you? Explain.

2. In what ways was Balthasar distinctively Catholic?

3. What does Balthasar add to theology by his emphases on prayer and God's glory? Do you agree with him?

4. Is Balthasar persuasive in his view of Holy Saturday? Why?

5. What are the strengths and weaknesses of Balthasar's hope for universal salvation?

6. Does Balthasar give you a new view of philosophy? How so?

7. How is Balthasar similar to John Henry Newman on non-Christian religions?

8. If you are in a group, share one thing that you find particularly interesting about Balthasar.

FOR FURTHER READING

Balthasar, Hans Urs von. "Why I Am Still a Christian." In *Two Say Why: "Why I Am Still a Christian" by Hans Urs von Balthasar and "Why I Am Still in the Church," by Joseph Ratzinger.* Translated by John Griffiths. Chicago: Franciscan Herald Press, 1973.

Kerr, Fergus. "Hans Urs von Balthasar." In *Twentieth-Century Catholic Theologians.* Malden, Mass.: Blackwell, 2007.

---

[41]Balthasar, *Grain of Wheat*, pp. 93, 19.

13

What These Theologians Teach Us
About Theology

At the end of each chapter I have teased out a few lessons to be drawn from each theologian. There's no need to rehearse those lessons here. But it might be helpful in this last chapter to think about how this book might help us understand the nature of theology itself. Here are seven observations we can safely make.

1. There are grand, unifying threads that run through the work of these great theologians. Three have shown up repeatedly in this book. The first is the *incarnational-redemptive core* of Christian theology. This is the predominant emphasis of Christian faith that God is a God of salvation, who has taken on human flesh to save. Put another way, we know God as a God who comes to save us when we cannot save ourselves. All that we know of the history of the Trinity (after the creation) is of the three Persons conspiring to redeem a creation that has gone astray. In other words, Christian theology is not about a static God who stands above the creation simply contemplating himself (as per Aristotle) or a God who lets the creation go its own way (as per deism). The true God, these great theologians have said in a variety of ways, is a God who in three Persons has directed all of history to save us, and in fact has come into history as a human being himself toward that end.

A second theme is related to the first: this God is a God of *love*, and his love is in its essence a giving of himself. *Self-giving* has always been in eternity, with the Father and Son giving themselves to each other in the unity of the Holy Spirit. Then it is seen in God giving of himself to the world by creating it with goodness and beauty. It takes more concrete form in the person of Jesus Christ and his suffering and rising from the dead (the incarnation, atonement and resurrection), and finds ultimate fulfillment in the completed kingdom of God when the Son gives a redeemed world back to the Father (eschatology).

The third theme is another aspect of the second: God's giving is most beautifully seen in giving his own life and being to us. This is the *mystical union* of Christ with his church, so that every believer is in union with Christ—because Jesus has given us his very own self. This is what Aquinas meant when he said that grace is God's action that leads us to union with him. It is the theme of deification or divinization, which we saw in Athanasius, Origen, Augustine, Luther (his "happy exchange") and especially Edwards. It is there even in Schleiermacher, who repeatedly spoke in his pietist voice of Christ assuming believers into the power of his God's consciousness.

2. All theologians work within a distinct cultural environment, which helps shape their thinking. Perhaps you have noticed that every theologian we studied seemed a bit constrained by the worldview of his culture. None was able to free himself completely from the intellectual milieu in which he was immersed. Another way of saying this is that all thinkers are shaped by the culture in which they are raised and live, and can never completely escape it. If it is true, for example, that Origen actually toyed with reincarnation and the preexistence of souls, it was undoubtedly a sign of his immersion in the Platonism that dominated the Hellenistic world. Augustine's doctrine of evil and God's immutability owe as much or more to Neo-Platonist conceptions of deity than to the Bible. His belief that even marital sex was sinful if its first purpose was not procreation owed principally to Platonism's view of the body as the "prison of the soul." Luther's view of justification and his conviction that this was the center of the biblical story can be traced as much to his sixteenth-century struggle with Rome as to first-century writings in the New Testament. Barth's refusal to concede revelation in nature was probably a function of his opposition to the Nazi religion of blood and soil. And so on.

This pattern in the history of theology should induce in us a certain humility. We should recognize that we too are blinded to some degree by the prejudices of our own age. This should make us all the more eager to read theology from other ages in an effort to uncover our own distorted perspectives. We should ask ourselves, for example, whether we should buy into our culture's presumptions that democracy is always the best polity, personal choice should trump the right to life, absolute equality is always the best social arrangement, hierarchy is always destructive and the individual is always supreme.

If this pattern reminds us of theology's limitations, it should not obscure the flip side—that over the history of the Great Tradition the church has corrected what was missing or deficient in the tradition. For example, the church as a whole did not emphatically recognize slavery as an egregious sin until the nineteenth century—despite the implied teaching of Scripture and the writings of more than a few Christian leaders. The value of seeing how one part of the long history of the Great Tradition supplements and develops and corrects other parts is all the more reason why we should learn from the whole history, in humility and with attention.

3. The cultural limitations of theologians do not prevent their opening up truth for the church. Not only have we seen the ways the prevailing culture affects the theologian's mind, but we have also no doubt been disappointed by what seem to have been egregious failures in theology that have had tragic social consequences. Augustine's theology of persecution helped open the door to mistreatment of Donatists. Luther's invectives against Jews were used by the Nazis to promote the Holocaust. Edwards's inability to see the evil of slavery enabled him to support "the peculiar institution."

But we must not make the mistake of dismissing their theologies in general because of these intellectual lapses. This is the mystery of all life in the church—that God chooses to display his "treasure in jars of clay" (2 Cor 4:7) that crack and shatter all too easily. God chose to give much of his revelation to the apostle Paul, who not only had participated in killing Christians (Acts 8:1) but continued to cause problems for the church after his conversion (Acts 15:39). Because every theologian is finite and sinful, we should not be surprised or disillusioned when we see serious flaws in the theological perspective or life of one of the "greats." They remind us that God is a God of grace who shares the mind of Christ with sinners. Besides, theologians of the Great Tradition often correct each other and learn from each other.

If we should not expect perfection in a theologian, neither should we imagine that any theological system is final or complete. Because the fullness of God always eludes our puny minds, we should never think that any theology can have all the answers. God will always shatter that illusion by showing a theology's gaps and the questions it cannot answer—especially when we compare one great theologian with another. But again, that's why it is wise to study the whole Great Tradition and not rest content with only one great, dismissing all the others. There are too many questions that one theology by itself cannot answer satisfactorily. We must remember that the church is a body with many members. The mind of Christ is never restricted to just one part of the body.

4. The Holy Spirit is at work in the history of the Great Tradition. I think we have to conclude, when looking at the history of Christian theology, that the Holy Spirit was guiding the church at key points. Sure, there have been plenty of heresies, but as John Henry Newman observed, the church over the long haul is steadily guided to identify and reject heresies and aim for the orthodox center.

Think of the Trinity, for example. The word *Trinity* is not in the Bible, but the story and pictures that point to the concept are. The precise formulation of the concept is not in the Bible either, but the church was led through several hundred years of debate to a formulation that has stood the test of time ever since. We can hardly doubt that the Holy Spirit was guiding that long debate until its concluding formulation in the creeds, which have also stood the test of time. In similar fashion, we must conclude the Spirit was leading Origen, for instance, to develop his fourfold sense that has brought light to the universal church for nearly two millennia, that the Spirit opened up to Calvin fresh perspective on divine sovereignty and to Edwards new insight into God's beauty and so forth. Most of the theologians treated in this book (Schleiermacher is a notable exception) have led the universal church to deeper understanding of our life in the Trinity. We could say that the Trinity's work in the incarnation and ever since was a blinding white light of revelation, and that this Great Tradition has diffracted this white light into a thousand different shades of color, each one displayed in the work of one or more of the great theologians—most of those in this book and many more besides. It takes the whole orthodox tradition to display the brightness of that original revelation, and if God permits we will see more as history proceeds.

This is not to say, however, that the Great Tradition stands by itself. It is simply reflection—orthodox at that—on biblical revelation, which culminated in the apostolic tradition. In other words, the Great Tradition is the Spirit-led development for the church of the meaning of what the apostles gave us—God's Word in both Testaments.

5. There has been development of understanding over time through the history of the Great Tradition. If the Spirit has been guiding the Great Tradition, there is a certain sense of development over time. I just mentioned the Trinity. Surely the movement from Athanasius's triumph over Arianism to a full elaboration of Christ's relation to the other two members of the Trinity was a development from a more basic understanding of Christ as God to a fuller understanding of Christ in the Trinity. We could say the same about gradually developing understandings of human nature in the first few centuries, culminating in Augustine's mature conclusions after his debates with the Pelagians. Much truth was known about justification in the early church, but after semi-Pelagianism got the upper hand in the fourteenth and fifteenth centuries, the Reformation debates brought more clarity. Even greater clarity came at the end of the twentieth century when Lutherans and Catholics finally came to agreement on basic principles in justification, and realized they had been talking past each other for centuries.

But this development is not always linear. For example, the church has now forgotten much of what the fathers knew and taught. Simply because we think we know more about, say, the role of women or spiritual gifts than some of the fathers does not mean our understanding of God is deeper than theirs. Even Barth, who brought the church back to a better understanding of theology and Trinity, cannot be said to have known more of the mind of Christ than Augustine or Thomas. Barth himself said he could spend the rest of his life with Calvin, and probably would have said the same for Augustine. (He didn't know Aquinas as well.) Therefore we can say, somewhat ironically, that the way for us to move ahead in theology is to move back—to the greats of the past. We will see further development only if we go back and sit at the feet of the great minds and hearts of the early and medieval church, or of those like Edwards who shared their spirit.

6. We will be able to discern the spirits today (which is the work of theology) only by studying afresh this long and rich Great Tradition. There are many traditions competing for our attention today: the Enlightenment tradition, the new postmodern tradition, the feminist tradition, the Marxist tradition and a host of Christian traditions such as liberation theology, emergent theology, environmental theology, black and womanist theologies, and so forth. If there is a thesis of this book, it is this: The best way to navigate our way theologically is to use the Great Tradition of orthodox theology as a lens through which to evaluate all competing traditions. Not that all competitors are to be thrown out lock, stock and barrel. For each contains truth in some measure. But their capacity to contribute to Christian theology should be gauged only by weighing them against the long history of the Great Tradition, led by the great orthodox theologians outlined in this book. This is the best way to discern the spirits.

It is also the best way to read the Bible. As we have seen a number of times in the preceding chapters, there is no way to read the Bible without some tradition shaping our reading. In other words, whenever we read the Bible we are reading through colored glasses tinted by some tradition that has shaped our thinking—whether we realize it or not. Jehovah's Witnesses claim *sola scriptura*—that they come at the Bible with no preconceptions and simply read their theology right off the pages of the Bible. Arius said the same thing. In hindsight, we would say that JWs and Arius have come to the Bible with cultural filters that have caused them to see what they see.

The question, then, is not *whether* we use tradition, but *which* tradition we are using as we interpret the Bible. Therefore it behooves us to learn the Great Tradition so that we can use it to critically evaluate the tradition we have already been using—knowingly or not—and every other tradition competing with Scripture or claiming to interpret Scripture. We should also use the Great Tradition to help lead us, when we read the Bible, to the inner subject that the great minds and hearts of that tradition have encountered—the Christ of the triune God.

7. We should read not only about *the great theologians, but the actual* writings *of these thinkers.* I will have failed in my task if your interest has not been whetted enough to lead you to read Augustine's *Confessions* or sermons by Origen or Luther's *Christian Liberty* or Edwards's *Personal Narrative.* It is one thing to read a travel guide to Greece, but quite another to go there. Without the latter, you can't say you really know Greece. By the same token, without reading the great theologians—or at least tasting their writings here and there—you can't know the beauty and drama of their visions of God. And perhaps to that extent, you will know a bit less of the great triune God whom they labored to bring to us.

FOR REFLECTION AND DISCUSSION

1. If you are in a group, have someone read each of the seven "observations" of this chapter out loud. Then let each person share which one spoke the most to him or her, and why.

2. In the group, have each person talk about what he or she has learned from this book.

3. Congratulate yourself for having done some serious reading and discussion—and for getting a handle on the history of theology.

Index